101 Accessible Vacations

TRAVEL IDEAS
FOR
WHEELERS
AND
SLOW WALKERS

101
Accessible
Vacations

TRAVEL IDEAS
FOR
WHEELERS
AND
SLOW WALKERS

Candy B. Harrington

PHOTOGRAPHS BY
CHARLES PANNELL

demos
HEALTH

Visit our website at www.demosmedpub.com

LIBRARY OF CONGRESS CATALOGING-IN-PUBLICATION DATA

• •

Harrington, Candy.
101 accessible vacations : travel ideas for wheelers and slow walkers / Candy B. Harrington ;
photographs by Charles Pannell.
p. cm.
Includes index.
ISBN-13: 978-1-932603-43-9 (pbk. : alk. paper)
ISBN-10: 1-932603-43-3 (pbk. : alk. paper)
1. People with disabilities—Travel.   I. Title.   II. Title: One hundred and one accessible
vacations.   III. Title: Travel ideas for wheelers and slow walkers.
HV3022.H36   2008
910.87'3—dc22
2007028496

Special discounts on bulk quantities of Demos Medical Publishing books
are available to corporations, professional associations, pharmaceutical companies, health care
organizations, and other qualifying groups. For details, please contact:

Special Sales Department
Demos Medical Publishing
11 W. 42nd Street, 15th Floor
New York, NY 10036
Phone: 800–532–8663 or 212–683–0072
Fax: 212–941–7842
Email: rsantana@demosmedpub.com

Book design by Steven Pisano

Made in the United States of America
10   5 4 3 2

TO
Charles

Acknowledgements

A project of this magnitude doesn't happen without a lot of help. The research for this book was, at best, daunting, and a big thank you goes out to every PR person who answered my questions, showed me a room, set up an itinerary, gave me directions, arranged an interview or otherwise granted my special access-related requests. Your cooperation is greatly appreciated and if it weren't for your help, I'd probably still be researching this book.

Several other people deserve to be singled out, and to them I'd like to offer a more personal word of thanks.

To PB, who helped put things into perspective when I had 75 more destinations to write about, no clean clothes, a broken telephone and a very big headache.

To Noreen, Phyllis and Steve for their encouragement, knowledge and assistance.

To Jenna, for encouraging me to use Alder Springs as my creative space. You gave me the final push I needed.

To Chet and the boys, for making the Alder Springs property a very comfortable place to write this book.

To Bonnie, for setting the bar high and always encouraging me to do things the right way instead of the easy way.

To all of the *Emerging Horizons* readers who have written or e-mailed me about an accessible destination, lodging or activity. Many of your suggestions were used in this book.

And, most importantly, to Charles, for taking and cataloguing thousands of photos for this project. And for tirelessly reading my text, choosing the right photos and captioning them. And for climbing that fence to get the cover shot! But most of all, for just being there.

Contents

The Great Outdoors

A Place to Rest Your Head

Road Trips

Historic Haunts

Family Friendly Fun

Off the Beaten Path

Candy's Picks

Preface

"Where can I go on vacation?"

As the editor of *Emerging Horizons*, I've been asked that question a lot over the years. A whole lot.

There I'd be, giving a presentation on accessible travel, and somebody would stick their hand up in the air. Since I was talking about air travel, I figured they had a question about seating or wheelchair assistance or even the boarding procedure. But no, the question was always the same.

"Where can I go on vacation?"

At first I didn't know quite how to answer it. I mean, here was this person who I didn't know from Adam, asking me where I thought he should go on vacation. What was I suppose to tell him?

So I usually answered it with my own question.

"Well, that depends," I'd say "What do you like to do?"

That usually just confused people more. It was routinely met with that standard deer-in-the-headlights stare and the dreaded, "What do you mean?"

"Well," I clarified "What kind of things do you like to do when you are on vacation? Do you like to visit museums, hike, shop, ski, gamble, drive, boat, enjoy nature, see plays, visit historical buildings or perhaps something else? Tell me what you like to do so I can give you recommendations based on your tastes After all, if you like museum hopping, my suggestion to visit the Everglades would be pretty useless to you. Give me something to work with here."

Again, the deer-in-the-headlights stare.

And so the dance continued, until one day I finally figured out the problem. All of a sudden it hit me when a business writer interviewed me for a piece on accessible travel.

"So, where can disabled people go on vacation?" he asked. "Well," I quipped, "They can pretty much go wherever they want. Last time I looked, there were no laws prohibiting them from crossing state lines.

"Dead silence."

"No," he said, "Can't you just list the accessible destinations for me—you know, like Disneyland. Everyone knows disabled people like to go to Disneyland, but I'd also like some other suggestions to share with my readers. I'll make it easy for you; just give me a list of accessible destinations in the US."

At that moment, the little light bulb went on in my head. This writer, like a lot of other people, thought there was this great master list of accessible vacation spots, with Disneyland at the top of the list. It never occurred to him that people should look for accessible vacation destinations the same way they look for any other vacation destination—based on their own personal tastes and preferences.

Now don't get me wrong; I don't have anything against Disneyland or any other theme park for that matter. Truth is, most theme parks have gone to great lengths to make their attractions as accessible as possible. My point is, just because you happen to be disabled doesn't mean that you automatically like theme parks. If you don't like theme parks, you just don't like theme parks.

Unfortunately, over the years, theme parks have usually been the top (and sometimes only) accessible recommendation by many travel professionals. Even today, if you happen to run across a travel agent who is not well versed in accessible travel, she or he will undoubtedly recommend a Disney World package the minute you mention the word *wheelchair*.

But that's not the way it has to be. Really. In fact, that's the reason for this book.

Over the past decade, I've spent a good deal of time on the road researching accessible destinations for *Emerging Horizons*. Truth be told, I've covered everything from accessible tide pools and sailing to museums, national parks, cruising and factory tours. Granted, some destinations took a little more research and legwork than others, but, in the end, I came home with some great resources and vacation ideas.

And this book contains many of those ideas, along with the resources, information and access details to make those ideas a reality. Think of it as an accessible-vacation idea book with substance.

Of course, once I got all this information together, the real challenge was putting it in a logical order. Most travel books arrange their chapters geographically, but that just wouldn't work for this book. After all, how do you know if you want to go to California or Texas or Indiana if you don't know what those places have to offer? Ultimately I decided to organize the book by activity, so people could decide where they want to go based on their specific interests and travel preferences. Truthfully, that's the way most people plan their vacations anyway— by interest, not necessarily by location.

Most of the sections in the book are self-explanatory, and they include a wide range of activities, from road trips and the great outdoors to family fun and cultural attractions. Admittedly some destinations can be classified a number of ways, and that's where I took a bit of artistic license.

For example, Chicago is listed in the "Bright Lights, Big City" section even though it boasts a good number of family attractions.

I just chose to emphasize a broader range of activities in that piece. Conversely, many of the destinations listed in the "Family Friendly Fun" section also have activities and sights appropriate for adults only. Again, it's just that I chose to emphasize the family attractions in those destinations.

And then there is the "A Place to Rest Your Head" section, which features some fun lodging choices, many of which can be considered destinations in their own right. And last but not least, there is "Candy's Picks," which is just a collection of some of my favorite trips, destinations and activities.

Regardless of how they are grouped, all of the chapters contain meaningful access information. As is the case in *Emerging Horizons*, I describe the access of the attractions, lodging options and tourist sights rather than just state that something is or isn't accessible. After all, accessibility is in the eye of the beholder; and what may be accessible to one person can be filled with obstacles to someone else. And finally, I've included resources at the end of each chapter, so you can do more research and plan you own accessible getaway.

It's important to note that, although this book does contain information on more than 101 destinations, entire books have been written about some of my chapters. So consider this book a starting point, albeit a very well-researched starting point. And don't forget to check out the Recommended Reading chapter for titles that offer more in-depth information on specific destinations. And of course, make sure and visit my Barrier Free Travels Blog at www.BarrierFreeTravels. com for the latest access news, new accessible travel resources, timely commentary and destination updates.

Where *can* you go on vacation?

After you read this book, just about anywhere you want.

Candy B. Harrington
candy@EmergingHorizons.com

101
Accessible
Vacations

TRAVEL IDEAS
FOR
WHEELERS
AND
SLOW WALKERS

Bright Lights, Big City

CHICAGO LIKE A LOCAL

S ome cities are perfect for walking tours. Take Chicago, for example. It's not only a very walkable city, but it's also very accessible as well — accessible in two ways. First, it's accessible because you can actually get around the city and out to the suburbs by public transportation. And second, because, for the most part, that public transportation system is physically accessible to people with mobility disabilities.

Of course not all Chicago walking tours are physically accessible. Some tour guides just don't have the time or the inclination to research the accessible routes. Terry Sullivan is not one of those guides; in fact, as the owner of Walk Chicago Tours, he makes sure all of his tours are wheelchair accessible. And Terry knows what he's talking about when he's talking about access. His daughter uses a wheelchair, so Terry truly understands that even one small step can be an access barrier.

Terry also knows Chicago, although he's far from what I'd call a typical tour guide. This retired English teacher and part-time scout for the Boston Red Sox founded Walk Chicago Tours in 2005 after a long volunteer stint with the Chicago Greeter program. Today his motto is "There's a story on every corner," and, given the opportunity, Terry will tell you all of them.

I first met Terry when I signed up for his "Tiffany Glass in the Loop" walking tour. The tour began at the Chicago Cultural Center, which is a hidden gem in itself. Built in 1897, this grand old building faced certain demolition until Mayor Daley stepped in and saved the day. Today it houses the Museum of Broadcast Communications, the Landmark Chicago Gallery and the visitor information center plus an art gallery, theater, restaurant and a concert hall. Of course Terry was quick to point out the real hidden gems of the building: a 38-foot Tiffany dome on the third floor and a collection of Tiffany mosaics near the stairway.

Our tour quickly moved to the street, where Terry showed us the underground walkways, known as pedways to the locals. They are very accessible and a great way to get around in inclement weather. Next we popped into Marshall Fields for another hidden gem. Terry quickly herded me past the jewelry counter. "No time for shopping," he quipped as we headed on to see another Tiffany dome. And so we continued for the next two hours,

Terry Sullivan, founder of Walk Chicago Tours.

discovering treasure after treasure. And, as promised, Terry had a story about each one.

Terry offers several other tours of the Loop, many of which focus on art and architecture. He also offers tours to Little Italy, Old Town and Wrigleyville, all of which use public transportation. Terry was also quick to brief me on the accessible L stops in the Loop, for future reference. Tours can be personalized to meet special interests, and, with a maximum of eight people per tour, you really do get personal attention. All tours must be booked at least 48-hours in advance.

If you are able to plan a little further in advance, check out the Chicago Greeter Program. Introduced in 2002, this volunteer-based visitor service gives Chicagoans a chance to show off their city. This free program is overseen by the Chicago Office of Tourism and is staffed by 180 volunteer greeters. Visitors are matched with a greeter based on their specific interests and needs. Currently the Chicago Greeter program offers more than 40 themed tours and visits 33 neighborhoods. A typical walking tour lasts two to four hours and is conducted on public transportation.

Chicago Greeter tours must be requested at least seven business days in advance, and, because of the individualized nature of this service, accessible tours are available. Remember, this is a volunteer-staffed service, so book as far in advance as possible to avoid disappointment.

And if you're an architecture buff, don't miss the Loop Tour Train. Presented by the Chicago Office of Tourism and cosponsored by the Chicago Architecture Foundation and the Chicago Transit Authority, this 40-minute architecture tour is narrated by docents from the Chicago Architecture Foundation. It is available on Saturdays throughout the summer.

General boarding for the tour takes place at the Randolph/Wabash L station; however, that station has no elevator access. Wheelchair users and slow walkers who cannot climb stairs should use the State/Lake Station, which has elevator access.

Although this tour is free, tickets are required. They are available on the day of the tour at the Chicago Office of Tourism Visitor Information Center. Tickets are available on a first-come basis, so come early, as this popular tour fills up fast.

- IF YOU GO
  - Walk Chicago Tours, (708) 557-5400, www.walkchicagotours.com
  - Chicago Greeter, (312) 744-8000, www.chicagogreeter.com
  - Chicago Office of Tourism, (312) 744-2400, www.cityofchicago.org/tourism

CLEVELAND ROCKS
· ·

Cleveland is well known for the Rock and Roll Hall of Fame, and, admittedly, you just can't visit Cleveland without spending at least a full day at this top-notch attraction. But, unbeknownst to most visitors, this Northern Ohio city also boasts a wide range of other less-publicized tourist haunts from museums and theaters to trendy restaurants and intimate comedy clubs. Indeed, Cleveland has something to satisfy just about every cultural taste. And the good news is, most of it is nicely accessible.

As noted in the previous paragraph, the Rock and Roll Hall of Fame and Museum is a Cleveland must-do. Known as the "Rock Hall" to the locals, this massive museum features excellent access, with a level entrance, elevator access to all floors and plenty of room to wheel around the spacious galleries. Throughout the museum you'll find interactive listening exhibits, films, memorabilia, guitars and stage clothing from all the great rock legends. And don't miss the excellent *Rolling Stone* archive. Die-hard fans will want to purchase a two-day pass, as there's really a lot to see.

If you'd like to have a peek at one of Cleveland's more traditional museums, then head over to University Circle. Located on Cleveland's east side, this community is home to Case Western Regional University and a number of cultural attractions. And exploring the area is easy, thanks to the wheelchair-accessible Circle Link shuttle. Called "greenies" by the locals, this free shuttle runs every 15 minutes and stops at the major University Circle attractions.

Your best bet is to spend the whole day at University Circle and hit the Cleveland Museum of Natural History in the morning and the Cleveland Botanical Garden in the afternoon.

You can't miss the Cleveland Museum of Natural History, just look for the Steggie II sculpture out front. Inside there's a wide variety of interpretive exhibits, typical of a natural history museum, but the real gem is the outdoor Wildlife Center and Woods Garden, which features a number of live specimens in natural habitats. There is barrier-free access throughout the entire museum, including level pathways in the outdoor section.

Access is equally impressive over at the Cleveland Botanical Garden, which includes 10 acres of outdoor gardens, the Eleanor Smith Glasshouse and a garden cafe. There is ramp access to the entrance, level access to the glasshouse and level pathways throughout the outdoor areas. Although there are a few uneven surfaces outside, a number of alternate accessible routes allow visitors to fully enjoy most areas of the gardens. Access inside the glasshouse is excellent, with barrier-free pathways on the main level and elevator access to the cloud forest canopy. Don't miss the daily butterfly release at 2 PM.

Cleveland is also home to a thriving theater community, and Playhouse Square Center has long been considered the heart and soul of Cleveland's lively theater district. Billed as the second largest performing arts venue in America, Playhouse Square Center features five stages: the State, Ohio, Palace, Allen and Hannah theaters. All of the theaters feature wheelchair-accessible seats next to companion seats; however, access varies depending on the theater.

Steggie II awaits visitors at the Cleveland Museum of Natural History.

The State and Ohio theaters feature accessible seating on the main level, whereas the Palace (where most Broadway shows are presented) offers the broadest range of accessible seating choices. The historic Allen Theater has stair-lift access to the main level, and the cabaret-style Hannah features accessible seating at almost every table. There is an accessible drop-off location in front of the theaters, and they have approximately 30 wheelchairs on hand to accommodate slow walkers. Just let the ticket agents know about your access needs when you make your reservation, and they will do their best to accommodate you.

For a taste of Cleveland's best musical entertainment, head over to Severance Hall, the home of the Cleveland Orchestra. The building in itself is an architectural treasure, complete with a 1930s vintage elevator. The accessible entrance is on East Boulevard, however there's a wheelchair drop-off zone at the parking garage entrance. Access is good throughout the theater building, including level access to the green room, where artists typically meet and greet patrons.

And finally, if you'd prefer a more intimate setting, then check out Pickwick & Frolic. Located in the heart of the 4th Street Entertainment district, this fun venue features a restaurant, a cabaret room, a martini bar and a comedy club. Access is excellent throughout whole complex, and it's a great place to spend the evening. Start with dinner, have a few laughs at the comedy club and then top it off with a martini. What better way to enjoy Cleveland?

- IF YOU GO
  - Rock and Roll Hall of Fame and Museum, (216) 781-7625, www.rockhall.com
  - Museum of Natural History, (216) 231-4600, www.cmnh.org
  - Cleveland Botanical Garden, (216) 721-1600, www.cbgarden.org
  - Playhouse Square Center, (216) 771-8403, www.playhousesquare.com
  - Severance Hall, (216) 231-1111, www.clevelandorchestra.com
  - Pickwick & Frolic, (216) 241-7425, www.pickwickandfrolic.com
  - Convention & Visitors Bureau of Greater Cleveland, (800) 321-1004 - Information Hotline, www.travelcleveland.com

COWBOYS AND CULTURE IN FORT WORTH

Fort Worth is a city of contrast, a contrast that's consistently reflected by the diversity of cultural offerings available in this former rough-and-tumble cow town. Today most of the steers are gone from the stockyards, however the cowboy heritage still lingers, as do a few straggling longhorns. And over in the cultural district, visitors can literally spend a whole week museum hopping. Culturally, Fort Worth has something for just about everyone.

As you stroll through the cultural district, it's easy to see why Forth Worth is considered the "Museum Capital of the Southwest." Truly if you have limited time here, some tough choices have to be made. The good news is, all of the cultural district museums have excellent wheelchair access. Even better, the major museums are all within walking distance of one another, and the cultural district features wide sidewalks and plenty of curb cuts. It's really a very pleasant area.

Must-sees in the cultural district include the Kimbell Art Museum, which is recognized as "America's best small museum," and the Amon Carter Museum, which is well known for its collection of Western and American masterpieces. The Modern Art Museum of Fort Worth is also worth a visit, as it houses one of the foremost collections of postwar art in the central states. And of course, don't forget the Fort Worth Museum of Science and History, which features hands-on science exhibits for all ages and a first-rate planetarium show.

The newest addition to Fort Worth's cultural district is the National Cowgirl Museum and Hall of Fame, a museum that honors women who embody the spirit of the American West. It's not all about cowgirls in the strictest sense but more about women who exhibit that feisty can-do cowgirl attitude. Honorees include painter Georgia O'Keeffe, Western sharpshooter Annie Oakley, author Laura Ingalls Wilder and Supreme Court Justice Sandra Day O'Connor. It is the only museum of its kind in the world and truly a highlight of the Fort Worth cultural district.

Sundance Square, the heart of the downtown entertainment district, is located just a short walk from the cultural district. Named for the Sundance Kid, who spent time in the Fort Worth area, this vibrant district features restaurants, galleries, theaters shops and hotels. It's a great place to stay, and the nicely accessible Renaissance Worthington Hotel is conveniently located within walking distance of all of the hot spots. Although this is a historic area, it has been renovated so there are wide sidewalks, level pathways and abundant curb cuts throughout the district. Like the cultural district, it's a very pleasant and accessible area to explore on foot.

For a look at a different side of Fort Worth, head over to the historic stockyards. Located just north of the downtown cultural district, this area was once the headquarters for Armour and Swift meatpacking companies. Today the meatpackers are gone, but the history of the stockyards remains.

A good way to get an overview of the area is to join one of the walking tours at the Visitors Information Center. The guides are very knowledgeable and, although the tour is fast paced, most of it (except for the catwalk over the pens) is wheelchair accessible. Tour stops include Stockyards Station, the Cowtown Coliseum, the Livestock Exchange Building and Billy Bob's Texas. Walking maps are also available at the Visitors Information Center, if you'd like to do the tour on your own.

The stockyards are designated as a National Historic Landmark, and, although there are curb cuts and sidewalks throughout the area, there are also

The Fort Worth Herd on its daily drive up Exchange Street.

spots that have high curbs and uneven brick pavement. The area is navigable in a wheelchair, but sometimes you have to find an alternate route.

Although there aren't a lot of accessible properties in the stockyards, the new Amerisuites Historic Stockyards is a perfect choice for wheelchair users and slow walkers. This five-story 102-room all-suite hotel is located right next door to the Visitors Information Center on East Exchange Avenue. Constructed in 2005, this affordable property offers wheelchair-accessible rooms with or without a roll-in shower. It's a very economical choice for people who travel with an attendant or caregiver and also a good choice for wheelchair users and slow walkers who want to explore the historic area at their own pace, without having to worry about finding accessible ground transportation.

The Texas Cowboy Hall of Fame, which pays tribute to the top Texas cowboys and cowgirls, is located just steps from the Amerisuites Historic Stockyards. The museum, which is located in the former horse and mule barns, features a level entry and good pathway access to all of the exhibits. Inside you'll find a collection of vintage carriages and wagons, plus memorabilia and personal items of the hall of fame honorees. It's definitely worth a visit.

And don't miss the Forth Worth Herd, the twice-daily cattle drive up Exchange Avenue. It's great fun and a good opportunity to get an up-close-and-personal look at some real Texas longhorns. Where else but Fort Worth could you find something like this?

- IF YOU GO
  - Renaissance Worthington Hotel, (817) 870-1000
  - Amerisuites Historic Stockyards, (817) 626-6000
  - Fort Worth CVB, (800) 433-5747, www.fortworth.com

MULTICULTURAL TORONTO
. . . .

As a melting pot for a plethora of cultures, Toronto is a true feast for all of your senses. And nowhere is this ethnic diversity more apparent than in Kensington, a small neighborhood just north of Chinatown off of Spanida. Suffice it to say that this Kensington is a far cry from the stately British palace of the same name.

Toronto's Kensington began life as a Jewish market in the 1920s and slowly evolved to include an eclectic mix of Portuguese, West Indian, Korean and Chinese merchants. Today you'll find everything from vintage clothing and herbal remedies to exotic produce and costumes in Kensington's colorful storefronts.

And although some sidewalks lack curb cuts, and it can get very crowded on weekends, Kensington is still doable for most wheelchair users. You won't be able to access all of the shops and vendors, but you will be able to savor the sights and sounds of this vibrant neighborhood. And for a real taste of Kensington, roll in to Global Cheese Market at 76 Kensington Avenue. Trust me, everything they sell is delicious.

Toronto is ground zero for a wide variety of multicultural experiences. Indeed the choices are mind boggling, as even the museums offer some very unique options. Take the Bata Shoe Museum for example. This kitschy offering includes more than 10,000 shoes and includes everything from ancient Egyptian sandals to Elton John's platforms. Access is good, with a level entry,

Wedding shoes at the Bata Shoe Museum.

automatic doors and elevator access to all floors. It's conveniently located right across the street from the accessible St. George subway station. You can't miss it; it's the building shaped like a shoe box.

Another unique museum is the Gardiner Museum of Ceramics. This museum houses an international collection of ceramics, including some very impressive pieces from Mexico, Central America and South America. Downstairs you'll find pottery, and upstairs you'll find European and Chinese porcelain. Access features include a level entry, elevator access and accessible restrooms.

Of course if you'd prefer the more traditional approach, just cross the street and check out the Royal Ontario Museum. This old standard includes a collection of more than six million objects that focus on art, archeology, science and nature. Access is excellent, with spacious galleries and elevator access to all floors. Wheelchairs are available for free loan at the front desk. And don't miss the golden mosaic ceiling just inside the main entrance. It's one of the jewels of the museum.

Toronto is also known for its lively entertainment district, home to the Royal Alexander and the Princess of Wales theaters. The elegant Royal Alexander was built in 1907 and restored in 1962 and features a level entry with accessible seating in the box seats. The Princess of Wales was built in 1993 and has great acoustics and a wider selection of accessible seating options.

And for a fun time and some great Italian food, head over to Leoni's Italian Kitchen on Blue Jay Way. There is level access to the restaurant, and (trust me) you won't go away hungry. After dinner, head upstairs to The Second City for an evening of comedy and improvisation. There is elevator access to the second floor, and wheelchair seating is available in the last row of this rather intimate theater. If you are a fan of *Saturday Night Live* or SCTV, this is the place for you, as many of those performers got their start at The Second City.

As far as hotels go, I strongly suggest you stay in the entertainment district, as this lively locale offers easy access to King Street restaurants, shops and theaters. And my top accessible lodging pick in that area is the Holiday Inn on King Street.

To be honest, I've never been much of a Holiday Inn fan, but the Holiday Inn on King changed my mind. It's just a block from the theaters and right across the street from restaurant row. And the newly renovated accessible rooms are excellent.

The accessible rooms are close to the elevator (they all end in the number 15) and feature wide doorways, lever handles, good pathway access, touch-control lamps and low-pile carpet. The accessible bathrooms each come equipped with a roll-in shower with a hand-held showerhead, a fold-down shower seat, a roll-under sink, a five-foot turnaround space and grab bars. And of course (just to make you feel at home) there's also a rubber ducky.

Getting around in Toronto is pretty easy, too, as there are a number of accessible transportation options. Airport Express provides accessible motor-coach transportation between the Lester B. Pearson International Airport and downtown Toronto. All buses are lift equipped, and you can purchase tickets on line or at the airport ticket booth.

Wheelchair-accessible taxis are available from Beck Taxi, Celebrity Wheelchair Accessible Taxi and Royal Taxi. These companies all have ramp-equipped vans with wheelchair tie-downs. Accessible taxis must be ordered by phone, although sometimes you can get another taxi driver to radio in your request.

And, if you'd rather drive yourself, wheelchair-accessible rental vans are available at Courtland Mobility.

Another accessible way to get around Toronto is on the metro; however, make sure and do your research before you head for the subway station. Right now, roughly 35% of the metro stations are accessible, so choosing the right route can save you time and trouble. Still, many attractions are near an accessible metro station, so with advance planning it is a viable transportation option. Updated station access information is available on the Toronto Transit Commission website, and an elevator status report is available on the Metro Elevator Hotline.

And don't forget to contact Tourism Toronto for free maps, tourist information and a comprehensive Toronto visitors' guide. It's the best way to start out your multicultural Toronto experience.

- IF YOU GO
  - Holiday Inn on King, (416) 599-4000, www.hiok.com
  - Beck Taxi, (416) 751-5555
  - Celebrity Wheelchair Accessible Taxi, (416) 398-2222
  - Royal Taxi, (416) 955-0564
  - Courtland Mobility, (800) 354-8138, www.courtlandmobility.com
  - Toronto Transit Commission, www.toronto.ca/ttc
  - Metro Elevator Hotline, (416) 539-5438
  - Tourism Toronto, www.torontotourism.com

THE STREETS OF SAN FRANCISCO

D on't let a few hills discourage you from visiting San Francisco," advises Bonnie Lewkowicz. "Just plan ahead and use public transportation to get around the hills." And Bonnie knows what she's talking about. As the founder of Access Northern California, she's the recognized expert on local access.

Indeed, she spends the bulk of her time inspecting hotels and performing onsite access evaluations for the annual San Francisco access guide.

And as far as public transportation in San Francisco goes, there are many accessible choices. San Francisco is one of a handful of US cities that has accessible taxi service. Several taxi companies, including Yellow Cab and Town Taxi, have taxi vans with ramp access and wheelchair tie-downs. The fares are the same for accessible taxis as for standard taxis, but they can be difficult to find on the street. The best course of action is to call the taxi company directly or have your hotel doorman get one for your.

BART operates an underground train system that runs along Market Street and serves the downtown tourist area. It also connects to several other BART lines and stops at the International Terminal at the San Francisco International Airport. All BART stations are accessible by elevator; however it's not uncommon for elevators to be out of service. Plan ahead, check with the BART elevator hotline and always have an alternate route or stop in mind, just in case of an elevator breakdown.

Additionally, San Francisco Muni operates a bus and train system. The trains feature roll-on access, and the buses have lifts, kneelers and wheel-chair tie-downs. A free *Muni Access Guide*, which details accessible services throughout the system, is available from the Muni Accessible Services office.

Of course you have to make some choices and decisions when visiting San Francisco, as it's literally impossible to see everything. Fisherman's Wharf tops my must-see list, as it offers a wide variety of food options, lots of street entertainment and the best people watching west of the Mississippi. You'll find plenty of curb cuts, accessible parking and level access throughout the wharf area.

Getting there is half the fun, too. Just hop on the historic F-line and enjoy a city tour, and stop off at Fisherman's Wharf along the way. The fare is a bargain at $1.50, and the F-line vintage streetcars offer roll-on access via boarding platforms and wayside lifts at all of the Embarcadero stops and several key Market Street stops.

Another San Francisco must-see is Alcatraz Island. It's a very popular attraction, so buy your tickets in advance, either on line, by phone or in person at the Pier 33 Hornblower Alcatraz Landing ticket office. Same-day tickets are rarely available, so plan ahead as tours usually sell out at least a week in advance. Transportation to Alcatraz Island is provided by Alcatraz Cruises, and, although all vessels have ramp access, the ramp slope is tide dependent. All Alcatraz Cruise ships also have accessible restrooms aboard.

The famous cell block is located at the top of Alcatraz Island and is accessed by a steep pathway. Anybody who cannot manage the 12% grade is welcome to ride SEAT, a wheelchair-accessible tram that departs from the dock area once each hour.

Bear in mind that Alcatraz is an old site, and it has some uneven patches of concrete and a few tight spots here and there, but, relatively speaking, the access is good. Accessible restrooms are located in the museum and near the cell block. Access to Alcatraz was upgraded in 2007, when another floor of the historic cellblock was opened, and elevator access to that floor was added. Be sure and opt for the new audio tour of the cell block. This excellent tour is narrated by former prison guards and inmates and it highlights the colorful history of Alcatraz.

Once you're back on the mainland, be sure and visit the Hyde Street Pier just west of Fisherman's Wharf. Here you'll find a sampling of vessels found on the Bay at the turn of the nineteenth century. You can get a good look at most of the ships from the pier, but the *Eureka Ferry* offers roll-on access. Be sure and have a look at the collection of vintage automobiles on her car deck.

For a different look at the waterfront area and a great view of the Golden Gate Bridge, catch a taxi down to Crissy Field, San Francisco's newest national park. As part of the Golden Gate National Recreation Area, Crissy Field offers visitors more than 100 acres of open space where the city meets the bay. This former airfield now boasts a restored tidal marsh, miles of hard packed dirt trails and a great bay view. Two all-terrain wheelchairs are available for free loan at the Crissy Field Center.

Of course no matter what you do in San Francisco, advance planning is a must. Says Lewkowicz, "Plan ahead, do your research and find out about the workarounds."

To that end, the most comprehensive access resource is ANC's *Access San Francisco*, a detailed guide with access information about San Francisco's hotels, restaurants, museums, shopping, recreation and transportation options. This helpful resource is packed full of useful information, and it's available free from the San Francisco Convention and Visitors Bureau or ANC. Updated access information can also be found on the ANC website.

. . . .

The lighthouse on Alcatraz Island.

So, don't let a few hills discourage you. Pack your bags and head for the city by the bay, and don't leave home without your copy of the *Access San Francisco*.

- **IF YOU GO**
  - Yellow Cab, (415) 626-2345
  - Town Taxi, (415) 401-8900
  - Muni Access Guide, (415) 923-6142
  - BART Elevator Hotline, (510) 834-5438
  - Alcatraz Island Tickets, (415) 981-7625, www.alcatrazcruises.com
  - San Francisco CVB, (415) 391-2000, www.sfvisitor.org
  - Access Northern California, (510) 524-2026, www.accessnca.com

VIVA LAS VEGAS!

Las Vegas has long been a favorite destination for wheelchair users and slow walkers. Somewhere along the way, casino owners realized that in order to make a profit they need to welcome *all* visitors. After all, money is money. To that end, they've done a great job making their casinos appealing and accessible to everyone.

The good news is there's no shortage of accessible hotel rooms in Las Vegas. In fact, most properties have gone well beyond the minimum Americans with Disabilities Act requirements. For example, Bellagio has 61 accessible rooms with roll-in showers, and the Imperial Palace has 85 such rooms. In both cases, this number greatly exceeds the minimum requirement of 30 and 27 rooms, respectively.

A few strip hotels, like Treasure Island, even have what they define as "high-needs accessible guest rooms." These guest rooms are equipped with ceiling track lifts and a number of other hard-to-find access features such as adjustable hospital beds, touch control lamps and draperies you can control with the flick of a switch.

Most of the newer Las Vegas hotels are like little cities, as they have everything from shops and restaurants to show rooms and movie theaters.

"High-needs accessible guest room" at Treasure Island on the Las Vegas strip.

All are nicely accessible. Many casinos feature accessible slot machines and lowered gaming tables. And, in most cases, dealers will place bets and take verbal commands from guests who have a mobility disability and cannot move their hands. Again, it's just a very accommodating destination.

This above-and-beyond access attitude extends well beyond the strip. Take public transportation for example. Currently there are 13 cab companies operating in Las Vegas, and all of them are required to have at least one accessible vehicle. The result is that you can actually hail a wheelchair-accessible taxi at the airport. In short, Las Vegas is one destination where you *can* have a truly accessible seamless travel experience.

The Las Vegas Monorail is also a good accessible option for some visitors. The monorail runs between six hotels and the Las Vegas Convention Center. Hotel stops include the MGM Grand, Bally's, the Flamingo, Harrah's, the Las Vegas Hilton and the Sahara. All of the stations are accessible and the monorail itself features roll-on access.

Unfortunately, some of the station names are pretty misleading. For example the Bally's station is called the Bally's/Paris station, when the monorail actually stops at Bally's (Paris is located next door). Likewise, the Flamingo station is called the Flamingo/Caesar's Palace station, even though Caesar's Palace is located across the street from this monorail station.

Considering the size of some of the casinos, next door or across the street can be quite a trek. To be honest, you could spend more time walking then riding on the monorail. On the other hand, if you are heading to the convention center from one of the six (true) monorail hotels, the monorail is usually a good choice. Check the map on the monorail website carefully before you buy your ticket.

Of course there's much more to Las Vegas than just the strip. If you'd like to see a different side of Las Vegas, consider staying in one of the new luxury hotels at the Lake Las Vegas Resort, located approximately 17 miles from the strip.

The Hyatt Regency is located on the west shore of the 320-acre lake that dominates the resort. This 496-room Moroccan-themed hotel features accessible parking, a level entrance and barrier-free access to all public areas. It has 14 accessible guest rooms, including five with roll-in showers.

The accessible guest rooms are located on the lobby level (which is actually the fourth floor) or near the elevator. Access features include wide doorways, lowered closet rods and good pathway access. The accessible bathrooms include grab bars around the toilet and in the shower (or tub), a hand-held showerhead, a full five-foot turning radius and a roll-under sink. A portable shower chair is available upon request.

Over on the south shore, you'll find the Mediterranean-styled Ritz-Carlton. Completed in February 2003, this 349-room luxury resort is the first Ritz-Carlton in Nevada. It features 15 accessible guest rooms, eight of which have roll-in showers.

The accessible rooms feature wide doorways, good pathway access and lowered closet rods. There are grab bars around the toilet as well as in the shower or tub area. Other access features include a hand-held showerhead, a roll-under sink, a portable shower chair and a five-foot turning radius.

Lake Las Vegas is the perfect place to relax and rejuvenate. Of course you can also shop till you drop at MonteLago Village, enjoy a concert on the resort's grand floating stage or linger over a gourmet meal.

Las Vegas truly has something for just about everyone, and the good news is, most of it is accessible.

- IF YOU GO
  - Las Vegas Monorail, www.lvmonorail.com
  - Lake Las Vegas Resort, www.lakelasvegas.com
  - Las Vegas Convention and Visitors Authority, (877) 847-4858, www.lasvegascva.com

WHEELING AROUND LONDON
· ·

L ondon is a top vacation choice for many first-time visitors to Europe. Viewed as a safe destination by Americans, the language, people and food are strikingly familiar to visitors from the colonies. And with nonstop flights from many American cities, London is also relatively easy to get to.

As far as access goes, the United Kingdom has national access legislation equal to the Americans with Disabilities Act. This legislation, know as the Disability Discrimination Act, was strengthened in 2004 to include even the smallest businesses. As a result, today many more UK attractions are now truly wheelchair accessible, which in turn makes London a very appealing destination for wheelchair users and slow walkers.

Ground transportation is always a prime concern for people who require accessible services. Fortunately London has a number of accessible transportation choices. Let's start at the airport.

Billed as the fastest option between Heathrow Airport and central London, the Heathrow Express provides high-speed accessible train service from Heathrow Airport to Paddington Station. Access features include a minimal gap between the platform and the train, dedicated spaces for wheelchair users, adapted toilets, and emergency call buttons near the wheelchair spaces.

The journey from Heathrow to Paddington Station takes just 15 minutes, and from Paddington you can catch an accessible taxi to your hotel. All London black cabs are required to be accessible, either by a portable ramp or a fold-down dickie transfer seat.

And although London is known for those big red double-decker buses (Routemasters), they are not accessible. The good news is, as of

January 1, 2006, the Routemaster buses were replaced with single-decker "bendy buses" with ramp access and lowered floors. On that same date, a new law went into effect requiring all London public buses to have working ramps when they leave the bus garage.

It should also be noted that, although there are many accessible ways to get around London, the much-publicized Underground is not one of them. In fact, the Tube is not recommended for wheelchair users because of the stairs, old elevators and large crowds. So, for the most accessible transportation options, stay above ground. For more information about accessible transportation in London, visit the Transport for London website.

A great place to begin your London adventure is in old Westminster, home of Big Ben, Westminster Abbey, and the Houses of Parliament.

As the site of royal coronations and the final resting place for monarchs and poets, Westminster Abbey is a must-see for tourists. The accessible entrance is on the north side, and an access guide is available at the information desk. Although there is level access to most of the Abbey, there are patches of uneven pavement throughout, and some parts of the sanctuary are only accessible by stairs or through narrow doorways. Additionally, some sections are accessible by a stair climber, but you must be able to transfer in order to use the stair climber.

The British Houses of Parliament are just a short walk from Westminster Abbey. During most of the year, visitors can queue up for a chance to visit the Stranger's Gallery and catch a glimpse of the action while Parliament is sitting. The good news is that, although the line for the Stranger's Gallery at the St. Stephen's entrance can be extremely long, there is rarely a wait at the accessible entrance down the street at the carriage gate.

Fall is the best time to visit the Houses of Parliament, as special tours are offered during the annual recess. All tours start at the Sovereign's entrance and follow the path of the Sovereign through Parliament. The majority of this excellent guided tour is wheelchair accessible, with two stair lifts along the route. Advance reservations are a must, and tickets are available through Keith Prowse Ticketing.

The State Rooms at Buckingham Palace are also open for tours from mid-summer to early fall. These 19 lavishly appointed rooms are used to entertain state guests on official occasions, and they are open to visitors only

· ·

Wheeling over the Thames River past the London Eye.

during the Queen's annual visit to Scotland. The accessible State Room tour bypasses the long lines at the tourist entrance and begins at the North Central Gate. It features stair-climber and elevator access to all floors. Advance reservations are a must, as space is limited on this very popular tour.

Tickets for the Queen's Gallery and the Royal Mews at Buckingham Palace can be purchased on site, and both buildings offer barrier-free access. There is no charge to watch the famous changing-of-the-guard ceremony, which starts promptly at 11:30 AM. The ceremony is presented daily during the summer and every other day in the winter.

Kensington Palace is also worth a visit. No doubt you'll find bouquets for Princess Diana at the main gate of the palace, since this was her residence. There is level access to the main level of Kensington Palace; however, the state apartments are only accessible by stairs. The sunken gardens also offer level access, and there is ramp access to the adjacent Orangery, where visitors can enjoy afternoon tea or a snack.

London is well known for two famous towers, but, to be honest, one is more accessible than the other. Truth be told, the Tower of London is best seen from afar, as the cobblestones, steps and narrow hallways of this London landmark make for some rough going for wheelers. An access guide detailing the obstacles is available at the ticket booth. If you do decide to give it a try, head straight for the crown jewels, as this is the most accessible part of the castle.

On the other hand, the Tower Bridge is nicely accessible. The main entrance to this attraction is located in the northwest tower; however, to avoid the stairs, approach the bridge from Tower Bridge Road rather than from The Tower of London. Inside, the Tower Bridge Experience features interactive displays that illustrate the history and explain the inner workings of the bridge. There is elevator access to all floors, but wheelchair access is limited to two wheelchairs per show. Visitors can also stroll across the walkways that connect the two bridge towers for a great view of London.

Of course, the best view of London is from the top of the British Airways London Eye. Billed as the world's highest observation wheel, the London Eye revolves very slowly, and it takes approximately 30 minutes to complete one revolution. There is ramped access to each London Eye capsule, which can accommodate up to 25 people. Additionally, wheelchair users are fast-tracked to the front of the line whenever possible.

The Original London Sightseeing Tour is also a good choice for wheelchair users, as the tour added 10 accessible tour buses to the fleet in 2005.

Operating 24 hours a day over several bus routes, these purpose-built, open-top buses are equipped with access ramps and dedicated wheelchair spaces. The buses make frequent stops at many of London's top sites and museums, and visitors can get on and off as they wish. The buses depart daily from Baker Street, Grosvenor Garden, Victoria Station, Marble Arch, Haymarket, Embankment Pier and Coventry Street.

Another great way to enjoy the sights of London is from the water, on a City Cruises tour up the Thames. City Cruises boats feature level boarding, preboarding for wheelchair users, barrier-free access to the main deck and an accessible toilet. Buy a day River Red Rover ticket and cruise from Westminster to Tower Hill to Greenwich, with unlimited reboarding privileges. All City Cruises' piers offer level access, although some assistance is required in a few places.

And finally, for a very accessible place to rest your head, check out the Copthorne Tara Hotel in fashionable Kensington. This four-star hotel features 10 wheelchair-accessible rooms with wide doorways, open-frame beds and automatic doors. Two of the rooms have ceiling track lifts, and six rooms have roll-in showers. Special equipment, including recirculating mattresses and trapeze assistance bars, is also available from housekeeping. The Copthorne Tara Hotel truly is one of the most accessible properties I've ever visited.

- IF YOU GO
  - Heathrow Airport Express, www.heathrowexpress.co.uk
  - Transport for London, www.tfl.gov.uk
  - Houses of Parliament, www.parliament.uk
  - Buckingham Palace, www.royalcollection.org.uk
  - The Original London Sightseeing Tour, +44 20 8877 1722, www.theoriginaltour.com
  - Copthorne Tara, +44 20 7937 7211, www.millenniumhotels.com
  - London Tourist Board, www.londontouristboard.com

Active Holidays

A BEACH OF YOUR OWN

Let's face it, wheelchairs and sand just don't mix. Sand isn't exactly compatible with canes or walkers either, and it can be downright dangerous for people who are unsteady on their feet. But that doesn't mean you have to rule out beach-combing on your next vacation because there *are* accessible choices out there. You just have to know how to find them.

There are many ways to make a beach accessible, including accessible boardwalks and beachside trails, beach mats and beach wheelchairs. Some beaches offer more than one option, so the best rule of thumb is to just keep your eyes open. With the aging US baby-boomer population, more and more recreational areas are making access modifications.

Boardwalks and paved beachside trails are the most common form of beach access. Generally speaking, these trails have level access from a nearby parking area and offer good views of the beach. Depending on the sand conditions, some trails offer direct access to the shore, but, for the most part, the boardwalks offer a good vantage point for ocean views.

For example, Half Moon Bay State Beach in northern California has a wheelchair-accessible beach boardwalk that extends into the snowy plover nesting area. This boardwalk is located at the northern end of Francis State Beach and it connects to the paved Coastside Trail. Visitors using the board-walk are treated to views of the ocean, dunes, plant life and the northernmost extent of the Santa Cruz mountains. Shorebird viewing from the boardwalk is also excellent.

But California is not the only place you'll find accessible beaches. Over in Hilton Head, South Carolina, the city has installed hard rubber beach mats at Coligny Beach Park, Alder Lane, Dreissen Beach Park, Folly Field Beach and Islander's Beach Club. These beach mats cross the sand and extend down to the high-tide water line and allow wheelchair users and slow walkers independent and safe access to the beach. In short, the beach mats prevent you from sinking into the sand.

Beach mats are really catching on in popularity, as they are easy to install and relatively inexpensive. They can also be found in Ala Moana Regional Park in Honolulu, Hawaii, and even on several of Chicago's Lake Michigan beaches.

Coastside Trail at Half Moon Bay State Beach.

Beach wheelchairs are also a popular way to access the beach. These specially made wheelchairs have wide plastic tires that are designed to navigate sandy beaches. Plus, if you want to cool off, you can just roll right into the ocean. The major drawback is that most manual beach wheelchairs are not self-propelling, so you need somebody to push you. The good news is, more and more public beaches have free loaner beach wheelchairs.

But how do you find them? Truth be told, there's no one universal directory for beach wheelchairs; however, it never hurts to inquire with beach wheelchair dealers. Since many state beaches, national parks and recreational areas purchase beach wheelchairs from these companies, once you know who their customers are, you'll know where to find the beach wheelchairs. Some companies, like De-Bug Beach Wheelchairs, even list their corporate customers on line.

Many public beaches have beach wheelchairs for loan; however they aren't widely advertised or readily visible. Make it a point to inquire at the lifeguard station or information kiosk when you visit a beach, as many times you will be pleasantly surprised by the availability of a beach wheelchair.

Independent access to the beach is also possible in the new Beach Cruzr power beach wheelchair. This self-propelled beach wheelchair is powered by two 24-volt electric motors and is outfitted with balloon tires and a high-torque gearbox. It's easy to operate from the joystick control and, because of the extra power, it's a snap to navigate over the sand. Of course, because of the power source, you can't take this chair into the water, but it's lots of fun to cruise along the beach in it.

Unfortunately because of the high cost of this model, it's hard to find on beaches; however you can try one out at San Diego's Mission Beach. Advance reservations are recommended, but you can just take your chances and show up at the lifeguard station near the roller coaster and see if it's available.

Still, it's best to call in advance, as availability varies depending on the season. Beach Cruzr availability is limited to weekends in the off season but expands to seven days a week during the summer months. And of course it pays to call in advance, as sometimes weather conditions force the closure of the beach.

There's no charge to use the Beach Cruzr at Mission Beach, and it's great fun. I highly encourage you to give it a try next time you are in the neighborhood. You won't be disappointed.

And finally, if you'd like to get a little more active and try out some water sports on the beach, check out Shared Adventures annual Day on the Beach, held every July on Cowell's Beach in Santa Cruz. Volunteers lay down 160 plywood sheets over the sand to create their own beach city, where participants can enjoy live music, free food and try out adapted water sports such as kayaking, scuba, surfing and canoeing. There's no cost to participate, but advance registration is required. Space fills up quickly for this popular event, so sign up early. Even if you've never tried a water sport before, you're welcome to participate at Day on the Beach. It's a great place to really get your feet wet.

- IF YOU GO
  - Hilton Head Beach Access Information,
    www.hhisleinfo.com/beaches.htm
  - Accessible Honolulu Beaches, (808) 692-5750,
    www.co.honolulu.hi.us/parks/programs/beach
  - De Bug Beach Wheelchair Locations,
    www.beachwheelchair.com/locations.htm
  - San Diego Beach Cruzr Wheelchairs, (619) 525-8247 (reservations)
  - Day on the Beach, (831) 459-7210, www.dayonthebeach.org

HIT THE SLOPES

. . . .

A s the snow and ice of winter settle in over the northern part of the US, many folks dream of sun, sand and surf and head for the southern beaches. It's the way of the snowbird. On the other hand, just as many folks pray for snow and head for the hills as soon as the ski areas open. But are winter skiing vacations really an option for wheelchair users? Gladly, they are.

Thanks to adaptive equipment and new techniques, just about anybody can learn to ski. And although you don't have to be an avid skier to enjoy a winter skiing holiday, it helps to know about the adaptive techniques, equipment and resources available before you hit the slopes. So here's a quick rundown of what you can expect to find at adaptive ski schools across the US.

The good news is, there are a lot of options, no matter what your ability. Skiers who can stand up can use standard snow skis and a set of outriggers. The outriggers, which are used in place of ski poles, are mini-skis attached to a pair of adapted forearm crutches. They help with balance and control and are ideal for people with lower-limb weakness.

Skiers who use one ski and two outriggers are called three-track skiers, whereas those who use two skis and two outriggers are called four-track skiers. The "tracks" refer to the number of ski marks left in the snow by the skier. Four-track skiers may also use a ski bra, a small tube attached to the tip of each ski, which prevents the skis from crossing. Four-track skiing is best suited for people who lack balance or have weakness in their limbs, whereas three-track skiing is a good choice for many amputees.

Those skiers who cannot stand up can use either a mono-ski or a bi-ski. A mono-ski works best for skiers who have a low-level spinal cord injury or good upper-body strength. It consists of a molded seat (bucket) mounted to a frame above a single ski. A shock absorber links the frame to the ski, and the skier uses two outriggers for balance and turning. Mono-skiers can use the chair lift with minimal assistance, as the bucket of the mono-ski raises when a lock is released. The chair lift comes up behind the skier and slides under the bucket.

People with higher-level spinal cord injuries or those with limited movement are better suited to the bi-ski. The bi-ski is a fiberglass shell mounted on two independently angulating skis. There is a handle or "power bar" inside that allows the skier to steer and two fixed outriggers near the

Adaptive skiing in Colorado. Photo courtesy of Andrea Jehn Kennedy.

base that give the bi-ski more stability. The bi-ski is usually tethered by a ski instructor, who is attached to the back of the bi-ski by a nylon strap.

So how do you know what equipment is right for you? Well, that's the great thing about it; you don't have to make that decision. Just find an adaptive ski school and talk with the employees about your access needs. They have a wide variety of equipment and their technicians are excellent at adapting and tweaking equipment. In truth, no two skiers are alike and adaptations are customized depending on specific access needs. Some adaptive ski schools charge a minimal fee for lessons and ski rental, whereas others are free. It's a very affordable way to get a good introduction to the sport, and, if you like it, you can always purchase you own equipment later.

There are a good number of adaptive ski schools across the US, and I've included some of the larger ones in the resource section at the end of this chapter. Granted it's not an all inclusive list, so check the Emerging Horizons database of accessible travel resources for more options. Additionally, check with your local CIL or other disability-related organization, as they may have a handle on some good local resources.

If downhill skiing isn't your cup of tea, then consider cross-country skiing. It's great exercise for both stand-up and sit-down skiers, and it can be adapted for a wide range of disabilities. It gets you "away from the maddening crowds" and, depending on your luck and location, allows for an up-close-and-personal glimpse of the local wildlife. Remember to pack your binoculars, as you never know what you will see.

Participants who can stand up use traditional cross-country skiing equipment: long narrow skis with bindings that attach to the toe of the boot. Skiers who can't stand up, can't walk or have problems maintaining their balance use a sit-ski. Sit-skiers propel themselves with shortened ski poles in this adapted sled-like device.

Not all resorts or adaptive ski programs offer cross-country skiing, so do your research to find one that suits your needs. Some areas are just more conducive to cross-country skiing than others.

No matter what your skiing preference or ability, it's still possible to have a fun and active skiing holiday. So don't be afraid to hit the slopes this winter.

- **IF YOU GO**
  - National Ability Center Park City, UT, (435) 649-3991, www.nac1985.org, downhill, cross country
  - Tahoe Adaptive Ski School, Truckee, CA, (530) 581-4161, downhill
  - Vermont Adaptive Ski & Sports, Sugarbush Ski Area, (802) 583-4283, www.vermontadaptive.org, downhill
  - Challenge Aspen, Roaring Fork Valley, CO, (970) 923-0578, www.challengeaspen.com, downhill, cross-country
  - Adaptive Sports Foundation, Windham, NY, (518) 734-5070, www.adaptivesportsfoundation.org, downhill
  - Maine Handicapped Skiing, Newry, ME, (800) 639-7770, www.skimhs.org, downhill, cross-country
  - Emerging Horizons Adaptive Ski School Database, www.emerginghorizons.com/resources/index.php3? viewCat=105

SAILING AWAY

S ailing is one of those great recreational activities that's pretty much accessible to everyone. Over the years, advances in adaptive equipment and teaching techniques have made the sport more physically accessible, but that's really only half the story. Sailing is also geographically and monetarily accessible. In other words, you don't have to invest big bucks or travel very far to give it a try.

Now don't get me wrong, a good number of sailors travel the world to enjoy the sport; however, just as many people prefer sailing close to home. Some folks build their yearly vacation around sailing, whereas others give it an initial try while visiting a new place. In the end, travel really isn't a requirement, but it's certainly a perk.

Still, getting on the boat is half the battle. Most marinas offer fairly level access; however, fluctuating tides, floating docks and older construction can present some serious access obstacles for wheelchair users. The good news is, there are a number of disabled sailing clubs around the world that have made their local docks more accessible.

Some groups have done this by working with marina management to permanently remove access obstacles, whereas others use portable ramps and lifts to solve the problem. In some cases, physical assistance is necessary to access the boats; however, disabled sailing clubs generally have a cadre of able-bodied sailors who are ready, willing and able to assist.

There isn't one official organization or regulating agency for disabled sailing clubs, but there's a good unofficial list on the Sailing Web website. Additionally, check with Disabled Sports USA or your local CIL to find clubs in your area. Many clubs offer lessons, informational meetings and even boat rentals. Even though you may want to venture out and buy your own boat later, disabled sailing clubs are a great place to learn about the sport, meet others who like to sail and try out a wide variety of adaptive equipment.

As far as adaptive sailing equipment goes, most keel boats are pretty easy to retrofit. The main adaptation for anybody with a mobility disability is a swivel seat with ample back support and some type of harness or safety straps. The swivel seat is mounted to the boat, and it allows sailors to rotate, face different directions and hold the tiller. The stock tiller can be adapted to accommodate sailors with limited arm movement, whereas sip-and-puff technology allows quadriplegics to control the rudder and trim the sails with their breath. Although sailing a keel boat requires some instruction, adaptive technology has made it a realistic option for wheelchair users, even those with a high-level injury.

If you are looking for instant gratification and want to enjoy sailing with a minimum of instruction, then look for disabled sailing clubs that have Access Dinghies. These fun little boats are very user friendly and, depending on the model, can accommodate one or two sailors. They are difficult to capsize and come equipped with a concave hull for additional stability. Best of all, they are designed to be operated by a person seated low in the boat, which is a very stable position for wheelchair users. Access Dinghies are also outfitted with a servo assist joystick to operate the electric winches. Even if you've never set foot on a boat before, you'll be able to enjoy sailing an Access Dinghy with a minimum of instruction.

Many clubs, like the Bay Area Association of Disabled Sailors (BAADS) have Access Dinghies as well as adapted keel boats. In fact, BAADS has eight Access Dinghies, three keel boats and a safety boat. This energetic group is composed of people who just love to sail, and they invite folks to join them every weekend at Pier 40 in San Francisco's South Beach Marina. BAADS sails usually last for four or five hours, although the length is dependent on the weather and sailing conditions. Everyone is welcome, but reservations are recommended. Check out the BAADS website for their weekend sailing schedule, as some days they sail the keel boats, whereas other days they work with the Access Dinghies.

Across the Big Pond, the Ro-Ro Sailing Project also offers instruction and has a variety of accessible vessels available for rent. Founded by Mike Wood, Ro-Ro was created to increase ocean sailing opportunities for disabled sailors. To that end, the organization designs, builds and rents out fully accessible ocean sailing vessels; in fact, the acronym Ro-Ro stands for roll-on, roll-off. They currently have two accessible yachts for rent, the *Verity K* and the *Spirit of Scott Bader*. They also maintain a list of volunteer skippers to accompany inexperienced sailors, so you truly can enjoy the thrill of ocean sailing with no previous experience.

And finally, if you're up for a little adventure, then consider crewing aboard one of the Jubilee Sailing Trust's two accessible tall ships, the *Lord Nelson* or the *Tenacious*. These two vessels were specifically designed for a crew of mixed abilities. Access features include wide decks, user-operated lifts, power-assisted hydraulic steering and wheelchair tie-downs.

Jubilee Sailing Trust voyages range from a short hop along the British Coast to a four-week transatlantic crossing. There are no passengers aboard these ships, as everybody is part of the working crew. Each ship is able to take a voyage crew of 40, including up to eight wheelchair users. No experience is necessary, and it's a fun way to meet new people and learn how to sail.

- IF YOU GO
  - Sailing Web, www.footeprint.com/sailingweb/clubs.htm
  - Disabled Sports USA, (301) 217-0960, www.dsusa.org

- Bay Area Association of Disabled Sailors, (415) 281-0212, www.baads.org
- Ro-Ro Sailing Project, +44 7734 246 385, www.disabledsailing.org
- Jubilee Sailing Trust, +44 870 443 5783, www.jst.org.uk

SCUBA 101

It's often been said that water is the great equalizer. As avid diver John Lawson puts it, "I don't need my wheelchair under water. I am released from the constraints of gravity to float weightless in a whole new world." In other words, you can do a lot of things in the water that you can't do on land. So, it's no big surprise that diving is a popular activity among wheelchair users. What may come as a surprise, though, is that even folks with high-level injuries or little movement can enjoy the sport. The key is getting the right instruction and assistance, and that's where the Handicapped Scuba Association (HSA) comes in.

Founded in 1981 by Jim Gatacre, the HSA offers diver education programs, instructor training courses, and accessible dive holidays. This nonprofit organization also educates the community on accessibility issues through their volunteer programs and works with rehabilitation hospitals to include HSA diving classes in their outpatient programs.

HSA's instructor training courses are intensive and are open to dive instructors eager to sharpen their teaching skills. In addition to attending 10 hours of lectures about disability issues, instructors participate in a variety of confined and open-water exercises designed to simulate different disabilities. By doing this, they are able to experience what it might feel like to dive with a disability, and as a result the instructors become more sensitive to the issues disabled divers face.

HSA's open-water dive certification programs are then taught at dive schools around the world by these well-trained instructors. Safety is a number one priority with all HSA-certified instructors, and no one ever dives alone. When disabled divers receive their HSA open-water certification, they are classified according to their ability, and this classification determines how many people must accompany the diver. For example, a Level A diver must dive with one other person, a level B diver must dive with two other people and a Level C diver must dive with two other people, including one who is trained in diver rescue.

As you can imagine, diving opens up all sorts of possibilities for travel, and, as luck would have it, the HSA also organizes yearly diving trips. These trips are a great opportunity to meet other divers and enjoy an exotic yet accessible vacation. All destinations are researched and evaluated for wheelchair accessibility, and a HSA-certified instructor is present on all trips. The HSA also maintains a list of accessible dive resorts and rates them according to their accessibility.

And, in some cases, the HSA actually improves the accessibility of the dive resorts they visit. Such is the case with the Divi Flamingo Bonaire, a favorite haunt of HSA divers. Back in 1984, when the HSA planned their first trip to Bonaire, Jim contacted the owner of the Divi Flamingo and requested that a few ramps be put in place for easier access to the resort. Since this was at a time when access in the Caribbean was almost nonexistent, nobody really knew what to expect. In the end, the group arrived to find ramps to nearly every section of the resort and an enthusiastic owner anxious to make more access improvements.

Over the years, additional access features have been added to the resort, including wheelchair-accessible guest rooms with roll-in showers. The Divi Flamingo also has a dive boat with roll-on access, so that divers who cannot walk don't have to be lifted aboard. Additionally, the small town of Kralendijk, which also has pretty good access, is just a short roll away.

Another Caribbean dive resort that gets high marks for access is the Bay Islands Beach Resort in Roatan, Honduras. In addition to having HSA-certified instructors on their dive staff, the resort itself features good access. The accessible guest rooms have wide doorways, ramped thresholds and bathrooms with roll-in showers, toilet and shower grab bars and hand-held showerheads. Additionally, there are accessible boardwalk pathways throughout the resort and ramps down to the beach.

And if you'd like to live, breathe and sleep diving, then sign up for a week aboard the very accessible *Fiji Aggressor*, a live-aboard dive boat. Built with input from the HSA the *Fiji Aggressor* has wheelchair-accessible staterooms with wide doorways, level thresholds and good pathway access. The accessible bathrooms feature continental showers with shower seats, hand-held showerheads and grab bars in the shower and around the toilet. Access is good throughout the rest of the boat as well, with lift access between decks. Additionally, the *Fiji Aggressor* staff includes HSA-certified instructors and dive buddies.

You can dive just about any time you want while aboard the *Fiji Aggressor*, and most dives are done from a high-speed skiff that is hydraulically lowered into the water. A monorail chair lift transfers divers from the deck of the *Fiji Aggressor* to the skiff, so divers who can't walk don't have to be manually lifted into the skiff. All in all, it's a great way to enjoy diving and a very accessible vacation idea. You only unpack once and you can dive till the cows come home.

- IF YOU GO
  - Handicapped Scuba Association, (949) 498-4540, www.hsascuba.com
  - Divi Flamingo Bonaire, +599 717-8285, www.diviflamingo.com
  - Bay Islands Beach Resort, (610) 399-1884, www.bibr.com
  - *Fiji Aggressor,* (800) 348-2628, www.aggressor.com

SUMMER IN WINTER PARK

I t's no secret that Winter Park is a playground for winter sports enthusiasts. After all, how do you think the town got its name? From downhill and cross-country skiing to snowboarding and snowshoeing, if it's a recreational activity that involves snow, Winter Park has it. The thing that comes as a surprise to many people, however, is that Winter Park is equally enjoyable in the summer. Indeed, a wide variety of recreational activities are available after the snow melts in this Rocky Mountain resort town. And the good news is, thanks to the advocacy efforts of the folks at the National Sports Center for the Disabled (NSCD), not only is the town nicely accessible, but so are many of the recreational activities.

Founded in 1970 by Hal O'Leary, NSCD was originally established to teach adaptive skiing to amputees from the Children's Hospital of Denver. Today this nonprofit organization remains the recognized leader in adaptive recreation. In addition to maintaining a top-notch adaptive skiing program, the NSCD staff also trains and coaches ski racers with disabilities for international competitions. Summer offerings at NSCD include rafting, kayaking, canoeing, horse pack trips, therapeutic horseback riding, mountain biking, overnight river trips, fishing, camping and rock climbing.

The whitewater rafting trips at NSCD are perennial favorites, and, yes, it's even possible for wheelchair users to enjoy a day of fun on the river. In fact, NSCD has accommodated people with disabilities from cerebral palsy to multiple sclerosis on these day-long and overnight whitewater rafting excursions. "Some people may believe it is impossible for an individual with a spinal cord injury to raft on the Colorado River," says Beth Fox, NSCD Operations Manager. "But at the NSCD, anything is possible. We make dreams come true all year long."

All activities at NSCD are customized to suit individual needs and abilities, so, in the end, it's really your choice how much you want to do. From a mild handcycle ride to a more adventurous rock-climbing expedition, NSCD offers a wide range of recreational activities. Instructors and volunteers return year after year to teach these popular programs, so there's really a family feel to the organization. And although NSCD encourages family participation and has a number of children's programs, most offerings are also suitable for adults. Bottom line, if you've ever wanted to try any type of adaptive recreational activity, NSCD is the place to give it a whirl.

NSCD programs are very affordable and, in fact, are priced below market so that everyone can participate. Scholarships based on financial need are also available. And if you are in need of accessible lodging, contact the folks at NSCD, as they maintain of list of local properties that can accommodate wheelchair users.

Of course you don't have to join an organized activity to have fun in Winter Park. If you'd like to enjoy the outdoors on a variety of trails, then visit the Bonfils Stanton Outdoor Center. Located just across the street from the Winter Park Ski Area, the outdoor center offers 1.2 miles of trails, ranging from an accessible boardwalk to the dirt-surfaced Challenger Trail.

The Challenger Trail has dips and bumps and a few short stretches of steep grades and was designed for wheelchair users who want a good work out, whereas the Discovery Trail is decidedly tamer and a better choice for people with limited upper body strength. And of course everyone can roll out and enjoy the view from the wide level boardwalk located near the trailhead.

Three accessible campsites are also available at the Bonfils Stanton Outdoor Center. Each campsite features level access and a wheelchair-accessible tent platform, which makes transfers easier. There is no charge to

. . . .

One of several accessible trails at the Bonfils-Stanton Outdoor Center in Winter Park.

use the campsites and they are available on a first-come basis. NSCD operates a number of group camps throughout the summer, so it's best to check with them to see if they will be using the facilities.

Be forewarned that the campsites are located about a mile from the trailhead, and individuals must pack in their own gear. NSCD will transport gear for their group camps, but individual campers are on their own. Although the first portion of the boardwalk trail is fairly easy, the Discovery Trail can be difficult with a lap full of heavy gear. Additionally, it may require several trips back to the car to get everything. The best advice on this issue comes from campers who have schlepped gear to and from the campsites, and the general consensus is to pack light, keeping in mind you will have to haul everything in and out. Taking along a few able-bodied friends doesn't hurt either. Still, it's a beautiful area, and one of the few places that offers raised tent platforms.

Bicycling is also a popular summer activity in Winter Park, and the 5-mile paved Fraser River trail is an excellent place to handcycle. Additionally, visitors can try tandem, mountain or hand-crank biking on the more than 600 miles of trails in the Arapaho National Forest and Fraser Valley. Although NSCD offers numerous handcycling clinics and trips, if you have your own handcycle, there are certainly enough trails to explore on your own.

And don't miss the town of Winter Park, as it's incredibly accessible. Because of the adaptive recreation programs available at NSCD, local business are used to seeing wheelers around town, and, as a result, they have made a concentrated effort to make sure their products and services are accessible to everybody. In the end, that's one of the great things about visiting Winter Park — the local attitude. It goes a long way to make everybody feel welcome.

IF YOU GO

- National Sports Center for the Disabled, (970) 726-1540, www.nscd.org

SWIM WITH THE DOLPHINS
. . . .

Some folks believe that dolphins react differently to people with disabilities. In fact, stories of special bonds, unusual dolphin behavior and of dolphins using echolocation to pick up physical differences, such as metal rods or plates, are not uncommon. In the end, dolphins seem to have an innate ability to differentiate a person's needs and then treat them accordingly. So it comes as no surprise that swim-with-the-dolphin programs are extremely popular among wheelers and slow walkers; in fact, many people plan their entire vacation around a dolphin encounter session.

But finding the right program is not as easy as it sounds. Even though there are more than 30 dolphin interaction programs across the US, only a handful of these offer any level of wheelchair access. Additionally, there are several types of dolphin programs, so it pays to understand the differences between them so that you can make an appropriate choice.

The three main types of dolphin interaction programs are therapy, lab and recreational swim programs. Both the therapy and lab programs last at least four to five days, but that's where the similarity ends. Therapy programs usually include work with occupational and physical therapists, whereas lab programs focus on education about dolphins and their environment. Both programs include scheduled dolphin interactions (including swims) throughout the week.

Recreational dolphin swim programs are by far the most popular vacation-time choice. These half-day programs begin with a workshop in which participants learn about dolphin behavior and culminate with a structured dolphin swim.

Although a few theme parks, aquariums and marine research centers offer accessible dolphin interaction programs, my top pick for both access and variety is the Dolphin Research Center in Grassy Key, Florida. Located in the heart of the Florida Keys, this nonprofit education and research facility provides a variety of accessible options, including mainstream access to most of their traditional programs and a five-day Special Needs Dolphin Pathways Program.

The special needs coordinator at the Dolphin Research Center works to remove physical barriers so that everyone can participate in their programs. Access modifications include private workshops, specialized equipment, and in-water or on-the-dock assistance. Says Mary Stella of the Dolphin Research Center, "If a person wants to participate in any of our programs, we do our best to make it possible."

The Dolphin Encounter is one of the Dolphin Research Center's most popular programs, and it's a good choice for vacation-time fun. This recreational swim program allows guests to interact with dolphins in a playful yet structured environment.

Participants begin with an educational workshop, in which they learn about dolphin biology and are taught some basic hand signals. These hand signals are used during the recreational swim to ask the dolphins for specific behaviors. The educational workshop lasts for about 3.5 hours and it's followed by a 20-minute recreational swim session.

During the recreational swim session, participants can ask the dolphins to display specific behaviors, including a hand shake, a dorsal pull, a foot push and a kiss. The entire program lasts approximately four hours, but participants are invited to stick around and watch other swim sessions.

The Special Needs Dolphin Pathways Program is a lab program designed for folks who'd like a more intensive dolphin encounter experience. It includes five dolphin interaction sessions (two swims and three dockside encounters) and five classroom sessions. All sessions are specially designed for each participant to make them as accessible as possible. Activities in the dolphin interaction sessions range from hands-on interactions with dolphins from the floating dock, such as painting or playing games, to in-water interactions, such as those offered in the Dolphin Encounter program.

Access is excellent throughout the Dolphin Research Center, with barrier-free access to the classrooms, public buildings and outdoor areas. The swim sessions take place in a special lagoon in the Gulf of Mexico, and an AquaLift chair is available to help wheelers access the water.

You don't have to be an expert swimmer to participate in the Dolphin Research Center's programs, but it does help if you are not afraid of the water. All participants wear life jackets, and assistance is available at all times. Participants must be at least five years old, and children ages five through 12 must be accompanied in the water by a paid adult participant. Guests must also be able to speak and understand English.

These dolphin encounter programs are very popular; in fact, they are so popular that reservations are only taken by phone and slots fill up almost as fast they become available. Reservations for all Dolphin Research Center programs can be made one month in advance by calling the reservations phone number. Payment is due at the time of the reservation. Access-related questions can be directed to the special needs coordinator before you make a reservation or at any time prior to your visit.

Suffice it to say that advance planning is essential to schedule a dolphin encounter session over your vacation; however the Dolphin Research Center offers excellent programs and the special needs coordinator works hard to remove barriers so that everyone can enjoy these programs. In short, it's a great vacation activity.

- **IF YOU GO**
  - Dolphin Research Center, (305) 289-0002 - Reservations, (305) 289-1121 ext. 232 - Special Needs Coordinator, www.dolphins.org

The Great Outdoors

A COLORADO BOARDWALK

So what's so special about a boardwalk? Granted it's a very accessible way to get an up-close-and-personal look at Mother Nature, but, in the end, it's just a boardwalk. Right? Well, not exactly. Take the Wilderness on Wheels (WOW) boardwalk, for example. Not only is this model wilderness project a destination in itself, but the nonprofit organization behind its creation continues to garner community support, encourage volunteerism and break down the physical and attitudinal barriers that so often prevent wheelchair users and slow walkers from truly enjoying the great outdoors.

And it all started with Roger West when he founded the Wilderness on Wheels Foundation back in 1986. His goal was to stimulate the development of accessible outdoor environments so that everyone could enjoy the great outdoors. Back then, there certainly weren't many (if any) examples for Roger to draw on, so he also resolved to share his design ideas and construction methods with other organizations so that more accessible facilities could be built. To date, more than 30,000 people have visited the WOW boardwalk, and Roger has provided access advice to both the US Forest Service and the National Park Service.

Located about 60 miles southwest of Denver on US 285, the WOW boardwalk winds through a secluded forest area and past picnic tables, accessible shelters, a fishing pond and numerous accessible campsites. Amazingly, it's all been created with donated funds, materials and labor; in fact, more than 116,000 hours have been invested in the project by some 3,500 volunteers. The eight-foot wide boardwalk features a steady but very doable rise to the upper terminus, with no railings along the way to obstruct the wildlife-viewing experience. There are a number of benches and picnic tables along the boardwalk, many of which were Eagle Scout projects, so there are plenty of spots to take a break.

There is also a spring-fed pond stocked with rainbow trout, which can be accessed from the boardwalk. And, although the folks at WOW don't like to refer to them as campsites, there are a number of accessible shelters with raised sleeping platforms, suitable for overnight stays. Most of the shelters are located near the parking area for easy access.

The WOW boardwalk is open from mid-April through mid-October. There is no charge for use of the facilities, but advance reservations are required, and donations are happily accepted. Additionally, all trash must be packed out to preserve the pristine wilderness environment.

And although WOW is not in the business of renting cabins, they do have two accessible cabins that are available to members. The WOW log cabin is located beside the trout stream and has two beds and a full-size couch hide-a-bed. There are no bathroom facilities in the cabin, but an accessible outhouse is located nearby.

The WOW ridge-top cabin has one king bed, one twin bed and a bathroom with an accessible tub and a hand-held shower. It also has a stove and a refrigerator.

Limited vehicle access to the ridge-top cabin is available.

As they say, membership has it privileges. Apparently this applies to accessible cabins as well as credit cards.

- IF YOU GO

  - Wilderness on Wheels, www.wildernessonwheels.org, (303) 403-1110

ON SAFARI
• •

Have you ever dreamed about taking an African safari but put it out of your mind because you just assumed safaris were not wheelchair accessible? Well, pack your bags and get ready for an adventure because, believe it or not, there are a large number of safari operators who actually specialize in wheelchair-accessible safaris.

Many of these operators have vehicles that you can roll on to and luxury tent accommodations with roll-in showers. Some operators specialize in Kenya and Tanzania, whereas others focus entirely on South Africa. Additionally, some private reserves even have accessible accommodations and safari vehicles. Prices and itineraries vary, but, the good news is, there are

• •

Wilderness on Wheels boardwalk.

many providers to choose from. Here's a roundup of companies that offer accessible safari options.

Green Leopard Safaris specializes in accessible Kenya safaris. This local outfitter can provide everything from oxygen and hospital beds to attendant care and medical supplies on their customized safaris. They have two lift-equipped safari vehicles and wheelchair users can either transfer to a seat or remain in their own wheelchair for game drives. Overnight accommodations are provided in a modified tent camp, which features accessible tents with private bathrooms and roll-in showers.

Southern Cross Safaris was established in 1957; however, they only recently began providing accessible Kenya safaris. In fact this African-based outfitter modified their existing facilities and vehicles to accommodate a wheeler guest. As a result, they now have two ramped safari vehicles and accessible accommodations at their tented safari camp in Tsavo East.

Endeavour Safaris provides accessible safaris in Botswana, Namibia, Zambia, Mozambique and South Africa. Game drives are conducted in a ramped Toyota Land Cruiser. Wheelchair users can stay in their own wheelchair or transfer to a vehicle seat. Overnight accommodations are provided in accessible tents with en suite bathrooms (toilets). The tents have level access, plenty of room to maneuver a wheelchair and wheelchair-height beds. Overnight accommodations are also available at hotels and lodges, but the tent camp is the most accessible option. Attendant care services are also available.

Epic Enabled provides accessible safaris in South Africa in their lift-equipped Mercedes Benz overland truck. Group participation is encouraged (meaning that everyone lends a hand with camp chores) and, as a result, Epic Enabled passes on the cost savings to their customers. A combination of tented camps, cottages and bungalows are used while on safari, all of which are accessible.

Go Africa Safaris focuses more on integrated adventures, resulting in a mix of able-bodied and disabled folks on their Kenya safaris. At last notice, they provided access to their safari vehicles via a rail-type ramp that consists of two metal planks rather than a solid platform. Although this works fine for many wheelchairs, it's not a doable option for scooters, so make sure and clarify the access if you have a scooter or a large power wheelchair.

On the plus side, this company seems very willing to work with folks to adapt its safaris, so they may be able to devise alternate access to their vehicle. They seem to do well in adapting accommodations as well, and, although they don't have accessible toilets in their safari camps, they do carry a folding commode chair for use while on safari. The same chair doubles as a shower chair where there are no adapted shower facilities. Attendant care and extra assistance is also available, and these folks seem real big on personal service.

Flamingo Tours offers a variety of accessible South African tours to the Western Cape, Namaqualand, the Garden Route and Kruger National Park. Their customized safari tours feature accessible accommodations in hotels, lodges and private game reserves. They can also arrange for rental of medical equipment while on safari.

And last but not least, there's Mala Mala Game Reserve, a private game reserve located in the eastern part of South Africa. It's an excellent game viewing site; in fact, more than 76% of Mala Mala guests report sighting the big five. This phenomenal rate of success is attributed to the fact that Mala Mala comprises 45,000 acres of pristine game viewing land, making it the largest privately owned game reserve in South Africa. Additionally, the unfenced border between Mala Mala and the Kruger National Park, allows animals to migrate freely to the perennial Sand River, which flows through the Mala Mala Game Reserve.

Photographic safaris at Mala Mala are conducted in specially equipped 4-wheel-drive vehicles. Wheelchair-users can either transfer to the front seat or remain in their own wheelchair in the back of the vehicle. Shoulder straps, waist straps and wrist straps are available to insure a stable ride. After dark, spotlight safaris provide the opportunity to view nocturnal creatures.

The Mala Mala Main Camp sits on the bank of the Sand River and features thatched roof buildings surrounded by shady trees. The camp has an accessible suite complete with ramps, wide doorways, wheelchair-height furniture, and a bathroom with a roll-in shower and shower seat. The facilities were designed with the assistance of the Quadriplegic Association of South Africa, in order to meet international standards for accessibility.

- IF YOU GO
  - Green Leopard Safaris, +254 20 3003365, www.greenleopard.com
  - Southern Cross Safaris, +254 20 884712 19, www.southerncrosssafaris.com
  - Endeavour Safaris, +27 21 556 6114, www.endeavour-safaris.com
  - Epic Enabled, +27 21 782 9575, www.epic-enabled.com
  - Go Africa Safaris, +254 40 320 2938, www.go-africa-safaris.com
  - Flamingo Tours, +27 21 557 4496, www.flamingotours.co.za
  - Mala Mala Game Reserve, + 27 11 442 2267, www.malamala.com

BEYOND CANNERY ROW

L ocated just two hours south of San Francisco, Monterey is well known for the outstanding Monterey Bay Aquarium. Granted, no visit to the area is complete without spending at least a day at this popular Cannery Row tourist attraction; however, Cannery Row is only a small portion of the whole Monterey Bay experience. Indeed, Monterey County is also an excellent destination for outdoor fun; in fact, from Moss Landing to Point Lobos, the scenic coastline is dotted with accessible trails and natural areas that showcase the natural beauty of the area. And in most cases it's the perfect place to ditch the tourist crowds, enjoy a secluded picnic lunch and get up close and personal with Mother Nature.

The best place to begin your Monterey County eco tour is on Cannery Row, as the coastal area to the south offers some great ocean views and several accessible trails. Just hop in your car and follow Cannery Row until it turns into Ocean View Boulevard, then head south toward Pacific Grove.

As you approach Asilomar State Beach on your right, Ocean View Boulevard becomes Sunset Drive and you'll notice a boardwalk trail along the beach. Although the trail runs the length of the beach, wheelchair access is only possible from the accessible parking spaces located near Jewell Avenue, Arena Avenue, Pico Avenue and the Asilomar Conference Center. It's easy to spend a whole afternoon on the boardwalk and hard-packed trails of Asilomar State Beach, as the scenery is absolutely gorgeous.

Across the street, Asilomar Conference Center also boasts a few accessible trails. Although this Julia Morgan-designed conference center is geared toward group retreats, they also have some guest rooms available for leisure travelers. And even though Asilomar Conference Center is a historic property, access upgrades have been added over the years.

The most accessible guest rooms (401 and 413) are located in the Stuck-Up Inn, and they feature bathrooms equipped with a roll-in shower, a hand-held showerhead and a fold-down shower bench. Accessible parking is located near the entrance and there is ramped access to the front door.

Additionally, there is an accessible shuttle to transport guests to and from their cabins, as some of the terrain is a bit hilly. Even if you can't stay at the Asilomar Conference Center, it's still worth a visit, as there are two

Accessible entrance to Stuck-Up Inn at Asilomar Conference Center.

accessible trails there, including a short boardwalk trail to Sunset Drive and a .25-mile trail up to the greenhouse.

Just up the road from Asilomar State Beach, you'll find another must-see: Pebble Beach's famed 17 Mile Drive. Use the Pacific Grove entrance off of Sunset Drive and head over to Spanish Bay to enjoy a romantic picnic and a stroll along the beach. Spanish Bay features accessible picnic tables with great views of the bay and a 1.8-mile boardwalk trail that follows the coastline to Bird Rock.

Another scenic trail is located at Point Lobos State Reserve, just three miles south of Carmel on Highway 1. Point Lobos' .6-mile Sea Lion Point Trail has a hard-packed dirt surface and features an accessible grade with lots of scenic overlooks along the way. At Headland Cove, you'll spot sea otters lounging on the rocks and shore birds skimming the waters' surface.

And if you really want to get off the beaten track, then head up to Moss Landing. Take Highway 1 north and turn right at the power plant on Dolan Road. Drive 3.5 miles and make a left on Elkhorn Road. You'll pass the Elkhorn Slough Reserve on your right. Continue along for another 2.5 miles and turn left into Kirby Park. This regional park isn't well marked and it looks like it's closed or off limits. Drive down to the bottom of the road and park. To your right, you'll see the Upper Slough Trail.

One of the best things about this trail is that it's relatively deserted, even during the peak season. Additionally, it's a great place to watch the shorebirds. The eight-foot wide paved trail and boardwalk is about a half-mile long. The pelicans are plentiful here and it's great fun to see them hit the water and dive for food. They aren't exactly the most graceful birds!

Although there are no services available at Kirby Park, the Upper Slough Trail still rates high on my list due to its remote location and the abundance of shore birds. Indeed, it's rare that you'll even see another person at this hidden gem in Monterey County.

- IF YOU GO
  - Asilomar Conference Center, (831) 372-8016, www.visitasilomar.com
  - Point Lobos State Reserve, (831) 624-4909, http://pt-lobos.parks.state.ca.us
  - Monterey County Convention and Visitors Bureau, (888) 221-1010, www.montereyinfo.org

BIG TREES AND WATER FALLS

The great outdoors has long been considered the last frontier as far as access is concerned. Although you can't exactly ramp Mother Nature, two of California's largest national parks have made significant access improvements over the past decade. As a result of this cooperative effort between the National Park Service and concessionaires in Sequoia and Yosemite National Parks, today not only do visitors have more accessible in-park lodging options, but they can also access trails and overlooks that were previously off limits to wheelchair users and slow walkers.

Access improvements in Sequoia National Park began with the opening of the Giant Forest Museum in November 2001. Housed in the former Giant Forest Market, which was built in 1928, the museum features interpretive hands-on exhibits that tell the story of the Giant Forest. Access is excellent in this rehabilitated building, as it has a level entry, hardwood floors

Spectacular views at Glacier Point in Yosemite National Park.

and plenty of room to maneuver. Accessible restrooms are located inside the museum, and there is plenty of accessible parking in the designated lot near the front entrance.

The Giant Forest museum also serves as a hub for a series of connected hiking trails, many of which have been regraded to meet accessibility standards. As Ranger Malinee Crapsey puts it, "We want to make it easy for everyone to enjoy the big trees." Although many trails have accessible sections, by far the crown jewel of accessibility is the Big Trees Trail.

Formerly the Trail for All People, the Big Trees Trail was lengthened and repaved to improve access in 2002. A little over a mile long, this interpretive trail circles Round Meadow and provides a good introduction to sequoia ecology. It's a great place to view wildflowers and to get an up-close-and-personal look at the giant sequoias. The nicely done five-foot wide paved trail features many benches and turnouts along the route, in addition to a few newly constructed boardwalk sections. Accessible restrooms are located near the end of the trail.

Sequoia National Park lodging was also given an access facelift in 1999, when Delaware North Companies Parks & Resorts built Wuksachi Lodge. Conveniently located in the Giant Forest area, this 102-room property features six accessible guest rooms.

The accessible guest rooms are located in the Stewart Building, and they feature wide doorways, lowered environmental controls and a 36-inch clearance space on both sides of the beds. The accessible bathrooms have a roll-under sink, grab bars near the toilet and in the shower and a low-step shower with a fold-down padded shower seat. There is a two-inch lip at the shower threshold; however, it's still possible to transfer to the fold-down seat.

Over in Yosemite National Park, major access upgrades began back in 1997 with the Glacier Point renovation project. Located just 45 minutes from the valley floor, Glacier Point is the place to get a spectacular view of the entire park. Prior to the access improvements, steep grades and inaccessible pathways made it impossible for wheelchair users to get much farther than the parking lot. All that's changed today, as the overlook is accessible via a 300-yard paved switch-back trail from the main parking lot. It's very nicely done.

Over the years there have been many access upgrades to Yosemite Valley accommodations. All Yosemite lodging is currently managed by Delaware North Companies Parks & Resorts. Accessible offerings with private bathrooms include seven rooms at The Ahwahnee, four rooms at Yosemite Lodge and two cabins and a hotel room at Curry Village. Eight of these rooms have roll-in showers. Accessible options with shared bath facilities include six cabins, seven canvas tents and two housekeeping units. All of these Curry Village units share community bathrooms with roll-in showers.

The newest access upgrade at Yosemite was unveiled in April 2005, and it's the culmination of the massive 10-year $13.5 million Yosemite Falls Restoration Project. Designed by the same landscape architect who worked on the FDR Memorial in Washington, DC, the project includes a new .75-mile paved trail to the bridge at lower Yosemite Falls. The gentle grade allows for wheelchair access, and this wide trail has many pull outs, resting spots and benches along the way. Indeed, for the first time there is barrier-free access to the base of Yosemite Falls. Not only does this new trail get high marks in the access department, but it also helps ease overcrowding at this popular valley landmark. It's a great reason to visit (or revisit) Yosemite.

And of course, no matter which national park you visit, don't leave home without your America the Beautiful – National Parks and Federal Recreational Lands Pass – Access Pass. Formerly named the Golden Access Passport, this free lifetime pass is available to any US resident with a permanent disability. Pass holders get free admission to all US national parks, monuments, historic sites, recreation areas and wildlife refuges. Pick one up at any national park entrance.

- IF YOU GO
    - Sequoia National Park, (559) 565-3341, www.nps.gov/seki
    - Wuksachi Lodge, (559) 253-2199, www.VisitSequoia.com
    - Yosemite National Park, (559) 372-0200, www.nps.gov/yose
    - Yosemite Lodging, (559) 253-5635, www.yosemitepark.com
    - America the Beautiful – National Parks and Federal Recreational Lands Pass – Access Pass, http://www.nps.gov/fees_passes.htm

DEATH VALLEY DAYS

Admittedly any destination that contains the word "death" sounds a little foreboding. Such is the case with Death Valley, and, unfortunately, because of this misunderstanding, many visitors completely overlook this southern California geologic treasure. Although you don't want to visit Death Valley in the middle of the summer, when temperatures have been know to top 120 degrees and many facilities are closed, it's the ideal spot for a winter break. Indeed, from December to April, the temperatures are mild and the desert is alive with color, especially when the wildflowers reach their peak blooms, usually in mid-February. And thanks to modern technology and access improvements, many of Death Valley's trails and tourist sites are now accessible to everybody.

The best place to begin your Death Valley experience is at the Furnace Creek Visitor Center, located about 12 miles from the park's eastern entrance. The Visitor Center features interpretive exhibits, an introductory slide program, a bookstore and an information center. The entire facility is barrier free with accessible parking, a level entry and accessible restrooms. The spacious theater offers a variety of wheelchair seating options, and the Desert Museum has a number of lowered exhibits and plenty of maneuvering room. Rangers are available to answer questions and to assist visitors.

The Furnace Creek Visitor Center is also the place to pay your park entrance fee. America the Beautiful – National Parks and Federal Recreational Lands Pass – Access Passholders are admitted free, but be sure to stop at the Visitor Center and get your receipt. And for a good introduction to the desert, check out the paved bike path that runs along the highway near the Visitor Center.

The Salt Creek Boardwalk in Death Valley.

One of the most accessible trails in the park, the Salt Creek Boardwalk, is located about 10 miles north of the Visitor Center, at the bottom of Cottonball Basin. The accessible half-mile loop boardwalk trail crosses the shallow creek in many places. One of the great things about the design of this boardwalk is that there are no railings or other obstructions to block your view. Instead, you'll find two-inch high safety bumpers along the sides of the boardwalk. Salt Creek is home to the endangered pupfish, which is said to live only in Death Valley. Pupfish are present in Salt Creek from February to May, with peak activity occurring in March and early April.

Another popular attraction in Death Valley is the Harmony Borax Works, located six miles south of Salt Creek. Here you'll find the ruins of the 1880 20 Mule Team Borax refinery, including borax wagons and antique mining equipment. This open-air museum is located along a paved inter-pretive trail, approximately one-half mile long. The trail does have a grade greater than 1:12 in a few places, but you can get a fairly good view of the borax works without going all the way to the top. If you are able to navigate past the first display, there are level patches near the top.

For a more accessible look at Death Valley's history, stop by the Borax Museum, located just a mile down the road at the Furnace Creek Ranch.

The museum is free and it's located right behind the registration building. There is ramp access to the museum building, which contains a pictorial history of early Death Valley. Outside, in the back courtyard, you'll find antique stage coaches, mining tools and even a railroad steam locomotive.

Access to the back courtyard from the museum is tricky because of the odd placement of some railroad ties near the back entrance. Best bet is to go around the side of the courtyard, pass the barn and access the courtyard from the side entrance. The paths through the courtyard are constructed of hard-packed sand, with some occasional loose gravel. It's quite doable for most folks, and it's a great exhibit of old equipment.

You can also see a good portion of Death Valley from you car, as there are a number of scenic driving routes throughout the park. At the top of the list is Artists Drive, located south of Furnace Creek on the east side of Badwater Road. This loop drive through the canyon is a good opportunity to see the alluvial fans of Death Valley. The highlight of Artists Drive is Artists Palette, where the mountains are covered in vibrant colors, from violet and red to yellow, red-brown, black and green. Some experts say the colors come from volcanic ash, but nobody knows for sure. It's a spectacular site, and a great photo opportunity, especially in the late afternoon.

And finally, make sure and save some time to enjoy the Death Valley sunset from Dante's View. Located about 25 miles southeast of the Furnace Creek Visitors Center at 5,475 feet, Dante's View overlooks the Badwater area and the adjacent salt flats. A paved road leads up to the overlook, and it's a very scenic spot to end your day, or your visit, to Death Valley.

- IF YOU GO
  - Death Valley National Park, (760) 786-3200, www.nps.gov/deva

EVERGLADES ADVENTURE

A t first glance, the Everglades doesn't appear to be the most accessible vacation choice; after all, wheel-chairs and swamps don't really mix. Upon closer examination though, you'll find that there are many boardwalk trails over the swampy areas, trails that are ideal for wheelers and slow walkers. Additionally,

Alligators along the Anhinga Trail.

it's a very nice driving destination, and a lot of the vegetation and wildlife can be enjoyed from the comfort of your own car.

Basically you have two choices when exploring the Everglades;: you can enter the park at the southern entrance along the road to Flamingo or at the northern Shark Valley entrance on US 41. Both areas of the park offer good wildlife viewing opportunities, however there aren't any roads connecting the two. There is also a Visitor Center on the northwest side of the park near Everglades City; however, it serves as a gateway for exploring the mangrove islands in the park, an area that by its very nature lacks accessibility. Generally speaking, if you only have a short time for a visit, the northern part of the park is your best bet, whereas the southern area is better suited for those folks who can stay a few days.

The southern entrance to the Everglades is located southwest of Florida City on State Highway 9336. The first building you will see after you enter the park is the Ernest Coe Visitor Center, which was constructed after Hurricane Andrew. There is plenty of accessible parking, barrier-free access to the building and lots of room to maneuver throughout the Visitor Center. Plan to stop here to pick up maps, get more information, ask questions and familiarize yourself with park.

Down the road, the Royal Palm Visitor Center features the most interesting, and perhaps the most accessible, trail in the park. If you have time to make only one stop on the way to Flamingo, stop here and explore the Anhinga Trail. This half-mile boardwalk winds through sawgrass pines and Taylor Slough and is home to a wealth of bird life. You will see blue herons, white ibis and snowy egrets, along with the "namesake" anhingas. The anhingas (also called water turkeys) can be seen in abundance drying their colorful wings in the sun or perched peacefully in trees along the trail. The Anhinga Trail is also an excellent place to get a close look at alligators, sometimes closer that you would like, as they have been known to cross parts of the trail leading to the boardwalk.

The half-mile Gumbo Limbo Trail is also located at the Royal Palm Visitor Center. This paved loop trail meanders through a hammock of gumbo limbo trees, royal palms and ferns. It's nicely accessible, fairly level and a good choice for wheelchair or scooter users.

Other accessible trails on the road to Flamingo are the Pahayokee Trail, the Mahogany Hammock Trail and West Lake Trail. These boardwalk trails are all less than three-quarters of a mile long, and each offers a slightly different view of the Everglades.

The Pahayokee Trail, located 12.5 miles from the park entrance, is a good place to see alligators hidden in the sawgrass and cypress vegetation. A short boardwalk leads to a ramped observation tower.

Seven miles down the road, the Mahogany Hammock Trail winds through a magnificent tropical mahogany jungle. There are a few slight inclines on this trail, but following the trail in a counter-clockwise direction helps minimize them.

West Lake Trail, located 30.5 miles from the park entrance, offers a nice stroll through the mangrove forest that surrounds West Lake. Raccoons, lizards and snakes are the prevalent wildlife along this trail. Mosquitoes can get quite heavy along this trail, especially in the summer, so be sure and pack plenty of insect repellent.

Lodging facilities are extremely limited inside the park, especially after Hurricanes Wilma and Katrina severely damaged Flamingo Lodge. Until the lodge is repaired, the best choice for overnighters is the Flamingo Campground, which has accessible campsites and restrooms.

On the northern end of the Everglades, the Shark Valley Visitor Center is located along US 41, 25 miles west of the SW Eighth Street exit on the Florida Turnpike. There is barrier-free access to the Visitors Center, which features interpretive exhibits, a gift shop and an information desk. The Bobcat Boardwalk, located behind the Visitors Center, offers visitors a very accessible glimpse at the native vegetation. This half-mile boardwalk winds through a sawgrass slough and tropical hardwood forest and is an excellent introduction to the park.

For a more in-depth look at the native flora and fauna, join one of the Shark Valley Tram Tours. Operated by a private concessionaire, these two-hour tours are led by park-trained naturalists and include a stop at a 45-foot high ramped observation tower. Views from the tower are fabulous; in fact, it's not unusual to have 20-mile visibility. Accessible tours on the Shark Valley Tram are available but advance arrangements are a must. Your best bet is to call at least 48 hours in advance to reserve your spot. It's a great tour and a very accessible way to get a good overview of the diverse Everglades ecosystem.

- IF YOU GO
  - Everglades National Park, (305) 242-7700, www.nps.gov/ever
  - Shark Valley Tram Tours, (305) 221-8455, www.sharkvalleytramtours.com

EXPLORING THE ADIRONDACKS

Located in upstate New York, the Adirondack Mountain region offers a wide range of accessible trails, recreational activities and lodging options. Known collectively as the Adirondacks, this area includes a patchwork of public and private lands dotted with backcountry trails, state parks, forest service lands, private homes, lodges and quaint villages.

Although many area parks offer some accessible campsites and trails, the shining star for accessibility is John Dillion Park, where *all* the trails, campsites and recreational areas are accessible. Located just 15 miles from Tupper Lake, this 200-acre accessible camping and recreation development is the result of a unique partnership between Paul Smith's College and International Paper. Named for the former International Paper CEO and Paul Smith's College alumnus, the park features nine Adirondack lean-tos, over three miles of hiking trails, a fishing pier, kayak and canoe docks, picnic areas and even a pontoon boat. And all of it is accessible.

Accessible lean-to at John Dillon Park.

Best of all, it's located approximately 1.5 miles off the main road, so it gives campers a real chance to get away from the maddening crowds. Composting toilets and potable water are available at each lean-to, and the welcome center has a flush toilet and a refrigerator for medication storage. Additionally, solar-powered battery chargers can be wheeled to the lean-tos upon request.

All of the lean-tos are either ramped or built at the appropriate wheelchair-transfer height, and they come equipped with a fold-down bed, a fireplace and a picnic table.

There is no charge to use John Dillon Park, but it's open only to people with disabilities and their companions. Proof of disability, such as an America the Beautiful – National Parks and Federal Recreational Lands Pass – Access Pass or a doctor's note, is required at registration. The maximum stay is 10 days and reservations are recommended. The park is open daily in the summer and on weekends after Labor Day.

If you'd prefer a few more creature comforts while exploring the Adirondacks, then head on over to The Wawbeek, located on Upper Saranac Lake, approximately 20 miles from John Dillon Park. This turn-of-the-century Great Camp property has been lovingly restored by owners Nancy and Norman Howard and features all of the amenities of an upscale resort on 40 acres of prime Adirondack forest.

The resort features two accessible rooms: Room 2 in the Lake House and Room 3 in the Carriage House. Both accessible rooms have wide doorways and excellent pathway access, and the bathrooms are equipped with a tub/shower combination with grab bars, a hand-held showerhead, grab bars around the toilet and a roll-under sink. A portable shower chair is available upon advance request.

As an added bonus, the Lake House room features a private deck with a fantastic view of the lake. Alternatively there is a large public deck in the Lake House, which can be used by all guests. And if you'd like a closer look at the lake, then sign up for the daily pontoon boat cruise. This hour-long cruise departs at 4 pm and the boat features roll-on access.

No visit to the Adirondacks is complete without a stop at the Adirondack Visitor Interpretive Center, located 15 miles from Saranac Lake on Route 30, near Paul Smith's College. There is accessible parking near the visitors center and level access to the building and the nearby picnic area. Inside you'll find interpretive exhibits about the wildlife and natural history of the Adirondacks.

Outside, the Barnum Brook Trail is a good choice for power wheelchair users and slow walkers; however some manual-wheelchair users may require assistance with the uphill sections of the trail. The trail winds through a stand of white pines and out to a boardwalk viewing platform over the marsh. From there it follows Barnum Brook, crosses over a fish dam and circles back up to the beginning. The .8-mile trail is rated as "accessible with assistance," and because of the dirt surface, it's not a good choice in wet weather.

For a good primer of Adirondack wildlife, check out the Wild Center in Tupper Lake. This natural history museum of the Adirondacks features interpretive exhibits, live animals and education programs about the flora and fauna of the region. There is excellent access throughout the museum, with a level entry, barrier-free access to all exhibits and accessible restrooms.

Outside, you can experience a real slice of Adirondack life on one of the three trails that dot the 31-acre campus. The interpretive trail that leads to the boardwalk over Blue Pond is wheelchair accessible, so save some time to enjoy it.

Finally, if you'd like to relax and enjoy the scenery, head on over to the Veterans Memorial Highway for a drive to the top of Whiteface Mountain.

This five-mile drive offers spectacular views of the Adirondacks and features several turnouts along the way. Up on top, there is elevator access to Whiteface Castle, which features a number of viewing platforms around its perimeter. The flagstone pathways that circle the castle are bumpy and uneven in places, but it's still possible to access most of the viewing platforms. The view is great and it's the perfect way to top off an Adirondack visit.

- IF YOU GO
  - John Dillon Park, (518) 524-6226 (summer), (518) 327-6266 (winter), www.johndillonpark.org
  - The Wawbeek, (518) 359-2656, www.wawbeek.com
  - Wild Center, (518) 359-7800, www.wildcenter.org
  - Adirondack Visitor Interpretive Center, (518) 327-3000, www.adirondackvic.org
  - Lake Placid Essex County Visitors Bureau, (518) 523-2445, www.lakeplacid.com

MAGICAL MAUI

Although Maui has long held the reputation of being a party haven, there is life beyond the bars and night spots on this scenic Hawaiian island. Truth be told, Maui has a lot of offer anybody who enjoys the outdoors, from scenic drives and garden walks to diving and kayaking. And the good news is, there are many accessible options.

A good way to get an overview of the island is from the air, and Sunshine Helicopters offers a number of accessible flight-seeing tours. Wheelchair users are transferred to a portable lift to board the helicopter and then transferred to the helicopter seat for the tour. The staff is excellent in regard to accessibility issues, so, if you've ever dreamed of flying in a helicopter, this is the place to give it a try. Flights range in length from 30 minutes to an hour and tour choices include West Maui, Hana/Haleakala or a Circle Island tour. Although other Maui helicopter services advertise accessibility, they are only able to accommodate wheelchair users because Sunshine Helicopter graciously lends

Sunshine Helicopters' portable boarding lift.

out their boarding device; so, in the end, it seems only fitting to patronize the business that invested the time and money in accessibility.

Back on the ground, if you'd like a look at the plants and flowers of Maui, then head over to the Maui Tropical Plantation. Although visitors are free to roam the gardens of this 60-acre plantation on their own, the narrated tram tour is a good option for slow walkers and wheelchair users, as it covers a lot of ground and offers an interesting commentary on Hawaii's native plants and most popular crops. The coconut-husking demonstration near the end of the tour is worth the price of admission by itself. There is ramp access to the tram and barrier-free pathways to most of the garden areas. Slow walkers can also take their manual wheelchairs with them; however the ramp on the tram cannot accommodate scooters.

Another interesting Maui attraction is the Sugar Cane Train, which departs from Lahaina. Billed as Hawaii's only day excursion steam train, it travels over 36-inch gauge tracks. There is lift access to the train and level access to the Lahaina station. Visitors can opt to get off in Kaanapali and return on a later train or just do the tour as a round-trip excursion. The narrated tour offers insight on the sugar cane industry and the Hawaii of yesterday. There are some great views along the way and it's really a must-do for train buffs.

If you'd like to get a little more active and have some fun in the water, then check out Lahaina Divers or Ron Bass's kayaking adventures. Lahaina Divers operates a variety of dive trips in their wheelchair-accessible *Dominion*. This vessel features good pathway access and a truly accessible (and very spacious) head. All staff members are certified as Handicapped Scuba Association (HSA) dive buddies and co-owner Akiyo Murata is a certified HSA instructor. Murata's top pick for disabled divers is their afternoon one- or two-dive trip to Turtle Reef.

If you'd prefer to stay in a boat (at least most of the time), Ron Bass offers personalized kayaking instruction and excursions. Even if you've never kayaked before, Ron can help you enjoy the sport with minimal instruction. Part of the secret to Ron's success is his location (which I've been sworn to secrecy on, so I can only say it's a "very special place") and part is because of his great way with people and his ability to adapt just about anything and everything at a moment's notice. Ron launches from a very accessible yet deserted stretch of beach, and he is truly the master at rigging up accessible modifications on the spot. Better yet, Ron is one of those very rare people who really loves what he does, and it shows in his attitude. If you've ever wanted to try kayaking, give Ron a call and he will work with you to make it happen.

Of course no visit to Maui would be complete with taking the legendary drive to Hana. This 55-mile road along the East Maui coast features some of the most scenic spots on the island, but be forewarned it does take at least eight hours to complete the round trip. Reason being is that it's a very popular route lined with buses and tourists, and because of the curves and a number of one-lane bridges you don't exactly zip along. But then again, that's part of the charm of the drive. Be sure to fill up your tank in Paia, as it's pretty much your last chance. It's also a good idea to pick up some sandwiches, water, snacks and "Road to Hana" CD before you set off.

As far as rental cars go, all the major rental car companies at the Kahului Airport will install hand controls with 48 hours' notice. Additionally, Wheelchair Getaways has a franchise on the island that rents self-drive lift-equipped vans. Advance reservations are a must for the rental vans, as they are in short supply.

And if you'd like an accessible place to rest your head, then check out Bruce and Amy Bernhardt's two-bedroom two-bath condo in Ma'alaea. Bruce is a C 5/6 quadriplegic, so he designed the condo to be truly accessible. It has lots of maneuvering room, a roll-in shower and an accessible lanai. It's a great place to relax and rejuvenate between your Maui adventures.

- IF YOU GO
  - Sunshine Helicopters, (808) 871-5600, www.sunshinehelicopters.com
  - Maui Tropical Plantation, (808) 244-7643,
    www.mauitropicalplantation.com
  - Sugar Cane Train, (808) 667-6851, www.sugarcanetrain.com
  - Lahaina Divers, (808) 667-7496, www.lahainadivers.com
  - Ron Bass Kayaking, (808) 572-6299, www.maui.net/~kayaking/access
  - Wheelchair Getaways, (650) 589-5554, www.wheelchairgetaways.com
  - Bruce & Amy's Accessible Condo, (800) 820-8220,
    www.mauiaccessiblecondo.com

SPRING MIGRATION ON LAKE ERIE

S pring is prime time for birding on the Lake Erie shore. Located at the junction of two major flyways, this area plays host to more than 340 species during the spring migration. Although a steady flow of migrants pass through the area beginning in late March, massive numbers of northbound warblers descend at the height of the migration in mid-May. It's truly a spectacular sight.

The good news is, most of the prime viewing locations offer some level of wheelchair access. Accessible choices are available on the Canadian and American shores, as well as on some Lake Erie islands. Additionally, many birding areas sponsor special events during this very colorful time of the year.

Located 30 miles southeast of Windsor, Point Pelee National Park is known as the warbler capitol of the world. The Point Pelee Visitor Center presents a good overview of the area, with interpretive exhibits, films, books and interactive displays. The Visitor Center has level access, barrier-free pathways and accessible restrooms. An access guide is available at the front desk, and an all-terrain wheelchair is available for loan.

Just outside the Visitor Center, you'll find the free shuttle to The Tip, the southernmost point in mainland Canada. You can also drive down to The Tip, but parking is limited there during peak birding times. The open-air shuttles, which are ramped and can carry up to six wheelchairs, are really the best transportation choice.

Accessible yurt on Kelleys Island.

Down at The Tip, you'll find more interpretive exhibits, accessible rest-rooms and a half-mile hard-packed dirt trail that leads out to a sandspit on Lake Erie. During the spring migration, the trees along this trail are filled with songbirds. At the end of the trail, there is a wheelchair-height viewing scope on an accessible deck at the sandspit. The Tip is a great area to explore, as it allows visitors an up-close-and-personal (yet accessible) nature experience.

During the spring migration, Friends of Point Pelee and Point Pelee National Park offer a number of special events with their annual Festival of Birds. Slated to run for the entire month of May, this migratory celebration features special workshops, speakers, hikes and even a birding breakfast. Shuttle hours are also extended during May (from 6 am to 8 pm) so birders have more time to enjoy The Tip.

Another option is to enjoy the migration from the middle of Lake Erie, on Kelleys Island. The Kelleys Island Ferry offers year-round service to the island from the Marblehead Peninsula in Northern Ohio. There is ramp access to the ferry; however, there is one step at the threshold to the passenger cabin. On the other hand, it's only a 20-minute ride, and it's really quite pleasant to enjoy the view from the open deck.

The best way to view the migration is from the campground on the north shore of the island. In fact, you can have a front row (yet very private) seat on the deck at one of the accessible yurts. These circular canvas structures have wood floors, electricity and even running water. Each yurt sleeps six people in the common main room and includes a full kitchen and a bathroom with a roll-in shower. Access features include a ramped entry to a large deck, wide doorways, level thresholds, and excellent pathway access. The yurts rent for $100 per night, with a seven-night minimum. It's a great way relax and enjoy the migration.

Of course if you'd prefer a day hike, head over to the Magee Marsh Wildlife Area on the Ohio shore. Located 17 miles west of Port Clinton on the Mississippi Flyway, this 2,000-acre area is considered one of the top ten birding spots in North America.

Your first stop should be the Sportsman's Migratory Bird Center, which is located near the entrance, just of Highway 2. The center features interpretive exhibits about the area, an information center and rangers on duty to field questions. Access is good throughout the center, with a ramped entrance, level thresholds and plenty of room to wheel around. Outside there is also a short paved path through the surrounding marshland.

The big attraction of the area during the spring migration is the appropriately named Bird Trail. This .6-mile boardwalk winds through seven acres of forested beach ridge and marshland, and, in the spring, it's home to large population of migrating warblers. The wide level boardwalk is shaded by trees and it features several viewing stations. Pack a picnic lunch and make a day out of it. It's an excellent place to view the spring migration.

- IF YOU GO
  - Point Pelee National Park, (519) 322-2365 general information, (519) 322-2371 migration update (recorded), www.pc.gc.ca/pn-np/on/pelee/index_e.asp
  - Friends of Point Pelee, (519) 326-6173, www.friendsofpointpelee.com
  - Kelleys Island Ferry, (419) 798-9763, www.kelleysislandferry.com
  - Kelleys Island Yurts, (866) 644-6727, www.dnr.state.oh.us/parks/parks/lakeerie.htm
  - Magee Marsh Wildlife Area, (419) 836-7758, www.dnr.state.oh.us/parks/parks/cranecrk.htm

YEAR-ROUND FUN IN WHISTLER, BC

Located just two hours north of Vancouver, Whistler has a solid reputation as a world-class skiing destination. But does this skiing hot spot have anything to offer travelers after the snow melts? Gladly the answer is a resounding yes. From hiking and handcycling to zip-lining and mountain biking, there's a variety of recreational offerings throughout the year. And as the venue for the 2010 Paralympic Games, look for Whistler to become even more accessible as the event approaches.

Whistler is largely a pedestrian village, which is a great bonus for wheelers and slow walkers. You can park at your hotel or in the day lots across from the main village and explore the shops, restaurants and galleries along on the paved Village Stroll. That said, different areas of the village have different levels of access, and, depending on your ability and stamina, you may prefer one over the other.

The most accessible area of the main village is located near Skiers' Plaza and the Whistler Village Gondola. In fact, local access experts advise visitors to find lodging near the gondola for the best access. That's not to say that other parts of the main village aren't wheelable; however, if you can't do distances, rest assured you won't have to go far to find a large selection of restaurants, galleries, pubs and shops in this part of the village.

North Village, which is located downhill from Skiers' Plaza and across the pedestrian bridge, also has a large selection of shops, restaurants and hotels; however, be aware that it's a sustained uphill trek back to the top. It's very doable for power wheelchairs and scooters, but it may present problems for some manual wheelchair users. Still there are lots of places to explore and take a break along the Village Stroll, so you can certainly take your time getting back up to Skiers' Plaza.

Most of the buildings in the main village have at least one accessible entrance; however, you may have to look around a bit to find the entrance. If you have questions or need assistance, then look around for a Village Host. These volunteer ambassadors are easy to spot in their red shirts as they roam the village offering assistance and information to visitors. They are very knowledgeable about accessible restaurants, shops, restrooms, walking routes and even outfitters.

The Village Stroll in Whistler, British Columbia.

And if you want to venture out beyond the village, then call Resort Cabs Whistler to order a wheelchair-accessible taxi. This is the first company in Whistler to offer this service, but, with the upcoming Paralympics, I expect it won't be the last.

No matter when you visit Whistler, a view from the top of Whistler Mountain is a must. In the winter, the Whistler Village Gondola transports skiers from the village up to the ski runs, whereas during the summer months the gondola is filled with mountain bikers and sightseers.

There is level access to the ticket booth at the Whistler Village Gondola and good pathway access to the boarding area. Wheelchair users can just roll on to the gondola cars, which can comfortably accommodate one wheelchair user and two or three able-bodied people (depending on how much ski equipment you have).

Up at the top, there is level access to the first floor of Roundhouse Lodge and elevator access up to the second floor. For the best view, head to the front patio on the second floor, which overlooks the mountain below. Dining options at Roundhouse Lodge include the casual lodge cafeteria and the full-service Steeps Grill, both of which are wheelchair accessible.

If you'd prefer a more active holiday, then contact the folks at Whistler Adaptive Sports, as they are the experts in Whistler's accessible outdoor offerings. Of course they operate their own programs, including an adaptive ski school, handcycling clinics, kayaking, canoeing and hiking trips; however they also work with local suppliers to make other activities accessible.

As Executive Director, Chelsey Walker, points out, "We consider ourselves a clearinghouse and referral service for adaptive activities in the area. We know we can't do everything personally, so we work with local outfitters so they can offer accessible activities."

And there are plenty of opportunities to get active in Whistler. For example, if you are interested in zip-lining, the folks at Whistler Adaptive Sports can refer you to a village outfitter who can accommodate wheelchair users. And if you'd like to try a handcycling tour, Chelsey suggests you contact Emma Bayliffe at Access Sea to Sky. Emma offers handcycle rentals as well as introductory handcycle tours of the Valley.

Truly there's something for just about everyone in Whistler. Additionally the focus is on integration at Whistler Adaptive Sports. "Our programs are not just for disabled people," emphasizes Chelsey. "We encourage able-bodied friends and family to join in on the fun, too." Adds Chelsey, "Our goal is to make Whistler the most accessible mountain community in the world." And from what I've seen, they have an excellent shot at achieving that goal.

- IF YOU GO
  - Resort Cabs Whistler, (604) 938-1515
  - Whistler Gondola, (604) 932-3434, www.whistlerblackcomb.com
  - Whistler Adaptive Sports, (604) 935-9406, www.whistleradaptive.com
  - Access Sea to Sky, (604) 905-2570
  - Tourism Whistler, (800) Whistler, www.whistler.com

A Place to Rest Your Head

BEACH COTTAGES ON THE OUTER BANKS

. . . .

Imagine the following scenario. You are charged with planning the perfect vacation for your family, but, the problem is, everyone wants to do something different. Your daughter wants to work on her tan, your son wants to play video games, your brother-in law wants to try out his new digital camera and your husband wants to fish. You just want to kick back and enjoy that new novel you've been meaning to read and maybe go out for dinner once or twice. Oh, and of course everything has to be wheelchair accessible. How in the world can you make the whole family happy?

Well, one solution is to rent a beach cottage on North Carolina's Outer Banks, a chain of barrier islands on the Atlantic Seaboard, 90 miles south of Norfolk, Virginia. It's the perfect place to unwind, enjoy a little natural beauty and just relax. Most of the larger beach cottages have pools, spas, gourmet kitchens, beach access, barbecues and games. And with up to nine bedrooms in the cottages, you can split the cost with another family or invite along some friends. There's lots of room to spread out, so everyone can do their own thing yet still be under the same roof. It's the perfect family vacation.

And with more than 14,000 units on the market, cottage rentals are big business in the Outer Banks. That's good news for wheelers and slow walkers because, with such a large inventory, there are accessible choices.

Seaside Realty has two wheelchair-accessible cottages: The Carolinian (7710) and Feelin' Good Again (7905). Both cottages are located on the beach in South Nags Head.

The seven-bedroom Carolinian features wide doorways, good pathway access and elevator access to all floors. The ground floor is the recreation area and kids floor, and it comes complete with a pool table, computer and kids bedrooms, plus a spacious patio with a lift-equipped swimming pool, wet bar and refrigerator. The whole patio area is fenced, so there's lots of privacy. It's a great place for a barbecue or a pool party.

The accessible bedroom is located on the second floor. It has a private bathroom with a roll-in shower, grab bars in the shower and around the toilet and a roll-under sink. There is sliding-door access to the second-floor deck

Accessible beach house SS19 in Nags Head.

from the accessible bedroom and a great view of the ocean from just about anywhere in the bedroom. The kitchen, living area and dining room are located on the third floor. There is also an accessible over-dune boardwalk out to the beach, with stairway access down to the beach.

Feelin' Good Again also has good pathway access, elevator access to all floors and a lift-equipped swimming pool on the ground floor patio. This nine-bedroom cottage features several bedrooms that are appropriate for slow walkers, but the most accessible choice is on the third floor. It has a private bathroom with a low-step shower (with a five-inch lip), a soaking tub and grab bars that are attached to the toilet. This home also has a wheelchair-accessible boardwalk out to the beach, with stairway access down to the beach.

Village Realty, another local company that handles rental cottages, also has one wheelchair-accessible property, Cottage SS19, located in the Village at Nags Head. This seven-bedroom cottage features elevator access to all floors, wide doorways and a roll-in sauna on the first floor. The accessible bedroom is located on the third floor, and it features a hallway bathroom with a roll-in shower, a hand-held shower head and grab bars in the shower and around the toilet. It also has a beautiful wrap-around deck that connects to a private ocean-view boardwalk. There is level access to the deck from the second floor, and it's a great place to enjoy the sunset.

As far as equipment goes, remember to bring your own shower chair or make arrangements to rent one locally, as none of the cottages come equipped with them. Additionally, for a little beach fun, you can rent a beach wheelchair at Lifesaver Rent-alls or borrow one from the Nags Head Fire Department.

A beach cottage is the perfect holiday solution for a diverse group, as there's plenty of room to spread out and you can do as little or as much as you want during your coveted vacation time. In the end, you really can please everyone.

- IF YOU GO
  - Seaside Realty, (252) 261-5500, www.seasiderealty.com
  - Village Realty, (252) 480-2224, www.villagerealtyobx.com
  - Lifesaver Rent-alls, (252) 441-6048
  - Nags Head Fire Department, (252) 441-5909
  - Outer Banks Visitors Bureau, (252) 473-2138, www.outerbanks.org

CABIN FEVER

Cabins are the ideal vacation choice for people who enjoy the outdoors yet cringe at the possibility of pitching a tent. And rental cabins, more specifically accessible rental cabins, come in all shapes and sizes. Indeed, you'll find them at national and state parks, recreation areas, forests and wilderness sites across the US. Some are privately owned whereas others are owned and operated by nonprofit organizations or the government. From rustic cabins to luxury chalets, there's something to fit just about every taste and budget. So if the thought of sleeping under the stars strikes terror in your very soul, check out these accessible alternatives.

West cabin at Dale Petkovsek's Sunset Pines Resort. Photo courtesy of Dale Petkovsek.

Located three miles east of Ely in northern Minnesota, Veterans on the Lake Resorts has 31 rental cabins, including seven that are accessible. The resort is in the heart of the Boundary Waters Canoe Wilderness on 25 acres of land with 2,700 feet of picturesque shoreline. Resort facilities include a day lodge, a dining room, boat rentals, campfire pits, a lift-equipped swimming pool and a sauna.

The one- to three-bedroom accessible cabins vary in configuration. Access features include hospital beds and bathrooms equipped with roll-in showers and fold-down shower seats. There are kitchen facilities in the accessible cabins, but an optional meal plan is available if you'd prefer to forego the kitchen chores while on holiday. And, as the name implies, booking priority is given to veterans or active-duty military personnel; however, everyone is welcome on a space-available basis.

Over in eastern Oklahoma, Greenleaf State Park boasts a fully accessible lakeside cabin available to anyone with a disability. Located three miles south of Braggs, on State Highway 10, this one-bedroom cabin was constructed as a volunteer project by the Oklahoma Chapter of the Telephone Pioneers of America. It's furnished with a hospital bed and a double bed, and it includes a Hoyer lift and a roll-in shower. The cabin features good pathway access, and it's outfitted with a fireplace, a full kitchen, a screened-in porch, a beautiful lakeside picnic area and a fully accessible floating fishing dock. Greenleaf State Park also has a miniature golf course, a children's fishing pond and a wetlands area, all of which are fully accessible.

If a mountain chalet is more your style, then check out Vicki Woods' Creekside Chalet near Watuga Lake in Butler, Tennessee. Technically this property is part of Vicki's Iron Mountain Inn; however it's really a stand-alone cabin, as it's located away from the main inn, between the mountain and a crackling creek. As they say, location is everything.

The three-bedroom cabin features ramp access, an open floor plan, an accessible bedroom and a bathroom with a roll-in shower. "Nearby Watuga Lake is simply beautiful," says Woods. She adds, "There are paved trails suitable for wheelchairs at Roan Mountain State Park. And Sycamore Shoals has a lovely two-mile long riverside trail. It's just a beautiful area."

Over in southeastern Maryland, just 32 miles from Washington, DC, Smallwood State Park has six accessible rustic cabins. Described as "wooden tents" by the park ranger, these mini-cabins are an affordable outdoor lodging option. Two of the cabins are located in the woods, two overlook the creek and two are close to the creek. All cabins have electricity, air conditioning, an accessible fire ring and a picnic table. A community bathhouse with roll-in showers is located nearby. Accessible facilities at Smallwood State Park include a floating marina, a boat launch, a shore side pedestrian walkway and an accessible fish-cleaning station.

And finally, if you'd like to steal away to the Wisconsin woods, then check out Dale Petkovsek's Sunset Pines Resort located near Willard, just 130 miles east of Minneapolis. Dale's purpose-built two-bedroom accessible cabins are furnished with open-framed queen- and full-sized beds, plus a sleeper sofa in the living room. The bathrooms have a roll-in shower, grab bars in the shower and around the toilet, a roll-under sink and a portable shower chair. The kitchen is furnished with appliances and utensils and the front patio allows a gorgeous view of the private lake.

Sunset Pines Resort is located on 40 wooded acres, with accessible paths, viewing blinds, fishing piers and a beach with a cement pad. A pontoon boat is also available for use by guests. As Dale points out, it's a truly accessible resort, as he took the outside features as well as the building designs into consideration when planning for accessibility. And from what I can see, he did an excellent job.

- IF YOU GO

  - Veterans on the Lake Resort, (800) 777-7538,
    www.veterans-on-the-lake.com
  - Greenleaf State Park Cabin, (918) 487-5196
  - Creekside Chalet, (423) 768-2446, www.creeksidechalet.net
  - Smallwood State Park Cabins, (888) 432-2267
  - Sunset Pines Resort, (715) 267-6989, www.sunsetpinesresort.com

EH, WHAT LODGE?

Some folks say it's all in a name, and when a friend of mine told me about the Eh Canadian Lodge, admittedly my first reaction was laughter. And who can blame me? But then I thought about it for few minutes, and I came to the conclusion that the innkeepers probably had a pretty good sense of humor. After all, would dullards name their property the Eh Canadian Lodge? Probably not. So, in my reasoning, it followed that the Eh Canadian Lodge was probably a pretty fun and welcoming place. I have to admit the fact that they advertised a fairly high level of accessibility for a somewhat remote region of British Columbia also piqued my interest. In the end, it was no contest — the Eh Canadian lodge was a must-see for me.

And I was not disappointed.

Actually getting there is half the fun, As if you approach the lodge from the west, you'll travel through Glacier National Park, whereas, if you come from the east, you'll pass through Jasper and Banff country. Both drives are very scenic, and the Eh Canadian Lodge makes a good base for exploring the natural beauty in either direction. The lodge itself is located in Blaeberry, approximately 15 minutes west of Golden.

Opened in 2005, the lodge was built by innkeepers Loren and Denise English, with wood harvested from their 300-acre private farm woodlot. Originally it was going to be a family home, but, with their kids off at college and starting lives of their own, it seemed a bit large for empty nesters; hence, the idea for the B&B was born.

The three-story lodge features five guest rooms and a common area on each floor. The main entrance, which is on the second floor, has ramped

Great Room at the Eh Canadian Lodge.

access, wide doorways and level access over the threshold. Accessible parking is available near the end of the ramp.

Inside there is barrier-free access to all of the common areas on the second floor, including the kitchen, dining area, living room and deck. There are wood floors throughout the lodge, which makes wheeling a breeze. The accessible guest room, Willow, is also located on this floor, and it's furnished with a queen-sized bed and a bathroom with a roll-in shower. Other access features include pocket-door access to the bathroom, a fold-down shower bench, a hand-held showerhead, grab bars in the shower and around the toilet and a roll-under-sink.

I was particularly impressed that the shower bench was set at a very convenient transfer height of 16 inches. This is something you don't usually see, and, in fact, many shower benches are installed dangerously high for a safe transfer. Upon further discussion, I learned that one of Denise's friends who is a quadriplegic helped her sort out some of the access issues in the lodge. And he did a good job, as he also let Denise know that there isn't one perfect access solution for everyone. Armed with that knowledge, Denise understands the diversity in needs and does her best to accommodate all of her guests on an individual basis. In short, Denise gets an A-plus for her attitude.

Admittedly Eh Canadian Lodge is a work in progress, and Denise and Loren are still working on the outside landscaping; however, when all is said and done, they hope to have an accessible path from the main parking lot down to the first-floor patio. Currently the only way to access the first-floor TV room is by a flight of stairs, so it's hoped that this new pathway will rectify that problem.

The Eh Canadian Lodge is a great spot for anybody who loves the outdoors, as you can simply relax and enjoy the view from the second-floor deck or pack a picnic lunch and head over to the accessible Hemlock Grove Boardwalk in nearby Glacier National Park. Or gather the family together and rent out the whole lodge for a family reunion, and enjoy the beauty of British Columbia together. No matter how you slice it, the Eh Canadian Lodge gets high marks for ambiance, access and attitude, and, in my book, that's a winning combination.

- IF YOU GO
  - Eh Canadian Lodge, (250) 344-2798, www.ehcanadianlodge.com

FLORIDA VILLAS

Although the term *villa* usually conjures up images of a palatial Italian estate complete with a butler, maid and cook, that's not the definition used in the Florida rental market. In the Sunshine State, the term has a much simpler meaning — a large rental house. In short, a Florida villa usually has at least three bedrooms (sometimes many more), two bathrooms, a good-sized living space and sometimes even a pool.

And villas are big business in Florida, as they are an extremely popular family vacation option. Prices vary depending on the size of the villa, but if you have a large family or if you split the cost with friends, it's still very affordable. Additionally you can cook your own meals or even have a pizza delivered to cut down on food costs.

As with other lodging options, only a small percentage of the villas are accessible; however, because of the large concentration of these rental properties in Florida, there are a number of accessible choices. Here are a few favorites.

Located on the Gulf Coast in Cape Coral, the three-bedroom Silver Star Vacation Home features wide doorways, level thresholds and good pathway access throughout the house. The large master suite includes a bathroom with grab bars by the toilet, a roll-under sink and a roll-in shower with a portable shower chair. Outside, there is level access to the large lanai and lift access to the pool. Information about the availability of local accessible transportation is also available from the owner. This German-owned property sleeps up to six people and it rents for $800 to $900 per week, depending on the number of occupants.

Over in the Orlando area, the four-bedroom Awayday Holiday Home is located just south of Disney World. There is barrier-free access throughout the property, and the home features a level entry and wide doorways. All three of the bathrooms have toilet grab bars, whereas two bathrooms have a roll-in shower. A portable shower/commode chair is available upon request. The heated pool is equipped with a water-powered pool lift that can also be used to access the spa. Owner Ian Day rents the home for $800 per week throughout the year.

Another accessible Orlando villa is owned by Roger Whittle, who resides in the UK but loves to vacation in Florida. He rents out his four-bedroom villa when he is not in residence, and he is particularly proud of the access features of his property. He is quick to point out that, as a wheelchair user, he designed the villa to be truly accessible. This four-bathroom villa includes two master suites and it's the ideal option for two families. One of the master bathrooms features a roll-in shower with a built-in shower bench, grab bars and a roll-under sink.

Pathway access is excellent throughout the home, including around the pool (which has a hoist) and the lanai. Roger's villa can sleep up to eight people and it rents for $790 to $1,140 per week, depending on the season. As an added bonus, the property backs up to an orange grove for extra privacy.

Finally, if you are looking for something a little beyond your standard villa, then check out this Key Largo Beach House. This executive bay-front home is located on Blackwater Sound in Key Largo, Florida. The five-bedroom four-bathroom property features a large screened-in patio with swimming pool, pool table, bar and BBQ, a private beach and a large dock. The master bathroom has a roll-in shower, a raised commode and a lowered vanity. There is elevator access to the upper floor, ramps to all outdoor areas and low-pile carpet throughout the home. Although the weekly rental rate of $4,000 is a little pricey, it's a great choice if you really want to pull out all the stops or if you'd just prefer a more exclusive vacation experience. Truly there's something to suit every taste in the Sunshine State.

- **IF YOU GO**
  - Silver Star Vacation Home, +49 231 49 48 12, www.capecoral-fl.de/ index_EN.html
  - Awayday Holiday Home, +44 1277 622 671, www.awayday-holidays.co.uk
  - Roger's Accessible Villa, +44 1242 573 233, www.accessiblefloridavillas. freeserve.co.uk
  - Key Largo Beach House, (305) 453-1900, www.keylargobeachhouse.com

HOME ON THE RANGE

D ude ranches are a great family vacation choice, as they offer kids the opportunity to have fun in the great outdoors, learn new skills and bond with family members. After all, there's something to be said for spending the evening around a campfire rather than a television set. Most dude ranches offer wholesome family fun, good food and a very attentive staff. And although access isn't exactly the cornerstone of the dude ranch industry, some properties feature accessible lodging options, whereas others go further and offer accessible riding and ranch activities.

Admittedly, finding a dude ranch that meets specific access needs can be quite a chore. Although there isn't a centralized database of accessible dude ranches, Gene Kilgore's "Ranch Web" website allows users to search for wheelchair-accessible properties. The problem is, there isn't a standard definition of wheelchair accessible for this site, and property owners are free to self-rate their accessibility. So, in some cases, the listed properties only have access to the main lodge or wide doorways on the guest rooms. Still it's a great starting point, but you need to ask a lot of questions to ferret out the truly accessible properties. That said, most dude ranch owners are very accommodating — after all it is a service industry — and they will do everything in their power to make their guests comfortable.

And, on the plus side, several dude ranch owners are making an concentrated effort to make their properties accessible to everyone. Here are a few of the more accessible choices.

Surrounded by the Trinity Alps Wilderness Area in northern California, Coffee Creek Ranch has one cabin (Boot Jack) and one ranch-house room (Half-Box) that are wheelchair accessible. Both rooms have wide doorways and are furnished with two open-framed twin beds. The bathrooms have a tub/shower combination with a hand-held showerhead and a transfer bench, grab bars in the shower and around the toilet and a roll-under sink. There are paved pathways around the ranch grounds, and owners Alicia and Shane Ryan are very accommodating and will do everything possible to make your stay a memorable one.

Over in Colorado, Bill and Krista Burleigh are just as accommodating at their Laramie River Ranch. Located just outside of the Rawah Wilderness and the Roosevelt National Forest, this property was renovated to be wheelchair accessible in 1995, when an accessible bedroom was added to the main lodge. The accessible guest room features wide doorways and plenty of room to maneuver a wheelchair. Access features in the spacious bathroom include a tub/shower combination with a hand-held showerhead and a shower seat. Guests can participate in a variety of accessible outdoor activities, including fishing and nature walks, and, although adaptive riding equipment or lessons are not available, there is full access to the barn and all of the ranch facilities.

Access is also a high priority for Dan and Ellen Morin at their Sundance Trail Guest Ranch in Red Feather Lakes, Colorado. As Dan puts it "Ramps are cheap, friendships are invaluable. I've really enjoyed many of our disabled guests, and, if our ranch wasn't accessible, I would have missed out on meeting some great people."

Sundance Trail Guest Ranch has two accessible suites, the Apache Suite and the Buffalo Suite. Both suites have wide doorways and plenty of room to maneuver a wheelchair or scooter. The two-bedroom Buffalo Suite is located on the first floor of the main lodge and it has a private ramped porch in the back. The Apache Suite has one bedroom (with a loft for kids) and ramped access to the private entrance from the adjacent parking area. Both suites have bathrooms with large roll-in showers and hand-held shower heads, roll-under sinks and grab bars in the shower and toilet areas. The roll-in showers have a small lip, but they are still doable for many people.

Most of the outdoor public areas are accessible, with the exception of the chicken coop and the rabbit hutch. There are level dirt paths to the corrals and the arena. The recreation barn, which has a pool table, ping-pong table, VCR and Jacuzzi, also has ramp access.

And finally, if you are looking for that total-emersion, accessible, dude ranch experience, then check out Stagecoach Trails Ranch in Arizona. Located in Yucca, just 45 minutes from Kingman, this barrier-free dude ranch offers loads of accessible activities. Guests can choose to take a horseback ride in the desert or putt around the accessible trails in a two-seater go kart. Accessible riding facilities include ramp access to horses. A variety of adaptive riding equipment is also available. And, in keeping with the access-for-all theme here, all guest rooms and public areas (including the swimming pool) are barrier free. It's truly a place where everyone can enjoy all of the ranch activities.

- **IF YOU GO**
  - Ranch Web, www.ranchweb.com
  - Coffee Creek Ranch, (800) 624-4480, www.coffeecreekranch.com
  - Laramie River Ranch, (970) 435-5716, www.lrranch.com
  - Sundance Trail Guest Ranch, (800) 357-4930, www.sundancetrail.com
  - Stagecoach Trails, 928-727-8270, www.stagecoachtrailsranch.com

HOSTELING

I f you're looking to reign in your lodging expenses and save a few bucks on your next trip, then consider staying in a hostel. This unique lodging option first gained popularity in the 1970s when college students backpacked across Europe and frequented easy-on-the-budget youth hostels. Today the whole hostelling industry has evolved, and, although hostels still present a very affordable option for young people, they are open to travelers of all ages.

There are many advantages to hostelling. The major perk is big savings on lodging costs. Rates vary depending on the location and the amenities of the property, so expect to pay more in the larger cities and less in the country. Another advantage to hostelling is that you can meet other travelers. And, finally, cooking your meals can cut down on food costs.

A painter captures the Pigeon Point Lighthouse, which houses an accessible hostel.

Hostels traditionally offer dormitory-style bedrooms, with separate quarters for males and females. Today many hostels also have private family rooms, which can be reserved in advance. Most hostels still have kitchens, and all have storage areas and public rooms. Some hostels even have swimming pools, barbecues and hot tubs. And today, many hostels are also accessible.

Most hostel managers are also very familiar with the access features of their property. As an added bonus, they are also incredibly honest about their access, as they don't want guests to be disappointed when they arrive. Even though this is a budget lodging option, it's still a service-oriented industry and hostel managers want all their guests to be happy. They rely heavily on repeat business, personal endorsements and word-of-mouth advertising to keep their properties full. In short, they don't want disappointed customers.

The best way to locate an accessible hostel is through Hostelling International (HI). You can search their on-line database, which lists more than 4,000 member hostels in 75 countries. Although accessible hostels are noted in the database, specific access details are not given. Your best bet is to contact the property directly to make sure it fits your access needs.

Accessible hostels come in all shapes and sizes. Some properties, like the HI Fisherman's Wharf Hostel, have even upgraded their accessible rooms. Says manager Rick Young, "We sought input from a number of local disability organizations during the construction of our accessible wing. It took a little longer, but it was well worth the effort." The new wing features an accessible kitchen, a bathroom with a roll-in shower and 2 dorm rooms. It's very nicely done. The location is hard to beat, too, with a great view of the Golden Gate Bridge. All this for only $23 per person.

Many hostels have great locations. For example, the HI Washington DC Hostel is located near the White House, the National Mall and the Smithsonian Museums. It's the perfect locatio n for sightseeing; at a very affordable $27 per night, it's a price that's hard to beat in downtown Washington, DC.

And some hostels, like the HI Pigeon Point Hostel, are housed in unique buildings. This northern California property is located on Highway 1 in Pescadero in the lighthouse-keeper's quarters, next door to the historic Pigeon Point Lighthouse.

The hostel includes the accessible Dolphin Dorm, which has level access, wide doorways and adequate pathway access. Guests have a choice of a dorm bed or a private room. Bathroom facilities are shared in all dorms, but the Dolphin Dorm also has an accessible shower and toilet room. The accessible toilet room includes a five-foot turning radius, a roll-under sink and grab bars around the toilet; the spacious roll-in shower comes complete with a fold-down shower seat, grab bars and a hand-held showerhead. All in all it's a fun place to stay, and, at just $24 for a dorm bed or $59 for a private room, it's also very affordable.

In the end, hostels can make for a very interesting lodging choice. After all, how often do you get to sleep in a lighthouse? And don't just limit yourself to hostels in the US, as there are some wonderfully accessible hostels around the world. It's a very affordable and accessible way to travel.

- IF YOU GO
  - Hosteling International, www.hiayh.org
  - HI Fisherman's Wharf Hostel, (415) 771-7277, www.sfhostels.com
  - HI Pigeon Point Hostel, (650) 879-0633, www.norcalhostels.org

LIONS AND TIGERS AND BEARS, OH MY!

. . . .

It all began with a quick white flash and a slight movement in the bushes off to my right. A few seconds later I was able to make out a couple of amorphous shapes. Just as I was about to query our guide, Sherry slammed on the brakes of our safari vehicle. With a thunderous roar, a herd of animals ran across the road in front of us and bounded up the adjacent hill. In a few seconds they were gone. "Thompson's Gazelles," quipped Sherry "Aren't they beautiful?"

Although this may be a common sight in Africa, we weren't exactly in the wilds of the Dark Continent. In fact we were just an hour from San Francisco, at a unique wildlife sanctuary that offers visitors an accessible and intimate taste of Africa.

The brainchild of Peter Lang, Safari West is a wildlife sanctuary with a twist; it also boasts an African-style tent camp. This 400-acre game preserve is home to a bevy of exotic animals and birds, most of which roam free inside the gated compound. Visitors can take a safari tour or stay overnight in a luxury tent cabin or both. It's almost like visiting Africa, except you don't get jet lag, you save about $3,000 and you can do it in a weekend.

The 2.5-hour safari tour is conducted in an open-air vehicle. Half of the tour is a driving tour and the other half is a ranger-led walking tour. The driving tour covers the gated compound, where Watusi cattle, Cape buffalo, gazelles, zebras, ostriches and oryxes roam free. Some animals approach the vehicle; in fact, one ostrich with an attitude took a peck at me. It's all part of the unscripted wildlife experience.

The standard tour is not technically wheelchair accessible, as you must climb up a few steps to transfer into the back of the high safari vehicle. It is suitable for slow walkers because you don't have to get out of the vehicle until it returns. Alternatively, if you can transfer out of your wheelchair and climb up one large step, you can sit in the front seat.

The walking part of the tour covers the enclosures near the tent cabins, in the main area of the preserve. The total distance covered is about a city block, and golf carts are available for visitors who cannot walk the distance. This part of the tour is excellent, as it includes a look at the cheetahs and

Accessible tent cabin at Safari West.

lemurs, some close-up giraffe interaction and a stroll though the spectacular open-air aviary.

Although the standard tour is moderately accessible, wheelchair users can request a modified tour if the standard tour does not suit their needs. The modified tour covers the same area as the walking part of the standard tour, but it includes transportation by golf cart and a private naturalist guide. The plus side is that it's a more personalized tour with your own guide, but the down side is that you don't get the driving tour of the compound. Advance reservations are required for all tours, so just explain your access needs when you call.

Of course the highlight of any Safari West experience is an overnight stay. Safari West has two accessible tent cabins and two additional tent cabins that are good for slow walkers. These luxury tents all have hardwood floors, canvas sides and tops, indoor plumbing and electricity — just like the upscale safari camps in Africa.

Cabin 1H is the most accessible choice. It has a paved parking area, a ramped entry, wide doorways, ample room to maneuver a wheelchair, a roll-in shower with a fold-down shower seat, a hand-held showerhead and grab bars in the shower and around the toilet.

Cabin 2H is located up a slight dirt grade. It has the same access features as cabin 1H except it has a grass parking area, and there are no toilet grab bars. Cabins 3 and 4 are located near the dining area, have steps at the entry and are a good choice for slow walkers. The other tent cabins are located up a rather steep incline. Golf-cart transportation is available to the tent cabins, but there are no phones to call for a downhill shuttle.

All four of these tent cabins have a roomy porch with great views of the giraffe enclosure. It's the ideal place to watch the sunset and enjoy a glass of wine. Plan ahead and bring the fixings for a picnic dinner. It's the perfect way to end your African safari day.

And of course, nothing beats sleeping with the animals!

• IF YOU GO

  • Safari West, (707) 579-2551, www.safariwest.com

MURDER, THEY WROTE

I had a few problems easing into my first murder mystery weekend. To be honest, I wasn't quite sure what to expect. There I sat in the parlor of Columbia's City Hotel trying to make small talk with a woman I had just met. I was expecting some instructions, or guidance, but that's not they way a murder mystery weekend works. In a sense, all of the guests are part of the show. Throughout the weekend, the plot slowly unravels as participants use their best detective skills to try and discover who is a guest, who is just playing a role and, of course, whodunit.

All murder mystery weekends have some type of a general plot and, of course, at least one dead body. At the onset we were told that we were all gathered at the City Hotel to welcome home Toni, the local gal who had made it big on the Broadway stage. Beyond that we were pretty much left to our own devices to figure out the rest. In the end, I just tried to go with the flow.

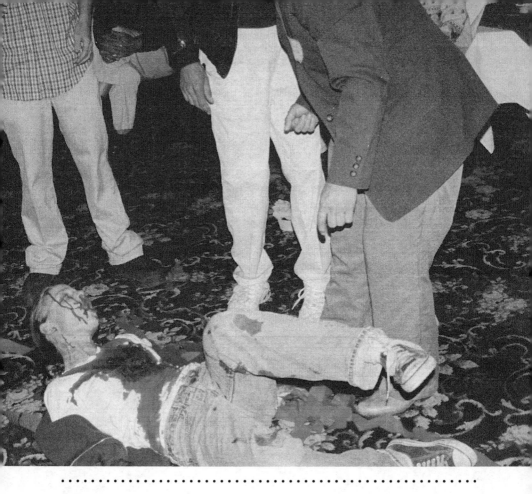

Who done it?

"So how do you know Toni?" the woman on my right asked. Caught off guard, I wasn't sure how to reply. I decided to go with an old standard. "She's an old high school friend," I stammered. "Really?" replied the woman. "Perhaps you'd like to browse through Toni's scrapbook." She handed the volume over and as soon as I turned the first page, I realized that Toni was half my age. I quickly corrected my error. "Did I say I went to high school with Toni?" I asked. "Silly me, I meant to say that my daughter went to high school with her," I added. "No more wine for me!"

Despite my clumsy beginning, my detective skills improved as the evening progressed. Soon Toni's father addressed the crowd and thanked us for coming out to welcome home his daughter. Then we all got into the spirit of things, had a few drinks and decorated the room with balloons and streamers in anticipation of Toni's arrival.

"Shhh," someone cried out "She's coming now." The lights were dimmed and we heard footsteps on the stairs. Very clumsy footsteps, I might add.

Then a woman stumbled down the stairs, clutched her chest and died right in the middle of the parlor. Stage blood oozed from her mouth as she lay twitching on the carpet for several minutes before she officially expired. At last, we had our body! And we would spend the rest of the weekend trying to unmask her killer.

Truth be told, we had an interesting cast of suspects from which to choose, from a whiskey-guzzling nun to three high school football buddies (Hank, Tank and Frank) who apparently shared one brain. Our assignment was simple; we were to comb the town, solicit clues from shopkeepers, build alliances, share information and in the end solve the mystery.

Best of all, the whole weekend was wheelchair accessible. In fact, according to City Hotel manager, Tom Bender, "If a wheelchair user signs up, we make sure all of the murder mystery activities are held in accessible locations."

Columbia provides an excellent backdrop for this popular event. Located just two hours northeast of San Francisco, in the heart of California gold country, Columbia was originally founded in 1850 as a tent town to house several thousand miners.

Today the town exists pretty much as it did during the boom days. Docents dress in period costumes and give visitors a real flavor for gold rush life. A stagecoach roars through town on a regular basis, children play with their hoops and sticks in front of the blacksmith shop and Dr. Jhon entertains Main Street visitors with a few tunes on his harmonica.

Access is varied throughout Columbia, and in many cases it is hidden in order to preserve the historic nature of the town. Some businesses have level access, some have hidden ramps, some have small thresholds and some have steps. On the plus side, vehicle traffic is prohibited in town, so it's perfectly safe to walk or roll in the streets. Boardwalk sidewalks line the streets, and although curb cuts are not the norm, there are some access points. All in all, most parts of town are at least partially accessible.

Although lodging in Columbia is extremely limited, the historic Fallon House has one wheelchair-accessible guest room (Room 14). It is located on the ground floor. It features wide doorways, good pathway access and it is the only guest room with a full bathroom. Access features in the bathroom include a roll-in shower with a fold-down shower bench and a hand-held showerhead, grab bars in the shower and around the toilet and a roll-under sink. It's simple but nicely done access wise.

Columbia murder mystery weekends are presented four times a year in January and February. They are priced at US$385 per couple and include two nights' lodging, a Friday night reception, three meals on Saturday, brunch on Sunday, entertainment, taxes and gratuities.

It's a great deal and lots of fun — even for beginners!

- **IF YOU GO**
  - Columbia Tourism Information, (209) 536-1672,
    www.columbiacalifornia.com
  - Murder Mystery Weekend Information, (209) 532-1479,
    www.cityhotel.com

SLEEPING IN PARIS
. . . .

Paris is a must-see on any European itinerary; however finding affordable and accessible lodging in the City of Lights can be quite a challenge. Budget lodging is a relative term in Paris, where rates at name hotels can easily top $300 per night. This further complicates the search for an accessible room, as the name hotels are usually the properties that offer the best access; however in Paris that access comes at a price. But it doesn't have to be that way, as with a little legwork you can turn up some accessible properties that won't break the bank.

Before you begin you search, it's important to understand something about lodging in Paris; rooms with roll-in showers are in short supply. They do exist, but, because of their limited availability, early reservations are a must. Additionally it's also important to understand that access terminology in continental Europe differs slightly from the language used in the US. In continental Europe, an accessible room is a room with adequate pathway access and doorway clearance, whereas an adapted room contains modified bathroom fixtures. So, if you need a room with a roll-in shower, ask for an adapted room rather than an accessible room. And of course always confirm that the room has a roll-in shower when you make your reservation.

It's also important to remember that in Europe the first floor is not at street level. If you want a room at street level, ask for a room on the ground floor. Some properties have tiny elevators or just stairway access to the first floor; so if you can't book a ground floor room, make sure the property has an elevator large enough to accommodate a wheelchair.

Although affordability and accessibility are important factors, location should also be considered when searching for a room in Paris. Many properties that appear to be great deals at first glance are actually located outside of Paris or far from any accessible public transportation. For the most part, the Metro is not accessible, so you will have to get around by foot, bus and taxi in Paris. And although G7 Taxis offer accessible service in ramped vans, taxi fares can add up quickly. With that in mind, here are my top Paris picks for affordability, accessibility and location.

As far as location goes, you just can't beat the Hospitel Hôtel Dieu Paris, conveniently located next door to Notre Dame Cathedral. Don't be surprised when your taxi driver drops you off at a hospital, as this 14-room property is located on the sixth floor of the oldest hospital in Paris. Don't let that put you off though, as it's hardly a sterile environment. Originally established to house friends and family of the patients, today this unique lodging option is quickly gaining popularity among tourists.

Access features include ramp access to the building, elevator access to all floors and wide doorways. Two guest rooms are designated as adapted rooms and they each contain a roll-in shower. A continental breakfast is included in the room rate, or a full breakfast can be ordered for an additional charge. One of the best features about this property is the very private classical courtyard, a great place to retreat from the hustle and bustle of the city. And at $145 per night for two people, it's a real steal.

If you'd prefer a traditional chain hotel, then check out the Ibis Tour Eiffel Cambronne. Also centrally located, this 523-room property has elevator access to all floors and eight adapted rooms. Each of the adapted rooms has a bathroom with a continental-style (roll-in) shower with a fold-down shower seat. Room rates range from $99 to $145, depending on the season.

Hostels are always a good budget option, and in Paris, the Residence Internationale de Paris tops my hostel list. It's located just east of the city, but it is near a bus stop. Be forewarned though, you need a sense of adventure to give the Paris bus system a shot. The main reason I'm including this property is because all 102 rooms are truly wheelchair accessible (complete with roll-in showers). Originally constructed by the French Federation Handisport to house disabled athletes, this property now welcomes tourists. Four people can share a room for under $100, and, in Paris, that's *really* a great deal.

- **IF YOU GO**
  - G7 Taxis, +33 1 47 39 47 39, www.taxisg7.fr
  - Hospitel Hôtel Dieu Paris, +33 1 44 32 01 00, www.hotel-hospitel.com
  - Ibis Tour Eiffel Cambronne,+33 1 40 61 21 21, www.accor-hotels.com
  - Residence Internationale de Paris, +33 1 40 31 45 45, www.residence-inter-paris.com

TIME FOR ROMANCE

Let's face it, when it comes to planning a romantic getaway, most wheelchair users entirely overlook the idea of whisking away their one-and-only to a cozy little inn or a secluded B&B. Truth be told, many folks think these properties are highly inaccessible.

Ironically, inns and B&Bs can be an ideal choice for wheelchair users. Many innkeepers have voluntarily made access modifications because they have friends or family members who need them. Additionally, most innkeepers are intimately familiar with the access features of their property. Plus, when you reserve an accessible room at an inn or B&B, you can rest assured that the room will be available for you when you arrive. This isn't always the case at larger hotels.

Indeed, sometimes access needs are more adequately addressed at smaller properties. With that in mind, here's a sampling of accessible inns and B&Bs that simply ooze romance.

First stop, Landis Shores, an eight-room luxury inn on romantic Miramar Beach, just 30 minutes south of San Francisco. The accessible San Francisco Bay room is furnished with a queen-sized open-framed bed and includes a cozy gas fireplace and a private ocean-view balcony. Access features in the bathroom include a full five-foot turning radius, a roll-in shower with a hand-held showerhead, a roll-under sink, grab bars in the shower and around the toilet and a portable shower chair.

There is barrier-free access to all of the public areas, including the living room, where wine and cheese appetizers are served every afternoon. Breakfast can be served in the dining area or delivered to your room. And for that

Bathroom in an accessible guest room (121) at The Inn at Honey Run.

romantic dinner, check out the Historic Miramar Beach Restaurant, located right next door.

Over in northern Arizona, the Lodge at Sedona offers an equally romantic setting, located on three beautifully landscaped acres and surrounded by Sedona's trademark red rock formations. The accessible Meadow Breeze Suite features barrier-free access through the front lobby and a private entrance on the back deck. Romantics take note — this private deck is the perfect place to enjoy a glass of wine and watch the sunset with your sweetheart.

This spacious suite is furnished with a king-sized bed, a fireplace and a two-person Jacuzzi tub. The continental-style bathroom includes a roll-in shower with a hand-held showerhead and grab bars in the shower and around the raised toilet. And breakfast is a grand affair here, with a full five-course meal served al fresco on the main deck.

Located in the heart of Ohio Amish country, The Inn at Honey Run is another surprising find, both in terms of access and ambiance. Far from your typical Amish inn, this unique property features sleek contemporary lines blended into a natural setting.

Room 121 has excellent pathway access and a great view of the adjacent woods, and it includes an oversized bathroom with a roll-in shower and a portable shower bench. The inn is surrounded by 60 nature-filled acres, and, although the trails aren't exactly wheelchair accessible, innkeeper Phil Jenkins is quick to suggest an appropriate solution. "We can easily take guests along the trails in our gator or golf cart," he offers. "It's a beautiful area and nobody should miss out on it."

I'd be remiss if I didn't include at least one New England property in this romantic roundup, and Vermont's Rabbit Hill Inn more than adequately fills that bill. In fact, I first learned of this property from a friend who spent a very romantic 25th-anniversary weekend there.

The wheelchair-accessible Turnabout Room at the Rabbit Hill Inn is furnished with a king-sized canopy bed, and it includes a gas fireplace in the sitting area and a whirlpool tub in the bathroom. Access features in the bathroom include a roll-in shower with a hand-held showerhead and a fold-down shower seat, grab bars in the shower and around the raised toilet and a roll-under sink. And for that perfect romantic touch, private in-room dining is available.

Last but not least, there's the Volcano Guest House, where I spent a very romantic Valentine's Day. Located on Hawaii's Big Island and surrounded by six acres of high-altitude rain forest, this unique property features three accessible units.

Claudia's Place shares the front porch with the main house, whereas Twin 1 and Twin 2 are located farther away from the main house and offer more privacy. All three units have a small kitchen, a living area and a separate bedroom. Access features include good pathway access, wooden floors, grab bars and a low-step shower in each unit. A shower chair is available upon request. Although it's not fancy, the secluded natural setting of this off-the-beaten-path property gets high marks in the ambiance department. After all, what could be more romantic than a secluded Hawaii retreat?

- IF YOU GO
  - Landis Shores, (650) 726-6642, www.landisshores.com
  - Lodge at Sedona, (928) 204-1942, www.lodgeatsedona.com
  - The Inn at Honey Run, (330) 674-0011, www.innathoneyrun.com
  - Rabbit Hill Inn, (802) 748-5168, www.rabbithillinn.com
  - Volcano Guest House, (808) 967-7775, www.volcanoguesthouse.com

Road Trips

A TASTE OF VERMONT

· ·

Vermont is the ideal choice for a summer or fall road trip, as the Green Mountain State offers some very scenic drives with a number of fun diversions along the way. One of my favorite Vermont drives begins in Waterbury near the junction of I-89 and Route 100 and circles in a counterclockwise direction over through Cabot, then across to Stowe before returning to Waterbury. Along this route you'll find quaint New England villages, local farms, rickety old barns and of course the requisite covered bridge.

Waterbury is also a good place to base yourself, and the Thatcher Brook Inn gets high marks for both access and ambiance. Even though this 22-room inn is listed on the Vermont Register of Historic Buildings, it still boasts two accessible guest rooms. The inn features accessible parking and level access to the front porch and all of the public areas.

The most accessible room is the spacious Luxury Suite, which includes a sitting room, a bedroom and an oversized bathroom. There is also a whirlpool tub and a fireplace in the bedroom. Access features in the bathroom include a five-foot turning radius, a roll-in shower with a hand-held showerhead and a built-in shower seat, grab bars in the shower and around the toilet and a roll-under sink.

Room 7 is also very spacious, but it's really better suited for slow walkers. It's furnished with a queen-sized bed and a sofa. The bathroom has a low-step shower with a hand-held showerhead, grab bars around the toilet, a roll-under sink and a full five-foot turning radius.

Whichever room you choose, there's no better way to begin your Vermont road trip than with a hearty breakfast prepared by innkeeper Lisa Fischer. You may even skip lunch!

Start your road trip by heading east on I-89 to exit 8 in Montpelier. Continue along until you hit 2 East to Marshfield, then go left on Route 215 for about 5 miles to Cabot Village. You'll find your first stop, the Cabot Cheese Factory, on your right.

The Cabot Cheese Factory features accessible parking and level access to the building. Inside you'll find the factory and a small cheese and gift shop. Guided tours are offered during the week, but it's best to call and make sure they are making cheese that day. There is a $2 fee for the tour, but its well worth it as you get a close-up look at the cheese-making process and the guides are very knowledgeable. The entire tour is level, so there's no problem maneuvering a wheelchair or scooter. And of course, cheese samples are available at the end of the tour.

After you've had your fill of cheese, continue along 215 to 15 West, then take Route 100 south to Stowe. The drive along this section of the route is particularly scenic, and Stowe Village is a nice place to stop and explore. Access varies throughout Stowe Village, but in some places there are sidewalks with curb cuts, whereas in others there aren't even any sidewalks. Don't be discouraged though, as many of the shops and restaurants feature level access; however the best bet is to park as close as possible to the business you plan to patronize.

The Vermont Ski Museum, located in the heart of the Stowe Village at the intersection of Route 100 and Route 108, is also worth a stop. Housed in the old Town Hall built in 1818, the museum focuses on the history of skiing in Vermont. The building, which is listed on the National Register of Historic Places, features ramp access from the parking lot and elevator access to all floors.

When you're done exploring Stowe Village, continue south on Route 100 and turn left on Gold Brook Road. Veer left after you cross the cement bridge, and continue along until you spot the covered bridge on your left. Known locally as Emily's Bridge, legend has it that Emily died there broken hearted, and it's said that her spirit haunts the bridge. There's no official parking place, but it's all fairly level, so just park alongside the road and wheel on over to the bridge. And watch out for Emily!

Back out on the main road, continue south on Route 100, turn right on Moscow Road and head over to 593 Moscow Road, where you'll find Little River Hotglass, the studio and gallery of glass blower, Michael Trimpol. There is a dirt parking lot in front of the studio and a small lip at the doorway, but the driveway is pretty level. Inside there is plenty of room to wheel around and observe the artist at work. Even if Michael is not there, it's worth the trip just to see his work, which features vibrant colors, original designs and unique shapes.

After you make your way back to the main road, continue south on Route 100 until you get to Waterbury. Although you've made a full circle on your road trip, you still have one more stop, Cold Hollow Cider Mill, which is located on the left side of the road as you enter town. There is plenty of accessible parking in the large lot and level access to the front entrance. Inside you

Emily's Bridge in Stowe, Vermont.

can see the cider press at work and have a sample of the cider. Free samples of jellies, mustards, fudge and other goodies are also available. Additionally there is a small store and a bakery in the building, so buy some goodies and enjoy them in the gazebo out front.

And once you've finished noshing, try a sample of some hard cider at the Grand View Winery tasting room, next door to the Cold Hollow Cider Mill. There is level access to the building and, after you've sampled some of their wines, you'll probably go home with a bottle or two. It's a great way to end the day.

- IF YOU GO
    - Thatcher Brook Inn, (800) 292-5911, www.thatcherbrook.com
    - Cabot Cheese Factory, (800) 837-4261
    - Vermont Ski Museum, (802) 253-9911, www.vermontskimuseum.org
    - Little River Hotglass, (802) 253-0889, www.littleriverhotglass.com
    - Cold Hollow Cider Mill, www.coldhollow.com

A HOCKING HILLS GETAWAY

. . . .

Located just an hour from Columbus in southeastern Ohio, the Hocking Hills area is noted for its natural beauty. Indeed, it's an ideal road-trip destination. The pace is slow, the people are extremely friendly and, because of recent access upgrades, more of it is now accessible.

As far as accessible lodging goes, The Inn at Cedar Falls is my top Hocking Hills pick. It's a great place to base yourself, as it's located just minutes from Hocking Hills State Park. Accessible choices at the inn include the two-bedroom Redbud Cabin and the one-bedroom Sumac Cottage.

The Redbud Cabin features ramped access to the front door, wide doorways and good pathway access to the first-floor kitchen, bedroom, bathroom, living area and back porch. The first-floor bathroom features a roll-in shower with a hand-held showerhead, grab bars in the shower and around the toilet, a roll-under sink and a portable shower bench. The second-floor bedroom and bathroom are only accessible by a flight of stairs, but it's a great option for kids, attendants or able-bodied friends.

The Sumac Cottage features ramped access to the front door, wide doorways and good pathway access throughout the living and sleeping area. The bathroom has a roll-in shower with a hand-held showerhead, grab bars in the shower and around the toilet, a roll-under sink and a lowered mirror. Other cottage features include an under-counter refrigerator, a spacious back porch and a whirlpool tub in the living area. A portable shower bench is available upon request. It should also be noted that, because of the bathroom configuration, scooter users will probably prefer the Sumac Cottage over the Redbud Cabin, as there is more room to turn and position a scooter in the Sumac Cottage bathroom.

Ash Cave tops the list of natural attractions in the area, and, as luck would have it, it's just down the road from the Inn at Cedar Falls. Named for the ash piles found nearby by early settlers, Ash Cave is not a cave in the traditional sense but, rather, a massive horseshoe-shaped recess. Today a nicely accessible trail leads into the recess.

There is accessible parking at the trailhead and a quarter-mile paved trail winds alongside the river down to the cave. The surrounding trees provide a nice shade cover and the level trail is easily navigable in a wheelchair

Redbud Cabin at The Inn at Cedar Falls in the Hocking Hills of Southeastern Ohio.

or a scooter. As an added bonus, there's a misty waterfall at the end of the trail right next to the cave. There are also a number of picnic tables at the trailhead, and it's a very pleasant spot for a picnic lunch or a midday break.

Just down the road, approximately 12 miles south of Logan on State Route 664, you'll find the equally scenic Conkle's Hollow State Nature Preserve. Known for its sandstone gorge, spectacular vistas and spring wildflowers, Conkle's Hollow had long been inaccessible to anybody with a mobility disability. All that changed in November 2004, when access upgrades were made.

Today the new Gorge Trail is a half-mile long and features a six-foot wide concrete path on approximately two-thirds of the trail. There are no railings along the trail, so there are some small drop offs on the sides. Although it's not technically billed as "totally ADA compliant," it's just as accessible as the Ash Cave trail. There are no steps at all along the trail and it's really a great improvement, as it allows wheelers and slow walkers a glimpse of some spectacular scenery.

Of course, you can't visit the Hocking Hills without stopping at Etta's Lunchbox Cafe, a local institution. Located south of Logan near the intersection of State Route 328 and State Route 56, this combination general store and cafe features a collection of more than 460 lunchboxes dating back to 1902. The brainchild of Tim Seewer and LaDora Ousley, the store was originally built to house LaDora's ever-growing lunchbox collection. And they are everywhere — on the shelves, the window sills, the counters and even hanging from the ceiling. It's a great walk down memory lane and, even though it's housed in a historic building, there is a level entrance at Etta's.

And then there's Tim. Suffice it to say he's a TV trivia king and a very engaging host. He's also a great cook, so order a picnic sandwich to go, or eat on the premises and enjoy the ambiance. Either way you can't miss.

And finally, a visit to the Hocking Hills just isn't complete without at least one gallery stop. Although there are a number of interesting galleries in the area, my top pick is Spirits of the Hills Gallery located on State Route 180 in Rockbridge. The gallery features the work of more than 60 Ohio artists and includes everything from stained glass items and wood carvings to photographs and watercolors. It's a small gallery but there is level access and room enough to navigate in a wheelchair. It's definitely worth a stop, as it represents the diverse range of artistic talent in southeastern Ohio.

- IF YOU GO
  - The Inn at Cedar Falls, (740) 385-7489, www.innatcedarfalls.com
  - Ash Cave, www.hockinghills.com/parks/p_ash.htm
  - Conkle's Hollow State Nature Preserve, www.dnr.state.oh.us/dnap/location/conkles_hollow.html
  - Etta's Lunch Box Cafe, (740) 380-0736, www.ettaslunchboxcafe.com
  - Spirit of the Hills Gallery, (740) 385-8245, www.sculpturebyspirit.com
  - Hocking Hills Tourism Association, (740) 385-9706, www.1800hocking.com

VIRGINIA'S CROOKED ROAD

Located in southwest Virginia, the Crooked Road is more than just a driving route. This 200-mile heritage music trail winds through Appalachia and connects music venues and heritage sites that highlight the traditional music

Get a feel of 19th century life at the Blue Ridge Institute's Farm Museum in Ferrum, Virginia.

of the region — the gospel, bluegrass and mountain music that's been passed down for generations by local families. Along the way, you'll find stage shows, outdoor concerts, festivals, Appalachian crafts, galleries and some great scenery; however it's the locals who bring the Crooked Road to life. Be it the banjo maker in Galax or the quilter in Floyd, they all have a story to tell. And part of the whole Crooked Road experience is simply taking the time to listen.

Technically the Crooked Road isn't just one road, but a route composed of many state routes and local roads. The best starting point is the eastern terminus, Rocky Point, which is located 25 miles south of Roanoke. Just take VA 40 west toward Ferrum and follow the Crooked Road signs. Not only is this the easiest access point, but Ferrum makes a great first stop, as the Blue Ridge Institute and Museum offers a good overview on the regional heritage.

Located on the campus of Ferrum College, the Blue Ridge Institute and Museum features indoor gallery space plus an outdoor heritage farm museum. The gallery space hosts exhibitions that highlight the people and heritage of the region. There is level access to the museum, barrier-free access throughout the galleries and plenty of accessible parking outside.

Across the street, take some time to look through the Farm Museum, which has gravel and dirt pathways, ramps up to the barns and a few steps up into the farmhouse. The pathways are doable for most people in dry weather, and, even though you can't access every display, you can still get a good feel for what Virginia farm life was like back in 1800.

Traveling west on the Crooked Road, you'll cross the Blue Ridge Parkway and enter Floyd County. Here's where a little diversion is in order. Although it's not on the official route, I highly recommend at least a short drive on the Blue Ridge Parkway, as it's very scenic. Either way, a stop in Floyd is a must, and, if you are looking for overnight accommodations, look no further than the Oak Haven Lodge.

Opened in 2003, this 10-room rustic lodge features ramp access to the front porch and office, with accessible parking available in a gravel parking area next to the office. Room 1 is located downstairs and has wide doorways, two double beds, good pathway access and a 5-foot turnaround in the bathroom. Access features in the bathroom include a low-step shower, a roll-under sink, grab bars in the shower and around the toilet and a portable shower chair. A commode chair is also available upon request. All this is available for a very affordable $65 per night.

Continuing west, you'll pass through Galax and Abingdon before coming to Bristol. Here you'll find the Birthplace of Country Music Alliance Museum, which features exhibits on the roots of country music and the musicians who helped shape the genre. Access is excellent throughout the museum, with a level entrance and barrier-free access to all the exhibits. Best of all, admission is free.

There's plenty of live music to be had in Bristol, too, with weekly concerts at the Birthplace of Country Music Mural on Monday, Tuesday and Thursday nights and a Thursday morning jam session at the Star Barbershop on State Street. All of these musical events are free and open to the public. And as far as access goes, there is good wheelchair access to the seating area at the mural and level access to the Star Barbershop.

Finally, no matter what you do on your Crooked Road adventure, save time for a visit to the Carter Family Fold for a Saturday night concert. Granted some advance planning is required to plan a Saturday night stay near the Hiltons, but fortunately it's only about 20 minutes from Bristol.

Located on the AP and Sara Carter homestead, the Carter Family Fold is actually a large theater and, in keeping with tradition, only acoustic instruments are allowed and no alcohol is served. That said, each week there's a different headliner, so no two shows are exactly alike. The energy, however, is ever present.

Accessible parking is located near the theater with level access to the entrance. Accessible seating (with companion seating) is available up front and it's the only reserved seating in the house. Indeed, the front seats are the ones with a close-up look at all the action because, once the music starts, the area in front of the stage turns into a massive dance floor. But again, that's all part of the show. All in all, it's great place to mix with the locals and an excellent opportunity to enjoy a real slice of Crooked Road culture.

- **IF YOU GO**
  - Blue Ridge Institute and Museum, (540) 365-4416, www.blueridgeinstitute.org
  - Floyd County, (866) 787-8806, www.floydcova.org
  - Oak Haven Lodge, (540) 745-5716, www.oakhavenlodge.com
  - Bristol CVB, (423) 989-4850, www.bristolchamber.org
  - Birthplace of Country Music Alliance Museum, (276) 645-0111, www.birthplaceofcountrymusic.org
  - Carter Family Fold, (276) 386-6054, www.carterfamilyfold.org
  - The Crooked Road, (866) 686-6874, www.thecrookedroad.org

EXPLORING ELKHART COUNTY

Located just 135 miles east of Chicago, Elkhart County makes a great destination for a fly-drive road trip. In other words, you can fly into Chicago, rent a car and then spend several days exploring this northern Indiana Amish enclave. Consider it an opportunity to lose yourself in the simplicity of the Amish culture, enjoy the peace and quiet of the country and learn to appreciate the simple pleasures of life. And because of the proximity of Elkhart County to several major airports, you can literally stow your tray table in the afternoon and enjoy a hearty Amish meal that same evening. What could be easier?

A good way to begin your Elkhart County road trip is by visiting a few local businesses to sample some traditional Amish food. Start your driving

The farmhouse at Amish Acres.

tour on CR 34, just east of Goshen, and continue on to the junction of CR 34 and SR 5. Here you'll find Fern's Country Foods. You can't miss it, as a large sign beckons visitors to "watch noodle making." Fern's has a gravel parking lot with no stripes, a two-inch step up to the entry and a 28-inch wide doorway. Still, if you can manage the obstacles, the noodle-making process is pretty interesting. Fern's is open for lunch from 11-3, but they only make noodles in the morning. They also sell noodles, picnic supplies, and country foods in their small country store.

After you've had your fill of noodle making, continue north on SR 5. Although this is a pretty modern road, you'll still see a few Amish buggies heading up to the Shipshewana auction. Turn left on CR 16 and head toward Middlebury. This secondary road is dotted with Amish farms and it's heavily traveled by Amish families who shop and do business in Middlebury and Shipshewana.

Deutsch Kase House is located on the right side of the road. There's plenty of accessible parking, ramp access and a level entry to this Amish cheese factory. Stop in and watch the cheese-making process and then taste a sample of the finished product. Deutsch Kase House is famous for its mellow Colby.

Aside from their food, the Amish are also well known for their craftsmanship; more specifically, the Amish women are famous for their beautiful handmade quilts. A good place to have a look at their handiwork is at Martin's Quilt Shop, located midway between Goshen and Nappanee at 25387 CR 46. This modest shop, located next to the carriage shed on the family farm, is run by the mother and daughter team of Bertha and Mary Alice Martin. There is level access to the shop, but you have to cross a short patch of grass and avoid a few stepping stones. If you're in the market for a quilt, Martin's is a required stop. Plan ahead, as they are closed on Thursdays and Sundays.

And if you're in the area on the fourth Saturday of September, don't miss the annual quilt auction at the Mennonite Relief Sale. Local crafters donate handmade quilts, which are auctioned off to the highest bidders, with proceeds directed to Mennonite relief efforts around the world. This popular event is held at the Elkhart County Fairgrounds in Goshen, which has accessible parking, restrooms and level access to the fair buildings.

You just can't leave Amish country without a visit to Amish Acres, located in Nappanee. Listed on the National Register of Historic Places, this popular attraction features 18 old-order Amish farm buildings on an 80-acre historic farm site.

Start your visit at the greeting barn, where you can purchase tickets and get general information about Amish Acres' ticket packages. There is level access to the Greeting Barn, and accessible restrooms are located near the ticket counter. A historic film is shown throughout the day in the Greeting Barn Theater, which offers wheelchair seating.

Outside, you can take a guided walking tour of the Amish Acres farm buildings. Since these are historic buildings, many have one or two steps at the entry and a few are two-story structures, so it's not possible to access every building. The good news is, some of the outlying farm buildings are accessible and you can see a lot of Amish Acres by just rolling around the wide level pathways that connect the buildings.

Top off your visit with a hearty threshers dinner at the Amish Acres Restaurant Barn and a play at the Round Barn Theater. There is level access to the restaurant and wheelchair seating is available at the Round Barn Theater. Amish Acres presents a unique opportunity for an intimate look at Amish farm life, and it's a must-see on any Elkhart County itinerary.

Accessible lodging is also available at The Inn at Amish Acres, which is connected to Amish Acres by a wide dirt driveway, and at the Nappanee Inn, just a half-mile down the road. Both properties feature accessible parking, level access and barrier-free pathway access in the public areas. The accessible rooms have wide doorways, lever handles and grab bars in the bathrooms. The accessible room at The Inn at Amish Acres has a combination tub/shower, whereas the one at the Nappanee Inn has a roll-in shower. Either property makes an excellent base for an Elkhart County driving tour.

- IF YOU GO
  - Fern's Country Foods, (260) 593-2222
  - Deutsch Kase House, (574) 825-9511
  - Martin's Quilt Shop, (574) 831-2256
  - Amish Acres, (574) 773-4188, www.amishacres.com
  - Elkhart County Convention and Visitors Bureau, (800) 262-8161, www.AmishCountry.org

FALL FOLIAGE IN OHIO AMISH COUNTRY

Although New England is a prime fall-foliage destination, there are *other* choices. Take Ohio Amish country for example, more specifically, Holmes County in east central Ohio. Generally regarded as Amish central, this rural county is home to more than 40,000 Amish people; in fact, it's billed as the largest Amish community in the world. With lots of things to see and do, Holmes County has all the makings for a great fall road trip. The fall colors in Holmes County are just as stunning as those on the East Coast, the prices are lower and it's a much less touristed area. And as far as access goes, well, admittedly, I've yet to find a ramped Amish buggy, however many shops, attractions, restaurants and accommodations offer at least some level of access.

Livestock in the barn at Yoder's Amish Home in Ohio Amish country.

Your first stop in Holmes County should be at the Behalt Amish and Mennonite Heritage Center just outside of Berlin. After all, if you are going to tour Amish country, you should learn a little bit about the local residents. Basically Behalt is an Amish information center of sorts, as it tells the history of the Amish people and helps eliminate many misconceptions about the faith. The center features a 15-minute informational video and a circular mural that illustrates the heritage of the Amish and Mennonite faiths. There is level access to the building and plenty of accessible parking in front. Local maps and information about Amish attractions are also available.

One of the most popular things to do in Amish country is to shop for handcrafted wares. If quilts are at the top of your shopping list, wander back into Berlin and check out the Helping Hands Quilt Shop. Accessible parking is available right in front of the store and there is barrier-free access to the main level. This very large shop features a good selection of quilts, quilting supplies, patterns and small quilted gifts. They even have quilters working on some days.

The Amish are also well known for their hand-crafted furniture, and a good place to get a look at some excellent examples of Amish workmanship is at Homestead Furniture in nearby Mt. Hope. Located approximately 15 miles northwest of Berlin, Homestead Furniture features accessible parking, level access to the first floor and stair-lift access to the basement.

They have a very wide selection — everything from end tables to bedroom furniture — and the good news is, they do ship.

One of the more popular attractions in the area is Yoder's Amish Home on State Route 515, between Trail and Walnut Creek. Make sure and save plenty of time for a leisurely drive along this scenic byway, as it's especially nice in the fall.

Yoder's Amish Home is located on 116 acres and it includes two houses, a barn, an old schoolhouse and a gift shop. There is level access to the gift shop from the gravel parking lot. All tours start in the gift shop area, and, although not all parts of the tour are wheelchair accessible, the staff is happy to make modifications for those who are unable to access all areas. There is level access to the big house from the porch, but the second floor is only accessible by stairs. Still, the main floor is very interesting, especially the cooking demonstration in the kitchen. Next door there are seven steps up to the smaller house, so it's not really doable for full-time wheelchair users.

The barn is also a must-see, as it was built in 1885. There is a four-inch step up into the barn, but you can still see a lot from the outside. From the barn, take the gravel path over to the one-room schoolhouse, which has ramp access. Schoolhouse tours are conducted several times each day.

As an added bonus, there are a number of special events, such as Apple Butter Stirring and Old Fashioned Butchering Days, held on weekends during the fall at Yoder's Amish Home. Check the Yoder Amish Home website for exact dates and times.

You can't visit Amish country without tasting some cheese, and, although there are several choices of cheese factories, Guggisberg Cheese, located just north of Charm on State Route 557, is a local favorite. There is level access to the building, with accessible parking close to the door. They have a very large selection, free samples and, if you visit on weekdays before noon, you can watch the cheese-making process.

As an added bonus, one of the most scenic drives in the county is located just south of Guggisberg Cheese, on State Route 557 between Charm and Farmerstown. Try and hit this drive in the afternoon, around 3 PM, when all the Amish children are walking home from school. Again, this is another drive that is especially scenic in the fall.

And if you're in the mood for a hearty Amish meal, then stop by Mrs. Yoder's Kitchen in Mt. Hope. Located right across from the auction grounds, this local favorite attracts big crowds on Wednesdays, when the local farmers wander over after the weekly farmers' auction. They all sit together in the back at a communal table. There is level access to the restaurant and plenty of room for wheelchair seating.

The food is ample and hearty, and it's all made from scratch. And I can guarantee you won't go away hungry. Best bet is to visit the auction in the morning and stop by Mrs. Yoder's for lunch. It's a great way to get a real taste of Amish culture.

- **IF YOU GO**
    - Behalt Amish and Mennonite Heritage Center, (330) 893-3192, www.behalt.com
    - Helping Hands Quilt Shop, (330) 893-2233
    - Homestead Furniture, (866) 674-4902, www.homesteadfurnitureonline.com
    - Yoder's Amish Home, (330) 893-2541, www.yodersamishhome.com
    - Guggisberg Cheese, (330) 893-2500, www.babyswiss.com
    - Mrs. Yoder's Kitchen, (330) 674-0922
    - Holmes County Tourism Bureau, (330) 674-3975, www.holmescountychamber.com

HIT THE ROAD IN YOUR OWN RV

RVing is fast becoming a popular vacation option for wheelers and slow walkers. There are several advantages to this type of travel, the main one being that you can travel in your own accessible space and you never have to worry about finding a hotel room or bathroom with appropriate access features.

Additionally, since your RV can be customized to fit your specific access needs, you can rest assured that you will be able to access everything in your rig. That's not always the case in hotel rooms, where the grab bars may be on the wrong side of the toilet or the bed may be too high. In short, RVing offers a certain peace of mind as far as access is concerned.

The down side to RV travel is that the initial investment can be expensive, so it's a good idea to rent one to see if you like the lifestyle before investing big bucks in your first rig. Unfortunately accessible rental rigs are difficult find, as dealers are reluctant to stock them. The best bet is to try and find a private rental from somebody who has purchased his or her own adapted RV. To that end, the Handicapped Travel Club (HTC) is a good resource for that purpose.

The HTC was formed to encourage RV traveling for people with disabilities. The majority of members have some type of a disability, and many own accessible rigs. Dues are a very reasonable $12 for the first year and $8 for subsequent years. It's a good organization to check out if you are considering RVing, as many members rent out their accessible rigs or can offer advice on adapting or purchasing a rig. The HTC website also has listings for accessible RVs for sale by members.

Once you've decided to join the RVing ranks, you then have to decide what type of rig to purchase. Most rigs can be ordered from the manufacturer with a bevy of accessible features, from wide doorways and wheelchair lifts to roll-in showers and even ceiling track lifts.

Truly you can spend as much as you want on your rig, but, generally speaking, travel trailers are more economical than motor homes of the same size. Travel trailers must be towed by another vehicle, whereas motor homes can travel under their own power. The advantage of a travel trailer is that you will always have a vehicle if you'd like to explore the surrounding area; of course, you can also tow a vehicle behind a motor home. In short, there's no one perfect rig for everyone, so it's best to look at a lot of sizes and styles before you make your purchase. The best place to do this is at an RV show, where you'll find a wide variety of rigs along with salespeople who are knowledgeable about the access features that can be added to them.

Once you get your new rig, it's best to try a few trips close to home before setting off across the country. It's also a good idea to carry a CB radio with you when you travel, as cell phone reception is spotty in some areas. Additionally, you should make a list of all the pertinent dimensions and measurements of your rig and keep it in the glove compartment. You never know when it will come in handy.

Finding an accessible campground is also a top priority. Most campground directories do not include access information, so, in order to find an accessible campground that meets your needs, you're going to have to get on the phone. And, just like when you are searching for an accessible hotel room, you have to ask specific questions when searching for an accessible campground.

In other words, don't just ask if it the campground is accessible, but also ask if they have wide level spaces that will accommodate a wheelchair lift. If the space isn't level, the lift will not work properly, and if it's not wide enough, you will be unable to deploy your lift. This is where those rig dimensions in your glove box will come in handy. Know how much space you need, so you won't be caught off guard.

You should also ask about the surface around the spaces — cement is good, sand is bad. And although most hook-ups are located at an appropriate height, there may be obstacles such as railroad ties or steps around them. Make sure and ask if there are any obstructions. Additionally, ask about the accessibility of the office, bathrooms and showers. And once you arrive at the campground, don't be afraid to drive through before you register. It never hurts to see what you are buying before you put down your money.

It should also be noted that most Wal-Mart, Costco, Kmart and Flying J locations offer free overnight camping for RVers. Some cities have enacted ordinances prohibiting overnight camping, so it's best to check with the store in advance to see if overnight camping is permitted at that location. Most of these sites are accessible because parking lots are generally flat and there are no hook-ups.

Additionally, don't forget to get your America the Beautiful – National Parks and Federal Recreational Lands Pass – Access Pass for free admission to all national parks and 50% off camping fees. It's available to anybody with a permanent disability at all national park entrances.

Finally, if you want to get the skinny on the accessible facilities at RV parks across the US, check out the on-line database compiled by the HTC. The parks are evaluated by members and are grouped by state. Each listing contains a short description along with access details. This database is continually updated, and new parks are added as members visit them and complete access surveys. It's an excellent resource.

- IF YOU GO
  - Handicapped Travel Club, www.handicappedtravelclub.com
  - America the Beautiful – National Parks and Federal Recreational Lands Pass – Access Pass, http://www.nps.gov/fees_passes.htm

SCENIC SOUTHEASTERN KENTUCKY

ummer road trips, scenic drives and state parks go hand in hand. Unfortunately so do the crowds. These days it's getting harder and harder to enjoy a piece of Mother Nature without tripping over hundreds of other tourists trying to do the same. Harder, but not impossible. The key lies in destination selection. So if you crave a little peace and quiet in a place where you can still see the stars, pack up the car and head to southeastern Kentucky. It's the perfect place to ditch the maddening tourist crowds, stretch your travel dollar and enjoy some very scenic state parks.

Natural Bridge State Resort Park is the perfect place to begin exploring the area. It's located just an hour from Lexington, yet it's a world away from the trappings and distractions of city life. As with most of the Kentucky state parks, Natural Bridge features a small lodge and a handful of rental cabins.

The 35-room Hemlock Lodge has two wheelchair-accessible rooms with wide doorways, level thresholds and good pathway access. Each room has a spacious private balcony that overlooks a scenic wooded area. The accessible bathrooms each have a tub/shower combination with a hand-held showerhead, grab bars in the shower and around the toilet, a roll-under sink and a portable shower chair. The lodge also offers one accessible cottage (209) with a tub/shower combination.

There is good access to the lodge public areas, including the lobby, gift shop and restaurant. The pool is quite a (downhill) hike from the main lodge, but it's beautiful and features a very accessible zero-step sloped entry. Best bet is to drive down, as there is plenty of accessible parking. There is also a pleasant boardwalk trail to the right of the main lodge; and, although the whole length is not accessible, there is a level 200-yard section that leads from the lodge to a waterfall.

The most accessible way to see the area is to hop in your car and explore one of the many scenic driving routes. At the top of the list is the Red River Gorge Scenic Byway, which follows the Red River on KY 715. Here you'll see stone arches, waterfalls and some great fall foliage, all from the comfort of your own car.

The historic Gladie Cabin at the Gladie Cultural Environmental Learning Center.

This scenic loop begins just north of the Hemlock Lodge at the one-lane Nada Tunnel on KY 77. Originally built for the railroad in the 1900s, this 900-foot tunnel is now on the National Register of Historic Places.

The byway follows the Red River to Gladie Creek Bridge, site of the new Gladie Cultural Environmental Learning Center and the historic Gladie Cabin. The visitors center houses a number of interpretive exhibits and has accessible parking, a level entry and good pathway access throughout the building. Gladie Cabin, a re-creation of an 1800s log cabin, is just a short drive away. There is one very large step up to the cabin, but it's still worth a stop, as you can get a good view of the cabin (and perhaps a few bison) from the parking area.

From the Gladie Cabin, the byway meanders south toward the Bert T Coombs Mountain Parkway and then loops back to the lodge. Make sure and stop along the way at the Sky Bridge, the largest arch in Red River Gorge. There is a level dirt trail to the top of the arch, which is doable for many wheelchair users.

After you've had a good dose of red rock country, head south to Buckhorn Lake State Resort Park for a little change of scenery. As the name implies, the big attraction here is the scenic lake.

Buckhorn Lodge, which is located on the lakeshore, features two accessible lodge rooms and one accessible cottage. Each accessible unit includes a tub/shower combination with a hand-held shower, grab bars in the shower and around the toilet, a roll-under sink and a portable shower chair. The accessible lodge rooms each have level access to a spacious balcony, where you can just sit back, relax and enjoy the lake view.

Access is good to all of the lodge public areas, including the lobby, gift shop, swimming pool and dining room. There is accessible parking at the marina and the afternoon pontoon boat rides are doable with a little assistance. Relaxing is the name of the game at Buckhorn Lake.

No matter where you travel in southeastern Kentucky, don't leave home without a good road map and remember to keep an eye out for changing road conditions. Also, just accept the fact that you will probably have to stop and ask for directions at least once. It's also worth noting than many parts of southeastern Kentucky are dry counties, so if you want to imbibe, you'll have to purchase your alcohol in a neighboring wet county. But, then again, that's just part of the charm of the area.

- IF YOU GO
  - Natural Bridge State Resort Park, (800) 325-1710,
    www.parks.ky.gov/findparks/resortparks/nb/
  - Buckhorn Lake State Resort Park, (800) 325-0058,
    www.parks.ky.gov/findparks/resortparks/bk/
  - Southern and Eastern Kentucky Tourism Development Association,
    (877) 868-7735, www.tourseky.com

WAY OUT WEST IN KANSAS

L et's face it, when you think of Kansas, you think of the tallgrass prairie, and there's no better place to get a glance at this disappearing habitat than in the Tallgrass Prairie National Preserve, located two miles north of Strong City on the Flint Hills Scenic Byway.

Musicians gather at the Emma Chase Cafe in Cottonwood Falls, Kansas.

The bulk of this 10,000-acre preserve occupies the land of the former Spring Hill Farm and Stock Ranch, which dates back to the late 1800s. At one time, this ranch had 7,000 acres of prime Flint Hills grazing land. Today it serves as the park headquarters, with several of the outbuildings and the ranch house open to the public.

There is accessible parking in front of the limestone barn, and, although the terrain is level, it's also a bit bumpy. Still it's doable for many people. There is level access to the limestone barn, where you will find a number of interpretive exhibits on early farming methods. Watch your step inside the barn, as there are one-inch thresholds here and there. Outside, there is a dirt path to the chicken coop and carriage house, which are both worth a look.

The ranch house is located at the top of a gravel driveway, so your best bet is to drive up and park near the back door. A portable ramp is available at the back door of the 1881 ranch house. Once you access the house, you can get a look at the second-floor bedroom and the dining room. The main floor of the house is only accessible by a flight of stairs, but there is a photo album available in the visitor center.

Of course the real gem of this site is the tallgrass prairie, and, since private vehicles are not allowed in the park, the best way to get a look at the prairie is on one of the ranger-led bus tours. There is lift access to the bus, which can accommodate two wheelchairs. The tour stops at a few places along the way, but there aren't any accessible pathways in the tallgrass. You can still get a great view from the bus, but, if you'd like to get out, you can certainly roll along the dirt road a bit. All in all it's an excellent, and very educational, tour.

And if you happen to be in the area in June, make plans to attend the Symphony in the Flint Hills, an annual concert presented in the Tallgrass Prairie National Preserve. This open-air concert features the Kansas City Symphony and chorus, and it's set in the middle of the tallgrass prairie. Accessible parking, seating and portable restrooms are available, along with accessible transportation to the concert site (which is about a mile away from the parking area). It's a very unique way to enjoy the prairie.

Accessible lodging is available at the Grand Central Hotel in nearby Cottonwood Falls, a town that residents proudly proclaim boasts 3,000 people and 250,000 cattle. This 10-room hotel has a definite ranch and cowboy theme to it; in fact, instead of names, all of the rooms carry the brands of local ranches on their doors. The accessible Crocker Ranch Room is located on the ground floor, and it features wide doorways, excellent pathway access and two double beds in the sleeping area. The bathroom features a roll-in shower with a built-in shower bench and a glass door that opens out, grab bars in the shower and around the toilet and a roll-under sink. A portable shower chair is also available upon request.

Save some time to explore Cottonwood Falls, too, as it's a cute little town, with a number of shops, small businesses and a historic courthouse. Access varies throughout town, and the brick streets may be difficult for some folks. Still, there are curb cuts at some corners and many businesses have level access. There isn't much traffic in town, so if the sidewalks don't work for you, you can always stroll out in the street. Walk down to the end of Broadway for the best view of the Chase County Courthouse, which was built in 1873.

The Emma Chase Cafe (known as "The Emma" to the locals) is also a required stop. Located just a few doors down from the Grand Central Hotel, the cafe has ramp access, but come early for the best seating. Friday is the best night to visit the Emma, as you can feast on a hearty catfish dinner and then enjoy a rousing set of music, which could include anything from blue grass and gospel to rock and silly songs. It's a great place to experience a real slice of rural Kansas life. As one waitress said, "I come here every Friday and volunteer because it's just so much fun."

- IF YOU GO
  - Tallgrass Prairie National Preserve, (620) 273-6034, www.nps.gov/tapr/home.htm
  - Symphony in the Flint Hills, (620) 273-8955, www.symphonyintheflinthills.org
  - Grand Central Hotel, (620) 273-6763, www.grandcentralhotel.com
  - Emma Chase Cafe, (620) 273-6020, www.emmachasecafe.com

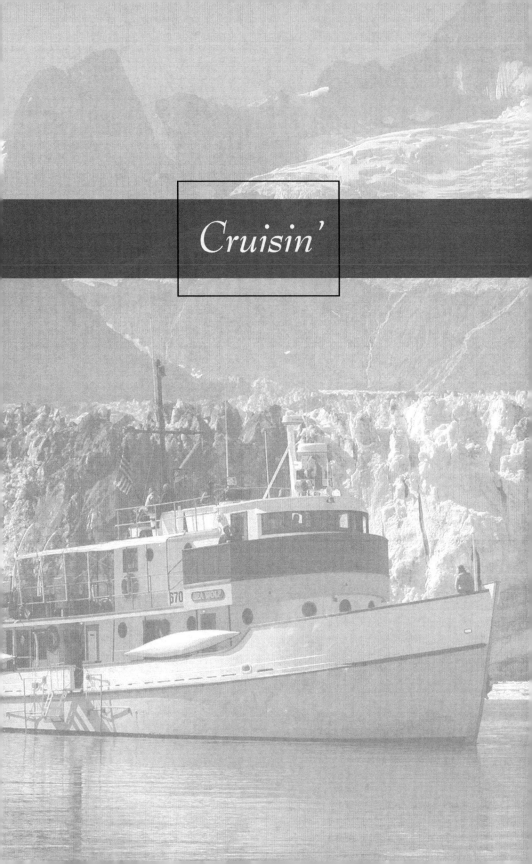

Cruisin'

ALASKA, EXPEDITION STYLE

Expedition-style cruises are all the rage these days as baby boomers turn out in full force for these high-energy sailings, which include activities such as kayaking, beach landings and up-close-and-personal whale-watching opportunities. Unfortunately, because of the very nature of their activities, most expedition cruise ships are not wheelchair accessible; in fact, many expedition operators claim it's a waste of time and money to make their vessels accessible because, as one owner puts it, "We only attract passengers seeking a physically challenging vacation." Granted, most expedition cruises require more physical activity than the average graze-and-guzzle cruise; however many wheelchair users and slow walkers actually prefer this heightened activity.

The good news is, one expedition cruise operator went above and beyond as far as access modifications are concerned. Kimber Owen, owner of Alaska-based Sea Wolf Adventures, which features itineraries around Alaska, British Columbia and the San Juan Islands, made her ship and excursions as accessible as possible, not an easy feat considering the *MV Seal Wolf* started out life as a US Navy minesweeper. The vessel was subsequently decommissioned, sold and converted to a private yacht. Kimber purchased the ship in 2003 and hired access consultant Mike Passo to oversee the access upgrades.

Make no mistake, the *MV Sea Wolf* is not 100% barrier free; however Kimber is very up front about the access limitations of the vessel. Additionally it's not a special ship that only accommodates disabled passengers; the focus on the *MV Sea Wolf* is on visitablity, inclusion and integration. Basically it's an expedition-style ship that happens to have physical access.

The focus is on usability on the intimate *MV Sea Wolf,* which can carry 12 passengers and six crew members. The three accessible staterooms (Wolf, Bear and Orca) are furnished with twin beds and each stateroom can accommodate one wheelchair user. The accessible bathrooms (heads, in nautical terminology) include a shower with a transfer bench, accessible controls and a hand-held showerhead. Although these units are not considered roll-ins, there is adequate space for a wheelchair user to roll alongside the shower and transfer to the 19-inch-high transfer bench. The accessible bathrooms also have roll-under sinks and toilets with plenty of room for a side transfer.

The MV Sea Wolf, against a backdrop of glaciers and mountains. Photo courtesy of Sea Wolf Adventures.

Access features throughout the rest of the ship include decks that are 32 inches wide, barrier-free access to all public areas and hydraulic lifts to all three decks. It should be noted that, because of space constraints, the lift to the lower deck cannot accommodate large wheelchairs; however since there are no public areas on the lower deck, it's not a major problem.

Of course the shore excursions aboard the *MV Sea Wolf* are the highlight of the cruise, and most include either a kayaking expedition or a beach landing in a skiff. An overhead sling-type lift is used to transfer wheelchair users into the kayaks, and the crew is happy to assist with paddling instruction and assistance. One of the double kayaks is completely open for easier access, and plenty of padding is also available. Even if you've never paddled before, it's easy to learn, especially in a double kayak.

The crew just loves to get folks on the water, and Kimber continues to receive rave reviews from wheelers about their kayaking experiences on the *MV Sea Wolf*. Generally, passengers go out in two groups, accompanied by guides. The kayaking expeditions allow passengers to explore the sloughs and rivers in search of wildlife, such as bears grazing along the beaches looking for salmon. Whale sightings are not uncommon and it's an incredible experience to view these giants up-close-and-personal from a kayak.

There is also lift access to the skiff, which has a drop-down bow for easy access to shore. There are also wheelchair tie-downs and fishing-rod holders aboard the skiff, so it's ideal for fishing. Beach access varies, and some shores are rocky whereas others are marshy; so a thin roll of plastic is carried abroad the skiff in order to make the inaccessible shores more wheelable. One wheelchair that can manage sand, mud and cobble is also carried aboard the skiff. Some beaches are only doable for short jaunts, but it's all still quite an adventure.

The *MV Sea Wolf* staff is also very accommodating and they are quick to lend a hand; however they are also quite mindful of folks who prefer to do things on their own. Says Kimber, "We are very observant as to strengths and possible weaknesses of all of our clients, and we gear their adventure to that ability." And she adds, "Where there are places where a shore excursion is not possible for some, we offer skiff or kayak alternatives so there is always an activity."

- IF YOU GO
  - Sea Wolf Adventures, (907) 957-1438, www.seawolf-adventures.com

ALOHA MATEY!

Although the Hawaiian Islands seem the perfect choice for a cruise, an obscure maritime regulation actually prevents many vessels from sailing a simple inter-island itinerary. Under the Jones Act, foreign-flagged vessels must call on a foreign port if they wish to call on any US port; so, in the case of a Hawaii itinerary, ships must either sail from Vancouver, stop in Ensenada, or make the four-day detour to Fanning Island. No matter how you slice it, all these options add up to more days at sea and less time ashore in Hawaii. But all that changed in 2004, when Norwegian Cruise Lines (NCL) rolled out their new US-flagged Hawaii fleet, under the NCL America brand.

The three ships that comprise the NCL America fleet are the *Pride of Aloha,* the *Pride of America* and the *Pride of Hawaii*. They all sail seven-night

The Pride of Aloha cruising along the Kauai coast.

inter-island itineraries from Honolulu and spend a whopping 100 hours ashore.

This new shore-intensive itinerary is especially good news for wheelchair users and slow walkers. First off, with more time in port, you don't have to rush. You can relax and take things at your own pace, yet still have plenty of time to see the sights. More importantly, since the Americans with Disabilities Act is the law of the land in Hawaii, there are many more accessible sights *to* see.

The *Pride of Aloha* was the first NCL America ship in the fleet. She entered service as the *Norwegian Sky* in 1999. After a short stint in dry dock for her Hawaiian makeover, she was reflagged and renamed on July 4, 2004.

The *Pride of Aloha* has six accessible staterooms located near the elevators on decks 8 and 9. These inside staterooms feature wide doorways, level thresholds and excellent pathway access. There is more than enough room (even with luggage and shopping bags strewn about) for a wheelchair user to navigate comfortably. Access features in the bathrooms include a roll-in shower with a fold-down shower seat, a hand-held showerhead, grab bars in the shower and around the toilet and a roll-under sink. Throughout the ship there is good access to most public areas, and, although not every route is barrier free, there is an accessible route to nearly every venue.

The *Pride of America* was christened on June 17, 2005, and she is the first newly built ship in the fleet. Access is excellent throughout the vessel, with 22 wheelchair-accessible cabins (including suites) in a variety of configurations. Each accessible cabin has wide doorways, good pathway access and a bathroom with a roll-in shower and a fold-down shower seat. There are also 11 accessible public toilets throughout the ship. As for the public areas, the spa has wheelchair-accessible showers and treatment rooms, whereas the pool and Jacuzzi feature hoist access.

The final ship to join the NCL America fleet, the *Pride of Hawaii*, was unveiled on May 20, 2006. Billed as the largest, most luxurious US-flagged cruise ship in history, the *Pride of Hawaii* boasts 21 accessible cabins in a variety of categories, including five inside cabins, eight cabins with an obstructed view, six ocean-view cabins with a balcony and two mini suites. All accessible cabins feature wide stateroom and bathroom doors and bathrooms with a roll-in shower, grab bars and a shower seat. There is good access to all public areas, including the 10 restaurants, on the *Pride of Hawaii*.

As far as dining choices are concerned, NCL America passengers can choose to eat whenever they want in the main dining rooms (there are no assigned seats or set dining times), opt for one of the many alternative restaurants, grab a bite in the bar or visit the buffet. And since NCL America ships overnight in Kauai and Maui, eating ashore is also an attractive option.

Ports of call include Kona and Hilo on the Big Island; Nawiliwili, Kauai; and Kahului, Maui, with Kona being the only tender port on the itinerary. According to NCL's official policy, wheelchair users must use a manual wheelchair in order to tender; so if you'd rather not hassle with it all, then consider staying aboard and exploring the ship on tender day. It should also be noted that, since the NCL America ships call on Kahului instead of Lahaina, Maui is not a tender port, so there are no delays or limitations going ashore there.

As with everything else on the NCL America ships, choice is the keyword for shore time. Whether you book an NCL shore excursion or head off on your own, there are many accessible choices. At least one accessible shore excursion is available in each NCL America port. This is partially due to the Americans with Disabilities Act, but it's also due to some good planning and employee training on NCL's part. First off, the shore-excursion employees are well versed in access issues. They can tell you in very simple (and honest) terms if a particular tour is suitable for you.

Additionally, NCL acquired Polynesian Adventure Tours in 2004, so lift-equipped transportation is available on all accessible shore excursions. The lift-equipped buses can accommodate two wheelchairs with 48 hours' advance notice.

The accessible shore excursions are clearly marked on the order form, but passengers are encouraged to inquire about accessibility if they are unsure about any tour. Planning ahead is also essential for ship-sponsored shore excursions, as many of the more popular options like the Pacific paradise luau or the Volcanoes National Park odyssey sell out early.

If you'd like to set out on your own, Hilo Hattie has free accessible shopping shuttles at all the ports. Additionally, the major rental car agencies can install hand controls with 48 hours' notice, but frequent travelers admit it's best to request them at least a week in advance.

With more than 100 hours in port, there's plenty of time to explore Hawaii on the NCL America ships. And, in the end, it's really the perfect way to get a good overview of paradise.

- IF YOU GO
  - NCL America, (866) 234-0292, accessdesk@ncl.com (access desk), www.ncl.com

BARGING THROUGH THE HEARTLAND

If you'd like to cruise along America's rivers, yet feel a riverboat cruise is too much of a structured or formal experience, then consider booking passage on the *River Explorer,* America's only hotel barge. The brainchild of Eddie Conrad, the *River Explorer* offers a safe, relaxed and very comfortable atmosphere, so relaxed in fact, that Eddie encourages passengers to take off their shoes in the

The River Explorer barge docked at St. Louis.

purser's lounge and catch a nap on the comfy couch. In short, he wants folks to feel like they are in their own living room. And from the number of repeat passengers on the *River Explorer,* it really is a second home to some.

Technically the *River Explorer* is made up of two 295-foot river barges: the forward *DeSoto,* which houses the public rooms, and the aft *LaSalle,* where the staterooms are located. Operated by New Orleans-based River Barge Excursion Lines, the *River Explorer* sails four- to 10-day itineraries on the Mississippi, Ohio and Missouri Rivers and along the Texas-Louisiana Intracoastal Waterway.

Access aboard the *River Explorer* is good, with elevator access to all decks, wide corridors, accessible public restrooms and plenty of room to navigate in a wheelchair or a walker. There are a few small steps here and there — at the end of the gangway and to some of the outside deck areas — but the crew is happy to assist. Additionally there is at least one level-threshold route to the outside public areas.

There are 98 staterooms on the *River Explorer*, including three that are wheelchair accessible (102, 103, 104). All of the accessible staterooms are identical, and they each feature a wide-entry door and a pocket door to the bathroom. The bathrooms have a low-step (4-inch) shower with a fold-down shower seat, a hand-held showerhead, grab bars in the shower and around the toilet and a roll-under sink.

The accessible rooms are furnished with a twin bed and a pull-out trundle bed. Although it's a bit cozy with both beds made up, it's navigable with the trundle bed stowed. As an added feature, staterooms 103 and 104 connect to nonaccessible staterooms.

There is barrier-free access to all of the public areas except the hot tub. Wheelchairs are available for loan for shore excursions, and the crew is happy to assist with boarding and disembarking. As a testament to the access aboard the *River Explorer*, it's worth noting that the vessel hosts several dialysis cruises each year.

Life aboard the *River Explorer* is indeed a very low-key experience. Daytime activities on nonport days usually include a lecture or film in the morning and an activity such as bingo or an ice cream social in the late afternoon. In between, there is plenty of time for what return passengers fondly refer to as *river time*: a time to just sit back, relax and watch the river go by.

There is no casino on board, but there is a library filled with books, puzzles, games and movies. There is also a bumper pool table in the library. Every evening, passengers are treated to a different show featuring regional entertainment, but things usually wrap up by 10 PM (at the latest). The *River Explorer* is definitely not a late-night party ship!

Like everything else, meals aboard the *River Explorer* are a casual affair. Breakfast and lunch are served buffet style in the galley. There is open seating for dinner, and the menu includes three main-course options, including one vegetarian choice. The food is plentiful, but it's light on the seasonings and spices.

The *River Explorer* crew also gets high marks; service is first rate but unobtrusive. Tips are not expected, as they are included in the cruise fare. In short, the *River Explorer* fosters a very casual and pleasant atmosphere where nobody really wants for anything. You just enjoy the river, explore the landings at your own pace and learn a little bit about America's heartland rivers and how they shaped the history of our nation. What could be simpler?

- IF YOU GO
  - River Barge Excursion Lines, (888) 462-2743, www.riverbarge.com

EXPLORING THE COLUMBIA RIVER
· ·

"Good morning fellow historians," boomed the NPR-like voice. Instinctively I rolled over to hit the snooze button. The voice continued, undeterred by my unsuccessful attempts to silence it. Frustrated, I continued to flail around in search of the coveted snooze button, only to send the contents of my bedside table crashing to the floor. Like the Energizer bunny, the voice kept on going and going and continued to rattle on about the Umatilla and Walla Walla tribes. Reluctantly I sat up, rubbed my eyes and assessed the situation.

At some point I realized I wasn't at home. Indeed, I was aboard the *Queen of the West* cruising along Oregon's Columbia River. The voice was coming from the ship's intercom, *not* my clock radio. In spite of this frustrating first encounter with the voice, I grew to love it over the next seven days. It belonged to ship historian, Junius Rochester; whose daily lectures, insightful musings and morning vignettes made the history of the region simply come alive.

As you might have guessed, the *Queen of the West* is not your average cruise ship. Built in 1994, this paddlewheel riverboat has just 71 staterooms, including two that are wheelchair accessible (109 & 111). Each accessible stateroom has a level entry, wide doorways and a bathroom with a roll-in shower. The bathrooms do not have a five-foot turning radius, but there is certainly enough room for a wheelchair user to enter and back out of the bathroom. Although cozy, these accessible staterooms fill the bill for many wheelchair users.

And then there are the shore excursions. Not only are they among the best I've ever taken, but they're also the most accessible. All shore excursions focus on the history of the region and are conducted on lift-equipped buses owned by Majestic America Line. Due to the retractable bow ramp on the *Queen of the West*, she can (and does) dock just about anywhere, and wherever she docks, the buses are waiting. It's a very accessible way to explore the area.

On our first shore excursion, we docked near Hood River and visited the Columbia Gorge Discovery Center and the Wasco County Historical Museum in The Dalles. These two museums are located side by side and present a comprehensive historic view of the area.

Paddlewheeling on the Columbia River.

The Columbia Gorge Discovery Center features interpretive exhibits about the geology, wildlife, vegetation and ancient ways of life along the river, whereas the Wasco County Museum focuses on the early inhabitants of the county. Outside there is a living-history park and an interpretive trail. The museum buildings offer barrier-free access and the level trail is composed of hard-packed dirt. The whole complex is very nicely done access wise.

After a short drive along the Columbia River Gorge, we returned to the ship for lunch. In the afternoon we visited Bonneville Dam and Multnomah Falls and returned to the ship in time for happy hour.

Another day we docked near Pendleton, Oregon, and visited the Pendleton rodeo grounds for a western show. I was expecting a rodeo demonstration, but instead we saw a Wild West show with lots of singing and comedy. The show was held in an indoor arena with level access and plenty of wheelchair seating up front.

One of my favorite stops was the Tamastslikt Cultural Institute, just east of Pendleton. This interpretive center tells the history of the Oregon Trail from the view of the Cayuse, Umatilla and Walla Walla tribes. There is barrier-free access throughout this very well done museum.

Actually Tamastslikt is more of a living history museum, as, in addition to the permanent exhibits, the tribal elders are on hand to share their memories with visitors. The highlight of the day was the afternoon dance performance at Tamastslikt.

We also covered the natural history of the area, with a visit to Mt. St. Helens. After docking in Longview, Washington, we traveled up the mountain to the Coldwater Ridge Visitor Center. Putting this all into perspective, this entire area was completely devastated by the 1980 eruption of Mt. St. Helens. It was ground zero. Gladly, today there is rebirth to the area, a rebirth that can be seen on the nearby Winds of Change trail.

Our final port of call was Astoria, Oregon, where we docked right next to the nicely accessible Columbia River Maritime Museum. Our morning shore excursion included a brief driving tour of the city and a chance to visit the museum in the afternoon.

So, although my *Queen of the West* experience got off to a rocky (and somewhat disoriented start), in the end it was an excellent (and very accessible) experience. If you enjoy history lectures, beautiful scenery and shore excursions that have nothing to do with shopping outlets, you'll love this cruise. It's a far cry from big ship cruising, and in my book that's a very good thing.

- IF YOU GO

  • Majestic America Line, (800) 434-1232, www.majesticamericaline.com

CRUISING EUROPE'S CANALS
. . . .

Although relatively unheard of in the US, narrowboat and canal boat holidays are gaining popularity in Europe. This self-drive or skippered cruise option allows passengers to cruise along at their own pace, stop wherever they want and see what they really want to see. It's a very relaxing experience and a great way to enjoy the sights and sounds of the countryside.

Canal boats and narrowboats are usually leased by the week, but some companies also offer half-week rentals and day trips. The vessels come in a wide variety of styles, from utilitarian to luxury, and, although standard models are generally not accessible, adapted models can be hired at a number of companies and charities throughout Europe. Here are a few accessible favorites.

The Lyneal Trust is a UK charity that provides accessible canal boat holidays on the Llangollen Canal, from their base at the Lyneal Wharf, near Ellesmere. They operate two accessible canal boats, the *Shropshire Lass* and the *Shropshire Lad*. The *Shropshire Lass* is a 70-foot residential canal boat that sleeps eight, and the *Shropshire Lad* is a 45-foot canal boat designed for day trips.

The self-drive *Shropshire Lass* can be leased for the week, but one passenger must have previous canal boat experience. The boat includes a hydraulic lift plus a lavatory and shower designed for wheelchair users. There is good pathway access throughout the vessel and it can accommodate wheelchairs up to 24.5 inches wide. A wheelchair is available for use aboard the vessel. The Lyneal Wharf also has accessible cottages for guests who wish to sleep on dry land and use the *Shropshire Lad* for day trips.

The *Waveney Stardust* is an adapted broads motor cruiser owned and operated by a UK charity of the same name. Based at Hippersons Boatyard at Gillingham Dam, it can be booked for day trips along the Waveney River from Beccles to Oulton Broad. There is lift access to the boat, and there is an accessible toilet and a patient hoist on board. The *Waveney Stardust* comes complete with a volunteer crew. These canal trips are available at greatly reduced rates, as operating costs are heavily subsidized by the charity.

Another UK charity, the Bruce Wake Trust owns the *Charlotte II* and the *Alice*, which are berthed at Upton Marina on the River Severn, approximately 10 miles south of Worcester. Access features on the vessels include hydraulic lifts, a disabled steering system, a ceiling hoist over the bed, and an accessible bathroom with a shower wheelchair. The maximum wheelchair width for access on both vessels is 28.5 inches. A 25-inch wide wheelchair is available for use on board.

The *Charlotte II* is a wide-beamed riverboat designed for use on the Severn and Avon Rivers and the Gloucester and Sharpness Canal. She can accommodate one wheelchair user and a maximum of seven passengers. The *Alice* is a narrowboat, which can accommodate a maximum of six passengers. Both vessels are available for lease by the week. This is a self-drive option; however a skipper can be hired for an additional fee.

Over in Ireland, you can cruise the waterways on the *Saoirse ar an Uisce* (*Freedom on the Water*). This fully equipped barge has central heating, a full galley and a large bathroom and shower. This barge is accessible to wheelchair users via a boarding ramp. Day cruises, which depart from Bell Harbor in Monasterevin, are available for groups and families. This is not a self-drive option.

If you'd like to explore Scotland's Lowland canals, then check out the accessible *Marion Seagull*. Owned by the Seagull Trust in Edinburgh, this purpose-built vessel can carry a maximum of six passengers. Access features include good pathway access throughout the boat, two lifts and a large bathroom with a low-step shower, a fold-down shower seat and a hand-held showerhead. The *Marion Seagull* can be hired for the entire week on either a self-drive or a skippered basis. The Seagull Trust also provides free day cruises on the Union, Caledonian and Forth & Clyde Canals.

And finally, if you'd prefer to see a bit of France by canal, Croisieres offers the Triton 10.50 handy canal boat, which sails on the canal du Midi in southern France. It can sleep up to six people and features a hydraulic platform lift between the corridor, the pilot area and the two front cabins. The bathroom has a continental-style shower and one of the front bedrooms is big enough to accommodate a wheelchair. There is level boarding via an adjustable gangway. This self-drive boat can be leased by the week or the half week.

- IF YOU GO
  - The Lyneal Trust, +44 1743 252728, www.lyneal-trust.org.uk
  - Waveney Stardust, +44 7817 920502, www.waveneystardust.co.uk
  - Bruce Wake Trust, +44 1572 822183, www.brucewaketrust.co.uk
  - Saoirse ar an Uisce, +353 45 529410, www.kildare.ie/FreedomOnTheWater
  - Seagull Trust, +44 1324 720096, www.seagulltrust.org.uk
  - Croisieres Canal Boat, +33 4 68 91 33 00, www.croisieres-handy.com

HAL'S SOUTHERN CARIBBEAN

A lthough there are a lot of accessible cruise ships to choose from, certain ships make better choices when matched with specific itineraries. Take Holland America Line's (HAL's) *ms Westerdam*, for example. When coupled with a southern Caribbean itinerary with port calls on Aruba, Curacao and Half Moon Cay, this Vista-class ship presents a very accessible yet exotic Caribbean cruise option. There are many reasons for this winning combination, but, in the end, it boils down to a very accessible ship matched with ports that have activities near the pier or accessible transportation on the island.

Christened in 2004, the *ms Westerdam* has 928 staterooms, including 28 that are wheelchair accessible. The accessible staterooms are available in a variety of classes and sizes, many of which have private balconies. Access features include wide doorways, good pathway access and zero-step access to the bathrooms. The accessible bathrooms have a roll-in shower with a fold-down shower bench, a hand-held showerhead, grab bars in the shower and around the toilet and a full five-foot turning radius.

The good access continues throughout the ship, with barrier-free access to all public areas. There are power doors to some outside decks and accessible unisex bathrooms on every deck with a public area. A portable pool lift was added to the ship in 2007 for access to the Lido pool and Jacuzzi, as well as the hydrotherapy pool. And access in the Vista Show Lounge is excellent, with a wide choice of seating for wheelers and slow walkers. You can sit close to the stage at a cocktail table or near the back in a row of designated accessible seats. And last but not least, the housekeeping staff uses hand-held caddies instead of those behemoth wheeled carts, which helps increase the hallway accessibility for wheelchair and scooter users.

The ports on the *ms Westerdam's* Southern Caribbean itinerary emphasize fun and sun, but all of them have accessible options. Located in the Bahamas, Half Moon Cay is HAL's private island, so you can use your ship card like cash everywhere on the island. Even though Half Moon Cay is a tender port, HAL uses its own accessible tender, which features roll-on access, to get passengers to and from the island. Passengers board the tender from the top deck while it's shipside and from the main deck on the island.

Shopping at the open-air market in Willemstad, Curacao.

There is level access on the gangways and lift access between the decks, so for a tendered port it's very accessible.

Once ashore, there is a paved pathway from the dock to Fort San Salvador, where you'll find a gift shop, a straw market, a bar, the first-aid station, an ice cream stand and an information booth. Beach wheelchairs are available for free loan at the first-aid station on a first-come basis. The sand on the beach is fairly hard packed, but you'll still need an able-bodied companion with a little stamina to push the beach wheelchair down to the water. Still, once you get there, you can take the beach wheelchair in the water and enjoy a refreshing dip in the Caribbean. There are also paved level pathways to the chapel and the picnic area (where a BBQ lunch is served), so, if you tire of the beach, take a stroll and enjoy the native flora and fauna.

Over on Aruba, you'll also find level access from the pier at Oranjestad; however the area around the dock is primarily of interest to shoppers. There are open-air markets, lots of jewelry stores and a number of small shops that feature native crafts. Access has greatly improved in Aruba over the years, and today the area around the dock is pretty accessible with wide sidewalks and curb cuts at most corners. Additionally, most of the shops along the main drag have level access.

Lite Life Medicab provides accessible tours of the island, but as the name implies it's also the local medical transportation provider. The tours are excellent and include stops at the California Lighthouse, Alto Vista Chapel and the Casibara Rock Formation; however, in order to provide local services, last-minute tour cancellations are very common. Still it's a beautiful island, so it's worth a shot, as I've had no reports of unrefunded money. The worst thing that will happen is that your tour will be canceled and you will be disappointed, but you'll get your money back.

Curacao, on the other hand, offers a very reliable and accessible tour option for wheelers and slow walkers. Tio Taxi Tours offers tours of the island in their lift-equipped Bluebird Bus. The bus normally holds 30 people, but capacity varies depending on the number of wheelchair users aboard. Advance reservations are a must and customized tours are available. As an added bonus, if you can't navigate the bus steps, you can just stand on the lift and use it as a mini-elevator.

Try to book a tour that includes a stop at the Ostrich and Game Farm, if possible. Tours of the complex are conducted in an accessible safari vehicle with roll-on access. It's great fun and the tour guides are very entertaining.

If you'd prefer to stick around the dock, then you are in luck too. There is excellent pathway access to the welcome center and a paved level pathway to a small shopping complex and an open-air market. A pontoon bridge leads over to Willemstad's popular Punda shopping area. A free water taxi operates when the pontoon bridge is out; however there is a three-inch step at the entrance. Your best bet is to browse through the colorful open-air market and use the pontoon bridge when it floats back into place.

Whatever you choice, there are lots of accessible options in Curacao, Aruba, and Half Moon Cay. And thanks to HAL, the *ms Westerdam* provides a nicely accessible way to get there.

- IF YOU GO

  - Holland America Line,
    (800) 547-8493 - Access & Compliance Department,
    www.hollandAmerica.com
  - Lite Life Medicab, +297 585 9764, www.litelifemedicab.com
  - Tio Taxi Tours, +599 9 560 5491, www.tiotaxi.com
  - Ostrich and Game Farm, +599 9 747 27 77, www.ostrichfarm.net

PADDLEWHEELING AROUND ALASKA

···

S ome folks claim that Alaska is overtourished, especially as far as cruises are concerned. Granted it's not unusual to pull into some ports only to find six mega ships already docked there; however that doesn't mean you should totally write off the Alaska cruise experience. Quite the contrary; in fact, since Alaska is covered by the Americans with Disabilities Act, you'll find a large number of accessible diversions there, so it's a great cruise choice for wheelers and slow walkers. Perhaps the best strategy is to cruise Alaska in a slightly different way — aboard a Russian-themed paddlewheel cruise ship, such as the *Empress of the North*.

Operated by Majestic America Line, the *Empress of the North* was launched in June 2003. Today she sails a number of Alaska itineraries, the most popular one being a seven-night Inside Passage cruise from Juneau. This itinerary is a great choice for first-time Alaska cruisers, as it features a different take on the more touristed ports as well a stop at some off-the-beaten-track gems. It's a very comfortable, intimate and relaxed way to cruise Alaska.

The *Empress of the North* can accommodate a maximum of 223 passengers. She has 112 staterooms, including two that are wheelchair accessible. The accessible staterooms include one BB Superior (#346) and one CC First Class (#341). Both rooms have wide doorways, level thresholds and adequate pathway access. The bathrooms in both staterooms are identical and each has a roll-in shower with a hand-held showerhead, a fold-down shower seat, grab bars in the shower and around the toilet and a full five-foot turning radius.

The BB Superior stateroom is the more spacious choice, with 228 square feet of area, 12 more square feet than the CC First Class stateroom. Some furniture may need to be removed from the rooms in order to comfortably maneuver a wheelchair or scooter, and most wheelchair users will need help with the heavy doors. Additionally, there are three-inch coamings (lips) on the balcony doors. Still, the rooms are nicely accessible, especially for a small ship.

Empress of the North at the entrance to Glacier Bay.

Access to the public areas is also good. There are two large elevators, accessible public restrooms, wide hallways and level access to most decks. The first deck has doorways with two-inch coamings, but, to be honest, this outside deck area is mainly used by the crew. The one tight spot on the ship is the dining room because, when the ship is full, it's quite crowded and very difficult for wheelers to navigate. Although there's no assigned seating, if access is an issue, ask if you can reserve a table near the door, as the crew is happy to accommodate special requests.

All shore excursions are included on the *Empress of the North*, and accessible transportation is available at all ports, with advance notice. Although all venues are not barrier free, the majority have a high level of access. *The Empress of the North* crew also gets high marks for their honesty in describing the access of the shore excursions, as they clearly point out possible access obstacles.

Of course, as with all Alaska cruises, boarding and disembarking can be difficult, due to the fluctuating tides. The good news is, the *Empress of the North* never tenders. That said, it's also important to note that sometimes the gangway can be very steep. Most wheelchair users and slow walkers will need assistance at some point. Additionally there is a six-inch step up to the gangway. The crew is happy to assist wheelers, and a manual wheelchair is available for slow walkers who need assistance getting from the ship to the bus. In the end, if you want to go ashore, the crew will work with you to make it happen.

The *Empress of the North* calls on the popular ports of Skagway and Ketchikan, docks (not tenders) at Sitka and stops at the less frequented ports of Petersburg and Wrangell. Memorable shore excursions along the way include Mendenhall Glacier in Juneau, the White Pass & Yukon Route Railroad in Skagway and the Alaska Raptor Rehabilitation Center in Sitka. And although all of the previously mentioned shore excursions feature good wheelchair access, exploring the port on your own or just wandering around near the dock is always an option.

In short, the *Empress of the North* is a very unique yet accessible way to cruise Alaska. Indeed, Alaska is a totally different experience on a paddlewheeler.

- IF YOU GO

  - Majestic America Line, (800) 434-1232, www.majesticamericaline.com

RCI'S ACCESSIBLE CARIBBEAN

Although cruising is often billed as the most accessible vacation option, all cruise ships are not created equal. Generally speaking, when you're talking about cruise ships, bigger is better as far as access is concerned. And when we talk big, the Royal Caribbean International (RCI) name inevitably comes up.

It all started when RCI introduced their Voyager Class ships: the *Adventure of the Seas*, the *Explorer of the Seas*, the *Voyager of the Seas*, the *Navigator of the Seas* and the *Mariner of the Seas*. Billed as the largest cruise ships in the world, these massive beauties shared a long-running five-way tie for that title. They each can accommodate 3,114 passengers, and, at the time they were built, they were up to a third longer than any existing ship.

Today they've been stripped of their title; however they still offer excellent access. Each Voyager Class ship has 26 accessible staterooms, including 16 outside staterooms, nine inside staterooms and one stateroom

that overlooks the Royal Promenade. All accessible staterooms have roll-in showers, fold-down shower benches, roll-under sinks, wide doorways and plenty of maneuvering room. Ten of the outside staterooms also have balconies with ramped thresholds.

The pathway access on the Voyager Class ships is excellent. All decks are accessible by elevator or stair-lift, and the ships are pleasantly devoid of those two- to three-inch coamings (door sills) that are standard on many old cruise ships. In place of those obstacles, you'll find threshold ramps, automatic doors and level access.

For a few years the "largest cruise ship" title bounced around among a number of cruise lines, until RCI reclaimed it in 2006, with the christening of their first Freedom Class ship, the *Freedom of the Seas*. This was followed in May 2007 with the launch of her sister ship, the *Liberty of the Seas*. Today these two vessels share the "largest cruise ship" title and they each can accommodate a whopping 3,634 guests.

Each of the Freedom Class ships has 32 accessible staterooms in a variety of categories. The accessible staterooms feature a level entry, wide doorways and good pathway access. The bathrooms are equipped with a roll-in shower with a hand-held showerhead and a fold-down shower seat, grab bars in the shower and around the toilet and a roll-under sink. And like on the Voyager Class ships, access throughout the public areas on the Freedom Class vessels is excellent. You just couldn't ask for better access on either class of ship.

Of course the ship itself is only half of the accessible cruise equation. Port access is equally important. So what's the most accessible itinerary among these RCI big ships? RCI access coordinator, Charles Newton and travel agency owner Connie George both agree, it's the eastern Caribbean itinerary. "Accessible shore excursions are spotty throughout the Caribbean, largely because most of the region is not governed by laws like the Americans with Disabilities Act," says Ms. George. "RCI's eastern Caribbean itineraries do however feature calls on St. Thomas and Puerto Rico, both of which fall under US law," she adds, "so you're more likely to find accessible shore options on those two islands."

Variety is the key word on St. Thomas, where a number of accessible choices await cruise ship passengers. For those passengers who don't want to venture too far, the Havensight Dockside Mall operates a free lift-equipped

· ·

The Promenade on Royal Caribbean's Adventure of the Seas.

shuttle to and from the dock. Approximately 80% of Havensight's shops have a level entry.

Alternatively, Accessible Adventures offers a 2.5-hour island tour in a lift-equipped open-air trolley, or, for a more customized tour of the island, contact St. Thomas Dial-A-Ride. Says Dial-A-Ride operations manager Lloyd Herman, "We offer everything from shopping to snorkeling, and we try and build the tour around the customer's interests." All tours are operated in lift-equipped air-conditioned vehicles and must be booked at least a month in advance.

Even though San Juan is a very old city, it's still possible to book an accessible tour in this port. Your best bet is to contact Rafael at Wheelchair Transportation and Tours. Rafael has been taking folks on tours of the island for years, first as the owner of a Wheelchair Getaways franchise and then when he opened his own tour business. Visitors can enjoy scenic views from the historic El Morro fort or opt to visit the Bacardi Distillery, El Yunque rainforest or Luquillo Beach. All are nicely accessible.

And although Philipsburg, St. Maarten, isn't a US territory, access is improving in this eastern Caribbean port of call. Previously the only option for wheelchair users was to use the stationery lift at the port to board a standard van for an island tour. Because the lift stayed at the port, wheelchair users were unable to stop and get out along the way. Thanks to the recent introduction of an accessible tour by Louis Jeffers, all this has changed. Wheelchair users can now enjoy a three-hour morning or afternoon tour in Mr. Jeffers' lift-equipped van. The van is clean, air-conditioned and equipped with tie-downs, and Mr. Jeffers is an excellent guide.

And no RCI Eastern Caribbean itinerary is complete without a stop in Labadee, RCI's private Haitian island. Although this is a tender port, passengers are transported ashore on an RCI accessible tender that features a track lift. Says Connie, "I've rarely had any wheelchair users report problems going ashore in Labadee." Once ashore, visitors can enjoy the beach in a beach wheelchair. RCI currently has nine beach wheelchairs on Labadee, and by all indications they are a very big hit. Admits Connie, "I have wheelchair users who keep cruising back to Labadee just because of the great beach access."

- IF YOU GO

  - Royal Caribbean International,
    (800) 327-6700, (800) 722-5472 ext. 34492 - Access Desk,
    www.royalcaribbean.com

- Accessible Adventures, (340) 344-8302 , www.accessvi.com
- St. Thomas Dial-A-Ride, , (340) 776-1277
- Wheelchair Transportation and Tours, (800) 868-8028
- Louis Jeffers Tours, +599 5249204, Bigjtx43@hotmail.com

THE MIGHTY MISSISSIPPI

L aunched in 1995 by the Delta Steamboat Company, the *American Queen* has long been billed as the world's largest river cruise ship. In 2006, after her parent company was liquidated, she reappeared as the flagship of the newly formed Majestic America Line. She was chosen as the flagship not only because of her size, but also because of her grand elegance. Indeed in some circles she is still known as the "grand" *American Queen*. Today she sails week-long itineraries on the Mississippi and Ohio Rivers, which highlight the natural beauty, regional cultures and vibrant history of the area.

It goes without saying that there's a huge difference between the *American Queen* and her ocean-going counterparts. For starters, there are no casinos, rock-climbing walls, golf courses, ice skating rinks or internet cafes aboard the *American Queen*. Instead you'll enjoy Victorian luxury in opulent public spaces such as the Gentlemen's Card Room, the Ladies' Parlor and the Mark Twain Gallery. And as you cruise along the mighty Mississippi, he pace is slow and the emphasis is on personal service.

The *American Queen* has 222 passenger cabins, including nine that are wheelchair accessible. Two elevators provide access to most areas of the ship (except the engine room and the Sun Deck), and wide decks make for easy maneuvering. Access to most of the public areas is excellent.

Pathway access throughout the ship is also very good. There are threshold ramps to most of the outside areas, and in the few places where there are high coamings (lips), there are also alternate accessible routes. Boarding is by a retractable bow ramp, and the pitch is dependent upon the river level. Assistance is always available.

Accessible cabins are available in a broad range of categories, from Category A (outside superior) to Category D (inside). All cabins are spacious, with plenty of room to maneuver. All of the outside accessible cabins have

The grand American Queen.

French doors that open to the deck, plus an inside hallway entrance. Some of the exterior thresholds are up to one-inch high, but most are quite doable. The interior entrance thresholds are all level.

The accessible bathrooms have either a roll-in shower or a tub/shower combination. Access features include grab bars in the shower and toilet areas, lever handles, a five-foot turning radius and a hand-held showerhead. A portable shower bench is available upon request. Even the Category D accessible cabin (381) is very spacious and includes a large bathroom with a roll-in shower.

The good access on the American Queen doesn't end when you go ashore. Many of the shore excursions are appropriate for slow walkers or wheelchair users. Accessible transportation (in a lift-equipped bus or van) can be ordered for most shore tours, and there is at least one accessible tour option in each port. You can also opt to explore on your own, as there is usually something to see or do near the port areas. If the American Queen docks away from the city center, a fee-based shuttle is available. An accessible shuttle can be ordered with 24 hours' advance notice.

It's also important to note that port access is dependent upon the river level. If the river is low, it's a greater distance to the top of the levee. A wheelchair transfer service is available for slow walkers, and crew assistance is available for manual wheelchair users. Power wheelchair and scooter users can transfer to a manual wheelchair for the trek up the levee, then transfer back to their own wheelchair or scooter at the top.

Ports of call vary depending on the cruise, but favorite Mississippi River stops include New Orleans, St. Francisville, Baton Rouge, Vicksburg and Memphis. And of course there's plenty of time for cruising down the river and watching the rest of the world go by. All in all the *American Queen* is a great cruise choice, as it offers good access and allows passengers the opportunity to slow down, relax and enjoy the charm of the mighty Mississippi.

- IF YOU GO

  - Majestic America Line, (800) 434-1232, www.majesticamericaline.com

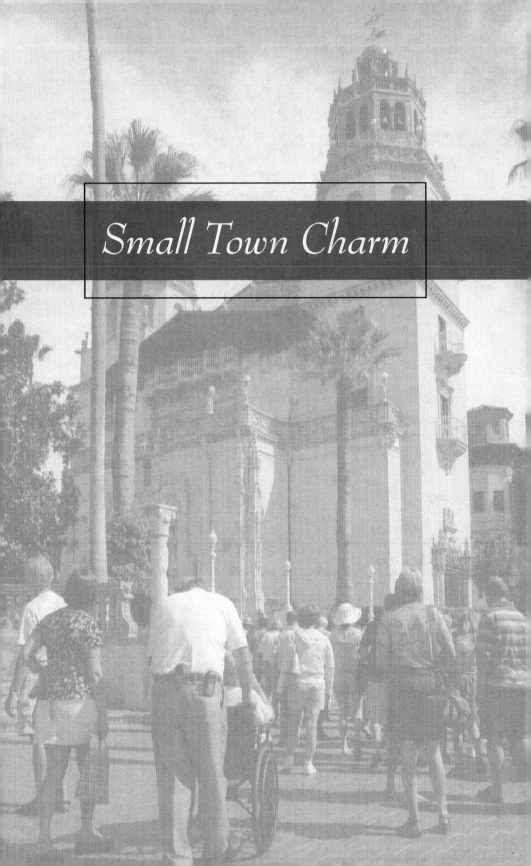

Small Town Charm

A REVITALIZED DUBUQUE

In the early 20th Century, the Port of Dubuque was home to heavy industry, a boat-building shop and even a lumber yard. Also known as the Ice Harbor, this Mississippi River port remained a bustling industrial area for many decades. All that changed in the 1970s when devastating floods and hard economic times hit the area. Most of the industries closed or relocated, leaving the port deserted and in disrepair.

But things turned around for the Port of Dubuque in 2002, with the introduction of a $188 million riverfront development project. Appropriately named, America's River, this unique project focuses on the historic, environmental, educational and recreational majesty of the mighty Mississippi River, and it turned the former Ice Harbor into a first-class tourist destination. The cornerstone of the project, the Grand Harbor Resort, was unveiled in 2002, followed shortly by the National Mississippi River Museum and Aquarium, the Mississippi Riverwalk and the Grand River Center. Today the completed project makes Dubuque a very accessible and affordable destination.

The Grand Harbor Resort, which is just steps away from America's River major attractions, features accessible parking, wide doorways, a level entrance, elevator access to the upper floors and barrier-free access to the resort facilities. This 193-room property has eight accessible guest rooms, including two with roll-in showers.

Access features in the accessible guest rooms include wide doorways, good pathway access and a five-foot turning radius in the bathrooms. The accessible rooms also include some often overlooked access features such as lowered closet rods and wheelchair-height robe hooks. All rooms include a refrigerator, a microwave and a coffee maker, and half of them feature stunning views of the Mississippi River.

The Grand Harbor Resort is just a short walk away from the National Mississippi River Museum and Aquarium, which highlights the cultural and natural history of the Mississippi River. Access at the museum is excellent, with a level entry, accessible restrooms, spacious galleries and elevator access to all floors.

An affiliate of The Smithsonian Institution, the museum features five large aquariums on the main floor plus an indoor wildlife exhibit that showcases the creatures of the Mississippi. Upstairs the focus is on the history

Access from the Woodward Wetlands Boardwalk at the National Mississippi River Museum and Aquarium.

of the river, with gallery space devoted to the early explorers, builders and inventors who made river trade and transportation a reality. Outside there's an elevated Woodward Wetlands boardwalk, which offers visitors an opportunity to see the native flora and fauna and also get a great view of the museum boatyard and the Mississippi River. It's all nicely accessible and the museum offers a pretty comprehensive look at the Mighty Mississippi.

Of course, there's no better way to get a real feel for the Mississippi River than to take a short cruise on it. To that end, consider cruising on the *Spirit of Dubuque*. Docked next to the National Mississippi River Museum and Aquarium, this paddlewheel riverboat offers lunch, dinner and afternoon sightseeing cruises.

Considering that the *Spirit of Dubuque* was constructed in 1976, the access on board is pretty good. Although the doorway to the main deck dining area is only 28-inches wide, there is plenty of room to maneuver a wheelchair once you get inside. Boarding of the vessel is via a ramp, and there is a two-inch lip at the entrance, but assistance is available. And once the *Spirit of Dubuque* sets sail, it's a calm and stable cruise experience. Unfortunately the on-aboard toilet is not accessible at all; in fact, you have to be able to stand to use it. Your best bet is to plan ahead and opt for the 1.5-hour afternoon sightseeing cruise.

Next door to the *Spirit of Dubuque*, you'll find the Diamond Jo Casino. Access is good throughout this riverboat casino, which is open 24 hours a day. It features a wide variety of slot machines and table games and there's also a deli on board, in case you work up an appetite from all that gambling.

If you'd like a breath of fresh air after your gambling excursion, then check out the Mississippi Riverwalk. This quarter-mile paved trail connects all of America's River attractions. It's wide, level and very accessible. A 5,000 square foot pavilion is located along the Riverwalk, and if you're lucky, you might even catch a glimpse of one of Majestic America's riverboats docked here. It's a very pleasant and accessible area, a great place for a leisurely walk and an excellent vantage point for a more intimate look at the Mississippi River.

- IF YOU GO
  - Grand Harbor Resort, (563) 690-4000, www.grandharborresort.com
  - National Mississippi River Museum and Aquarium, (563) 557-9545, www.rivermuseum.com
  - Spirit of Dubuque, (563) 583-8093, www.spiritofdubuque.com
  - Diamond Jo Casino, (563) 690-2100, www.diamondjo.com

ARTFUL BOISE

Boise surprised me on a number of levels. With a population topping 185,000, it's not exactly what you'd define as a small town; however that small-town ambience is ever present in this high-desert community. And that's a very good thing. Couple that with a high level of community involvement and a top-notch arts and culture scene, and you can begin to see the attraction. It's a very walkable city, with a lot of public art, unique shops and family-owned restaurants. In short, it's just a very pleasant (and accessible) place to visit.

The best way to get your feet wet in Boise is to hit the streets and explore the downtown entertainment district, known as BODO to the locals. From the state capitol to Capitol Boulevard, it's a very accessible area with wide level sidewalks and curb cuts at every corner. The best plan of action is to pick up the Public Art Map at the downtown Visitors Center (on the Grove Plaza located on the east side of Boise Centre), and start exploring. Think of it as a public art treasure hunt.

The great thing about the art walk is that you can do it at your own pace, expand it beyond BODO or just do a portion of it. The whole downtown area is filled with cozy cafes and unique gift shops (most of which offer level access), so there are lots of places to take a break along the way. Must-see pieces in the downtown area include the Basque history mural on the side of the Fronton Building, the murals on the fourth floor of the Capitol Building and the windows on the Egyptian Theater. And for a good chuckle, check out *Sidney's Niche*, a whimsical mural of a rat on a treadmill operating the escalator. It's located on the wall under the 8th Street escalator, between Main and Idaho Streets.

Save some time to explore the Basque Block (Grove Street), marked at the entrance by *Laiak*, a stone and steel sculpture erected to celebrate Basque history and culture. The Basque Museum is also worth a visit. This museum features level access and it houses interpretive exhibits on the Basques and their history in Idaho. Next door you'll find the historic Cyrus Jacobs-Uberuaga Boarding House. Although this building is not open to the public, the facade is worth a quick look. According to local historians, this 1864 building housed Boise's first indoor bathtub. Today it's the oldest surviving brick building in the city.

Located near downtown Boise, Julia Davis Park is also a must-see for visitors. Truth be told, you could spend several days exploring this 86-acre regional park, as it's more than just a park, it's also the cultural, historic and artistic gateway to the heart of the city.

Culturally speaking, Julia Davis Park has it all, starting with the Idaho State Historical Museum, located near the Capitol Boulevard entrance. The museum features level access, spacious galleries, elevator access to the second floor and a loaner wheelchair at the front desk. The focus of the museum is on Idaho history, from the Oregon Trail to the Victoria era, and the permanent collection features artifacts from Native American tribes of the area, early settlers and 1920s residents.

Next door, the Boise Art Museum features a permanent collection of 2,300 works, with an emphasis on Pacific Northwest art, American Realism and ceramics. Access is excellent throughout this building as well, with a level entrance, good pathway access and plenty of room to wheel around in the galleries.

• •

"Boise Totems" by Rod Kagen on Boise's Art Walk.

Another must-see in the park is the tiny Idaho Black History Museum located in the historic St. Paul Baptist Church, just across the street from the Rose Garden parking lot. There is ramp access on the side of this one-room museum, which features exhibits about the culture and history of Blacks, with a special emphasis on Blacks in Idaho. It's one of only a handful of Black history museums in the nation.

And for a trip back in time, hop on the Boise Tour Train, which departs from the ticket booth in front of the Black History Museum. You have to be able to transfer to the open-air car to ride the train, but assistance is available and folding wheelchairs can be carried on the train. This one-hour narrated tour travels through downtown Boise and focuses on local gold rush history. It's a fun way to see some of the historic haunts of the city and a great way to get a good overview of one of America's most livable cities.

- IF YOU GO
  - The Basque Museum, (208) 343-2671, www.basquemuseum.com
  - Idaho State Historical Museum, (208) 334-2120, www.idahohistory.net/museum.html
  - Boise Art Museum, (208) 345-8330, www.boiseartmuseum.org
  - Black History Museum, (208) 433-0017, www.ibhm.org
  - Boise Tour Train, (208) 342-4796, www.boisetours.net
  - Boise Convention & Visitors Bureau, (208) 344-7777, www.boise.org

CAMBRIA GEMS

Located on the central California coast, Cambria is a bit of gem itself. With a population of some 6,000 people, it's just a very comfortable place. It's not trendy or busy but simple, down-to-earth and pretty laid back. The big attractions in the area are the scenery, the coast and Hearst Castle. And of course some folks visit Cambria just to escape the maddening crowds.

And there's no better place to relax and escape than the Cambria Pines Lodge. Set on 26 garden-filled acres, this 126-room property borders on an undeveloped natural area filled with native wildlife. The ground-floor accessible suite (Room 611) features a living room, a small dining area, a kitchen area and a separate master bedroom. There is a Murphy bed in the living area, and the suite can accommodate up to six people, although it would be cozy for a wheeler. The suite has two fireplaces, one in the living area and one in the master bedroom, plus a private garden porch off of the master bedroom.

The bathroom features a full five-foot turning radius, a roll-in shower with a built-in shower bench, a hand-held showerhead, grab bars in the shower and around the toilet and a roll-under sink. There is excellent pathway access throughout the suite and parking is available just steps from the front door.

And if you have a green thumb, or just wish you did, then be sure and stop by the Cambria Nursery, located right next door to the Cambria Pines Lodge. Although a pathway connects the two properties, wheelchair users should drive, as there are a few steep sections along the trail. The nursery itself is nicely accessible, with wide level pathways and accessible parking near the entry.

The Cambria Nursery holds a number of gardening workshops throughout the year, the most intriguing being the Living Birdhouse Workshop. During this three-hour class, participants construct a miniature garden in a birdhouse, complete with a drip watering system. It's very unique and makes a great addition to any yard. The nursery also features a wide selection of plants and yard art, and it's a great place to get landscaping ideas, even if you don't purchase anything.

No visit to the area would be complete without a visit to Hearst Castle, located just up the highway in San Simeon. Make no mistake about it, Hearst Castle was not constructed to be accessible, and in order to participate in one of the standard tours you must be able to climb and descend anywhere from 107 to 404 stairs. The good news is, the Castle staff also offers an accessibly designed tour (ADT) for anyone who cannot manage the standard tours.

The ADT includes transportation to the hilltop castle in a lift-equipped bus, a visit to most of the first-floor rooms in the main house, a peek at the Casa del Mar guest house and a spin around the grounds in a ramped golf cart for a look at the gardens, the guest houses, the Neptune Pool and the tennis courts. This excellent tour offers an intimate look at the Julia Morgan-designed masterpiece; however be forewarned that the ADT must be booked at least 10 days in advance. Plan ahead to avoid disappointment.

Another coastal must-see, Piedras Blancas Elephant Seal Rookery, is located just 4.4 miles north of Hearst Castle. There are two accessible parking spaces in the small dirt lot at the rookery. A hard-packed dirt trail leads from the parking area to a wide boardwalk, which offers great views of the elephant seal colony. There are several viewing spots along this short boardwalk, and it's wide enough to accommodate pedestrian traffic and wheelers.

Although the rookery has a small number of year-round residents, peak activity begins near December 1, when the males begin to return to mate. Most of the births occur between the end of December and February, and by March the colony once again dwindles. It's easy to miss the rookery, as it's not well marked from the road, so look for the second "vista point" turnout north of Hearst Castle. If you reach the lighthouse, turn around, as you've missed the rookery.

And finally, save some time for a look at the other "castle" in the area, known fondly by the locals as Nitt Witt Ridge. Constructed in 1928 by local trash hauler Art Beal, this California State Historical Landmark was crafted entirely of discarded objects — otherwise known as junk. Known as the poor man's Hearst Castle, today Mr. Beal's creation sits behind a locked chain link gate at 881 Hillcrest Drive in Cambria. Tours are offered by appointment, however they are not accessible. Still it's worth a look while you are in the area, and you can get a pretty good view of the home from Hillcrest Drive. Just park across the street in the small dirt area — you don't even have to get out of the car to get a gander at Art's creation. It's definitely worth a stop, as it gives new meaning to the word, "eclectic."

- IF YOU GO
  - Cambria Pines Lodge, (805) 927-4200, www.moonstonehotels.com
  - Cambria Nursery, (805) 927-4747, www.cambrianursery.com
  - Hearst Castle, (805) 927-2115, www.hearstcastle.com
  - Piedras Blancas Elephant Seal Rookery, www.elephantseal.org

HOP OFF THE FAST TRACK IN COLUMBIA

Want to get away from it all? Then consider hopping off the fast track and enjoying the simple pleasures of life in Columbia, Missouri. Located halfway between Kansas City and St. Louis, Columbia sports all the essential trappings of Main Street USA; however, as an added bonus, it also boasts a

Touring Hearst Castle.

Wide paths and level walkways make Shelter Gardens nicely accessible.

cultural and intellectual diversity typically only found in larger metropolitan areas. Perhaps it's because Columbia is home to three universities, or maybe it's just because the locals have a broader world view. Whatever the reason, Columbia offers visitors the best of both worlds, everything from small-town festivals to upscale eateries. Additionally, thanks to local advocacy efforts, the access in Columbia is excellent.

Another plus about Columbia is that it's near the Katy trail, the nation's longest developed rails-to-trails project. This multiuse trail runs from Clinton to St. Charles along the abandoned rail bed of the former Missouri - Kansas - Texas Railroad. The Katy Trail offers a great opportunity for wheelers and slow walkers to explore Missouri's natural side, as the grade rarely exceeds 5% and the surface is covered with crushed limestone. Indeed, it's very rollable.

Although the Katy Trail doesn't pass directly through Columbia, it's connected to downtown by the nicely accessible MKT Trail. This 8.2 mile multiuse trail spur begins at 4th and Cherry Streets in downtown Columbia and connects to the Katy Trail near McBaine.

The MKT Trail is wide, flat and smooth, just perfect for wheelchairs and slow walkers. Once the trail moves out of the downtown area, it's sheltered by a dense canopy of trees as it winds toward the Katy Trail. MKT trailheads are located at Stadium, Forum and Scott Boulevards. All trailhead parking lots include accessible parking spaces. The Stadium Boulevard trail-head also features the Martin Luther King Memorial Garden. Emergency telephones are located along the MKT Trail, and it's patrolled regularly by a volunteer safety patrol.

Another good place to enjoy Missouri's natural beauty is at Shelter Gardens. Located on the grounds of Columbia-based Shelter Insurance company, this five-acre garden space features a wide selection of native and exotic plants, including a shade garden, conifer garden, rock garden and sensory garden. Wide paths and level walkways make Shelter Gardens nicely accessible. Don't miss the free summer concerts on Sunday evenings in June and July.

In truth, the best way to enjoy the ambiance of Columbia is to stroll through the downtown area. Don't miss the Candy Factory at 7th and Cherry Streets. This Columbia mainstay is nicely accessible with a zero-step entry and lift access to the upstairs area. The Candy Factory is much more than just a chocolate-lovers' paradise, as the upstairs production area features a series of unique candy-themed murals. It's best described as a subtle blend of Candy Land meets Willy Wonka, and it's a definite must-see.

Downtown Columbia also hosts a wide variety of festivals throughout the year. The Downtown Twilight Festival is a local favorite. It features musical performances, artistic demonstrations and fun for all ages on Thursday evenings in June and September. Then there's the September Festival of the Arts, which features over 40 live performances, followed by the Christmas-themed Downtown Holiday Festival held in early December. All downtown festivals are held in the streets of Columbia and are wheelchair accessible.

Another popular Columbia event is the annual Ramp Art exhibit. This visual arts exhibit and sale is held every May at Columbia College. Ramp Art showcases the artistic talents of people with disabilities and includes an art exhibit and sale, silent auction, food and live entertainment. The proceeds raised from this popular event help Columbia Services for Independent Living construct residential ramps for low-income individuals. It's a fun event, and yet another way to enjoy Columbia's small-town charm.

- IF YOU GO
  - MKT Trail, Columbia Parks and Recreation Department, (573) 874-7460
  - Shelter Gardens, (573) 445-8441
  - Columbia Visitors Bureau, (573) 875-1231, www.visitcolumbiamo.com

ESCAPE TO THE SPRINGS

P eople have been escaping to Palm Springs for decades. It all started in 1934 when Charlie Farrell and Ralph Bellamy founded the exclusive Racquet Club of Palm Springs so their fellow movie stars would have a place to play tennis and rub elbows with their own kind. Today Palm Springs has evolved, and, although celebrities still visit and even reside in this desert community, it's not the exclusive enclave of yesteryear. Indeed, these days, Palm Springs is an attractive escape for just about everyone.

Located just 114 miles east of Los Angeles, Palm Springs boasts a regional airport, however the best way to get there is by car. Many of the popular attractions are located outside of the downtown area, so, if you fly in, you'll need to rent a car to visit them.

At the top of the list of Palm Springs must-sees is the Palm Springs Aerial Tramway. Located on the north edge of town in rugged Chino Canyon, the tram ride begins at the Valley Station and travels 2.5 miles up the canyon to the Mountain Station in Mt. St. Jacinto State Park.

The Valley Station features accessible parking near the entrance and access to the station via a funicular-like lift device called an inclinator. The inclinator can accommodate scooters, power wheelchairs and anyone who can't manage the three flights of stairs up to the entrance. Inside the station there is barrier-free access to all areas and roll-on access to the tram.

And the view from the tram is simply spectacular. The tram cars have rotating floors, which allow visitors an unobstructed 360-degree view of the canyon, without moving around the car. If you are unsteady on your feet or tire easily, don't worry; there are also a few places to sit down inside the tram.

Up at the top you can grab a bite to eat and enjoy the view. There is also a small museum and a movie about the tram. Access at the Mountain Station is pretty good, with level access to most of the viewing areas, shops and facilities.

Another popular Palm Springs attraction is the Palm Springs Air Museum, appropriately located near the airport. Most of the World War II vintage aircraft in this museum are in working order and are flown on a regular basis. In fact, a number of the museum's planes have been used in

View from the Palm Springs Aerial Tramway Mountain Station in Mt. St. Jacinto State Park.

Hollywood productions, such as *Pearl Harbor*, *Forever Young* and *The Black Sheep Squadron*. As an added bonus, most of the docents are World War II veterans who love to share their stories, and they really make the museum come to life.

Access is excellent throughout the museum, with accessible parking near the door, level access to the building, barrier-free access throughout the hangars and a wheelchair available for loan at the front desk.

Another unique Palm Springs find is Moorten Botanical Garden, located just south of the downtown area on Palm Canyon Drive. It's pretty intimate for a botanical garden, but then again, that's part of its charm. Established in 1938, this historic landmark is part of the Moorten family estate. Over the years, they've turned their large yard into a living museum that showcases more than 3,000 desert plants from around the world.

In truth, this attraction is best suited for slow walkers; however the good news is, if you can get past the entrance, you'll probably be able to access most of the hard-packed dirt paths throughout the garden. Parking is only available on the street, and there is a very short and steep driveway at the entrance. Additionally there are no accessible restrooms on the premises. Still if you plan ahead and can make do with the access, it's a very interesting stop.

Finally, if you'd like to catch a great musical performance while you're in town, don't miss The Fabulous Palm Springs Follies. Billed as a Broadway-caliber celebration of the music, dance and comedy of the 30s and 40s, the follies features performers from 57 to 82 years old. But don't get the wrong impression; it's not just a bunch of retired amateurs putting on a community theater-type production. Nothing could be further from the truth, as most cast members are lifelong professional dancers, and the production is reminiscent of a Las Vegas review, complete with elaborate headdresses, skimpy costumes and millions of sequins.

Located in the heart of downtown Palms Springs, the Plaza Theater is home to The Fabulous Palm Springs Follies. Built in 1936 and renovated in 1991, the theater now features ramp access, wide doorways and a selection of accessible seats. The staff is very accommodating, and you can stay in your own wheelchair or transfer to a seat for the performance. Just let them know about your needs when you make your reservations. They even have a scooter and wheelchair check.

The Fabulous Palm Spring Follies offers matinee and evening performances from October through May. As an added bonus, the Plaza Theater is within walking distance of a wide variety of restaurants in the very accessible downtown area, so come early and enjoy a bite to eat before the show. You just can't visit Palm Springs without seeing the Fabulous Palm Springs Follies.

- IF YOU GO
  - Palm Springs Aerial Tramway, (760) 325-1391, www.pstramway.com
  - Palm Springs Air Museum, (760) 778-6262, www.palmspringsairmuseum.org
  - Mooten Botanical Garden, (760) 327-6555
  - Fabulous Palm Springs Follies, (760) 327-0225, www.psfollies.com
  - Palm Springs Bureau of Tourism, (800) 347-7746, www.palm-springs.org

FURNITURE CITY, USA

Once hailed as America's Furniture Capital, Grand Rapids. Michigan, was home to 44 furniture companies at the peak of the furniture production boom in the 1880s. In fact, if you purchased furniture back then, chances are it was manufactured in Grand Rapids. But times change, and today the Grand Rapids furniture boom is a thing of the past. The good news is, these days Grand Rapids is experiencing another boom: a rebirth and revitalization of the downtown area. That's great news for travelers, and excellent news for accessibility.

Today the revitalized downtown area is a wonderful place to wander about and enjoy the public art, linger over a good meal, listen to some live music and then stop off for a nightcap before heading back to your downtown hotel. Indeed, everything you need is within rolling distance.

Accessible lodging options range from quiet and comfortable to glitzy and glamorous. On the quiet side of things is the Marriott Courtyard. Located on the corner of Monroe and Fulton Streets, this 207-room property features accessible rooms with either a roll-in shower or a tub/shower combination. There is level access to the lobby and all of the public areas, including the small cafe. This is not your typical busy Marriott, as part of this complex houses apartments whereas the other part is devoted to the hotel. It has a very quiet residential feel to it.

On the grander scale of things, the 682-room Amway Grand Plaza Hotel is located just a few blocks away, in the heart of the lively business and entertainment district. Billed as a "destination" rather than just a hotel, the property features spacious public areas, a large shopping arcade and six restaurants. All of the public areas are wheelchair accessible, and the accessible guest rooms (which are called barrier-free rooms) are equipped with either a roll-in shower or a tub/shower combination.

Of course the great part about staying downtown is that you can just walk to dinner; and with more than 60 restaurants in the area, the hardest part about dining out in Grand Rapids is making a choice. Your best bet is to download the Downtown Dining Map from the Grand Rapids CVB website. This handy map features 37 downtown restaurants, with contact information listed on the back. Although most restaurants have a level entry, some have one or two steps, so it's best to call before you go, or just hit the streets and see what strikes your fancy.

Victorian room in greenhouse at Frederik Meijer Gardens and Sculpture Park.

If you just can't make up your mind, then head over to the BOB (which stands for "big old building"). Located across the street from the Marriott Courtyard, this renovated building is home to a steakhouse, an Italian restaurant, two bars, a seafood restaurant and a comedy club. It features ramped access to the front door and elevator access to all floors. Truly it has something for just about every taste.

Art and architecture also abound in the downtown area, and the best way to enjoy it is to pick up the Outdoor Art Inspirations map from the Grand Rapids CVB. This must-have resource highlights a walking tour of the public art and historic buildings in downtown Grand Rapids. It contains information about the better-known pieces (such as La Grande Vitesse on Calder Plaza), as well as details about some of the more obscure architectural finds (like the terra cotta peacocks that grace the Willard building). You can take the self-guided walking tour at your own pace and do as little or as much of it as you want. If your energy level is running low, you can even break it up over several days.

If you'd like a larger does of historic architecture, head on over to Heritage Hill. This historic neighborhood is located just a few minutes from downtown and features more than 1,300 properties dating back to 1848. The Grand Rapids CVB has an excellent map of the neighborhood, which highlights 77 of the more prominent structures. You can do the tour in your car or on foot, but I highly recommend the latter option as it's a very quiet and quaint neighborhood. As an added bonus, there are curb cuts and wide sidewalks throughout the area.

Last but not least, no visit to Grand Rapids is complete without a stop at Frederik Meijer Gardens & Sculpture Park. Located just 10 minutes from downtown, this 125-acre sculpture park is the ultimate integration of art and horticulture.

Access is excellent throughout the park, with level access to the front entrance, wide pathways, level access to the greenhouses and a veritable stable of loaner wheelchairs. The best way to experience the garden is to hop on the tram and enjoy the narrated tour. The wheelchair-accessible tram makes several stops throughout the garden and you can get on and off as you please. Take some time to enjoy some of the very pleasant paved trails near the tram stops.

You can even enjoy the garden in inclement weather, as it includes a large number of greenhouses and conservatories. And if you visit during March or April, don't miss the annual Butterflies Are Blooming exhibit in the 15,000 square foot Lena Meijer Conservatory. During this time, chrysalides from 40 to 50 species are placed in an "emergence area" where visitors can witness their magical transformation into butterflies. It's truly an amazing sight and reason enough to plan a Grand Rapids visit.

- IF YOU GO
  - Marriott Courtyard, (616) 242-6000
  - Amway Grand Plaza Hotel, (616) 774-2000, www.amwaygrand.com
  - Frederik Meijer Gardens & Sculpture Park, (616) 957-1580, www.meijergardens.org
  - Grand Rapids Convention and Visitors Bureau, (616) 459-8287, www.visitgrandrapids.org

SOCAL SOJOURN

Beach vacations are a popular commodity; however that popularity in itself can detract from the whole vacation getaway experience. After all, it's kind of hard to relax and unwind when you only have four square feet of sand between three people. But it doesn't have to be that way. Truth is, you can still enjoy a relaxing beach experience if you choose a relatively untourted

destination, a place like Oxnard, California. Located just 60 miles northwest of Los Angeles, this beachfront community offers accessible lodging, a nicely developed marina, a wheelchair-accessible beach and a quaint downtown area — all the ingredients for a relaxing, low-key beach getaway.

The major component for a perfect beach vacation is accessible beachfront lodging, and in that respect the Embassy Suites Mandalay Beach Resort fills the bill nicely. Located near the Oxnard marina on a lovely yet somewhat secluded beach, the resort features seven wheelchair-accessible suites, including one with a roll-in shower. The spacious suites feature two full bathrooms, a dining area, a wet bar, a living area and a separate master bedroom. The sofa in the living area converts to a bed, so it's an ideal arrangement if you travel with an attendant.

The accessible suites are located near the elevator and feature good pathway access, wide doorways and lever hardware. The master bathroom in the accessible suites is equipped with either a tub/shower combination or a roll-in shower and includes grab bars in the shower and around the toilet, a hand-held showerhead and a roll-under sink.

Most of the public areas are wheelchair accessible and the nicely landscaped grounds are very wheelchair friendly. Several accessible paths wind around the pool, spa and outside bar area, and there is ramp access to a wide paved pathway along the beach.

If you'd like to do a little more than just stroll along the beach, be sure and check out Rehab Point, located next door to the resort. The brainchild of Ed Hunt, this accessible beach area features a 900-foot paved beach path and a picnic area equipped with wheelchair-accessible picnic tables. A boardwalk runs from the picnic area down to the ocean, so you can either sunbathe or, at high tide, go into the water. It's a great place to play on the beach or just sit back and enjoy the view.

Another Oxnard must see is the excellent Ventura County Maritime Museum. Located on Fisherman's Wharf near the visitors center. This excellent museum contains historic ship models, maritime artwork and even some salvaged pieces from a local shipwreck.

One of the most unique exhibits is a collection of model ships made by POWs during the Napoleonic Wars. The museum also features the work of Ed Marple, a dental technician turned model builder. He is well known for his historic model warships built with instruments with which he was

Ventura County Maritime Museum on Fisherman's Wharf.

very familiar — his dental tools. Ed's tools, workbench and the model he was working on when he died are also on display. The museum also features a new exhibit of marine artwork every month, along with a permanent collection of John Stobart's well-known maritime paintings.

Access is excellent at the museum, with a level entry, good pathway access and accessible restrooms. Docents are on hand to answer questions, and there is no admission charge.

Another museum worth a look is the Carnegie Art Museum. Located next to Plaza Park, this community museum is housed in a 1906 neoclassic building, which towers over the adjacent park. Don't be intimidated by the front stairs, as you'll find a small elevator on the left side of the building. The elevator is unlocked during business hours and it goes directly to the main-floor gallery.

The majority of the exhibits are on the main floor, but there is also a small mezzanine area that is only accessible by a flight of stairs. It's a small museum but definitely worth a stop, as the exhibits change frequently in order to rotate items from the large permanent collection and showcase new visiting exhibits.

And for a look at the historic side of Oxnard, be sure and visit Heritage Square. Located in the downtown area between 7th Street and 8th Street, this square block of late 1800s and early 1900s buildings highlights Oxnard's rich agricultural, historic and cultural heritage. The buildings were relocated from other places in the county, restored and then leased out to local businesses. In short, Heritage Square became a sanctuary for endangered buildings.

Free docent-guided walking tours of Heritage Square are available every Saturday from 10 am to 2 pm. The tours last approximately 45 minutes and begin at the Heritage Square Visitors Center at 715 South A Street. There is level access on the Heritage Square pathways and all of the buildings included on the tour have ramped access. Even if you can't make the Saturday walking tour, Heritage Square is still a pleasant place to explore on your own, as the facades of the restored buildings are very nicely done. It's a nice way to get a look at another side of this historic beach community.

- IF YOU GO
  - Embassy Suites Mandalay Beach Resort, (805) 984-2500, www.mandalaybeach. embsuites.com
  - Ventura County Maritime Museum, (805) 984-6260
  - Carnegie Art Museum, (805) 385-8157, www.vcnet.com/carnart

- Heritage Square, (805) 483-7960
- Oxnard Convention and Visitors Bureau, (800) 269-6273, www.visitoxnard.com

THE HOME OF LL BEAN

Located on Maine's midcoast, Freeport is a well-known shoppers' paradise. This pedestrian-friendly village is home to outlets aplenty, including outdoor clothing giant LL Bean. And although shops and restaurants are all the rage along the main drag, the charm of Freeport extends well beyond the retail experience. In fact, just minutes away you'll find another side of Freeport filled will scenic drives, accessible trails and outdoor activities. This quaint community represents the best of both worlds — it's a place where you can shop for hiking gear in the morning and road test your purchases on an accessible trail in the afternoon.

Of course Freeport wasn't always factory outlet central; in fact it was once a manufacturing town filled with shoe factories. As the factories shut down, workers moved away, businesses closed and the historic buildings fell into disrepair. In a last-ditch effort to save the historic district and stimulate the local economy, the city invited outlet stores to locate in Freeport. In 1982 the Dansk Factory Outlet opened its doors, and today more than 125 retail shops are housed in the renovated buildings that line Main Street. In short, Freeport is a redevelopment success story.

Access is fairly good in downtown Freeport with wide sidewalks and ubiquitous curb cuts. The area along Main Street is level, but there is a downhill grade to the south. Accessible parking is available on Main Street or down the hill in the LL Bean Outlet parking lot. About 75% of the shops have level entries and access to at least one floor. Many of the shops are housed in historic buildings and have a few steps or narrow doorways; however, there are still plenty of accessible shopping choices in downtown Freeport.

Located on the far end of Main Street, The Harraseeket Inn is an excellent lodging choice for a Freeport visit. This 84-room inn includes two period buildings, which were built in 1795 and 1850, plus a new wing which was

The Harraseeket Inn in Freeport, Maine.

added in 1989. And although the inn is a historic property, owner Chip Gray is very aware of access issues and has gone to great lengths to make his property accessible. Says Chip, "We have discovered that the American with Disabilities Act rules are actually only the tip of the iceberg."

The inn features two accessible rooms: Room 107 and Room 204. Both rooms have a level entry, wide doorways, good pathway access, lever handles and a lowered closet rod. Access features in the bathrooms include a hand-held showerhead, a roll-under sink and grab bars around the toilet and in the shower area. Room 107 has a tub/shower combination, whereas Room 204 has a roll-in shower.

If you'd like a closer look at the great outdoors, then head on over to Wolfe's Neck Woods State Park. Located just five minutes from the Harraseeket Inn on Route 1, this 200-acre park features white pine and hemlock forests, a salt marsh estuary and great views of Casco Bay and the Harraseeket River. And considering it's a nature area, the access is excellent.

Accessible parking is located near the picnic area, and designated picnic spaces are reserved for "wheelchair users only." These accessible spaces feature roll-under picnic tables and wheelchair-height grills. The whole area is level and a hard-packed dirt trail leads over to the nearby accessible restrooms.

The accessible White Pines Trail starts on the other side of the picnic area. This hard-packed dirt trail winds through the forest and alongside the Harraseeket River. It's four feet wide, level and very easy to navigate in a wheelchair or scooter. And according to Chip Gray, "It's one of the few accessible trails in the area that actually takes you right down to the water."

Don't forget your binoculars, as the trail offers a great view of the osprey sanctuary on nearby Googins Island. And if you visit during the late spring, be on the lookout for Lady's Slippers in the shady areas on the forest floor. These pink orchids are a protected species in Maine, and they bloom from late May to early July. They are quite beautiful. And no matter when you go, don't forget the insect repellent!

- IF YOU GO
  - Freeport Merchants Association, (207) 865-1212, www.freeportusa.com
  - Harraseeket Inn, (207) 865-9377, www.harraseeketinn.com
  - Wolfe's Neck Woods State Park, (207) 865-4465

WILMINGTON'S RIVERFRONT

F lanked by an urban wildlife refuge on one end and a riverfront park on the other; Riverfront Wilmington features a bevy of shops, restaurants and entertainment venues connected by a 1.3-mile accessible riverfront walkway. Once home to a bustling shipyard, this redeveloped riverfront area now houses factory outlets, restaurants, a farmers market, an art museum and even a baseball stadium. It's a great place to stroll along the river and enjoy a piece of maritime history or shop till you drop and then sample some culinary delights. Variety is definitely the key word at this unique Delaware attraction.

For a look at the cultural side of Riverfront Wilmington, check out the Delaware Center for the Contemporary Arts. Dedicated to the advancement

Wilmington's riverfront walkway.

of contemporary art, this 35,000-square foot museum houses seven galleries and 26 artists studios. Access is excellent throughout the building with a level entrance and barrier-free access to all gallery areas. Although the center does not have a permanent collection, it does host more than 30 exhibitions a year, which feature contemporary artists from around the world.

Down the street from the Delaware Center for the Contemporary Arts, and kitty-corner from the Chase Center, is the core retail area of Riverfront Wilmington, the Shipyard Shops. This single-story retail outlet center features a variety of favorites such as LL Bean, Coldwater Creek and Nautica. There is level access throughout the complex, plenty of room to maneuver in a wheelchair and lots of accessible parking. And, best of all, there's no sales tax in Delaware, so the price you see on the tag is the price you pay at the register.

Walking along the riverfront walkway, you'll pass the giant Kahunaville Restaurant before you arrive at the bustling Riverfront Market. This public market is housed in a riverfront warehouse, which features vaulted ceilings, heavy timber construction and exposed brick walls. It's a great place to grab a sandwich or a quick snack, buy some produce or pick up fresh ingredients for dinner.

Sports buffs will want to save some time to visit the Delaware Sports Museum and Hall of Fame in nearby Frawley Stadium. The 5,000-square foot interactive museum features barrier-free access and includes sports memorabilia and artifacts dating back to the Civil War. The museum focuses on sports history, whereas the Delaware Sports Hall of Fame highlights the accomplishments of more than 230 athletes, coaches, officials, administrators and journalists who have been inducted. Thanks to technology, the museum offers visitors a unique opportunity to actually hear Delaware sports figures describe their experiences.

History lovers will enjoy the interpretive displays along the nicely accessible riverfront walkway, which traces the history of Wilmington's riverfront history. Just north of the Shipward Shops, two large cranes overlook Dravo Plaza and serve as a reminder of Riverfront Wilmington's shipbuilding past. And don't miss the Kalmar Nyckel, a hand-built replica of the Swedish ship that brought the first permanent European settlers to Wilmington in 1638. This unique ship is docked near the plaza and you can get a good glimpse of her from the riverfront walkway.

If you'd rather cruise along the river, then hop on board one of the wheelchair-accessible river taxis, operated by the Christina Riverboat Company. Although the pontoon boats are very accessible, some of the smaller docks are difficult to access at low tide. You'll find the best access at the larger docks, such as the Shipyard Shops dock.

And finally, save some time for a stroll through Tubman-Garrett Riverfront Park. Located on the far north end of Riverfront Wilmington, this 2.5 acre urban park features wide level pathways and plenty of room to navigate in a wheelchair. Not only is this urban park a great place to relax and enjoy the scenery, but it's also a popular venue for concerts, festivals and special events. It's just a fun place to enjoy the natural side of the Wilmington riverfront.

- IF YOU GO
  - Wilmington Riverfront, (302) 425-4890, www.riverfrontwilm.com
  - Greater Wilmington Convention & Visitors Bureau, (302)-652-4088, www.visitwilmingtonde.com

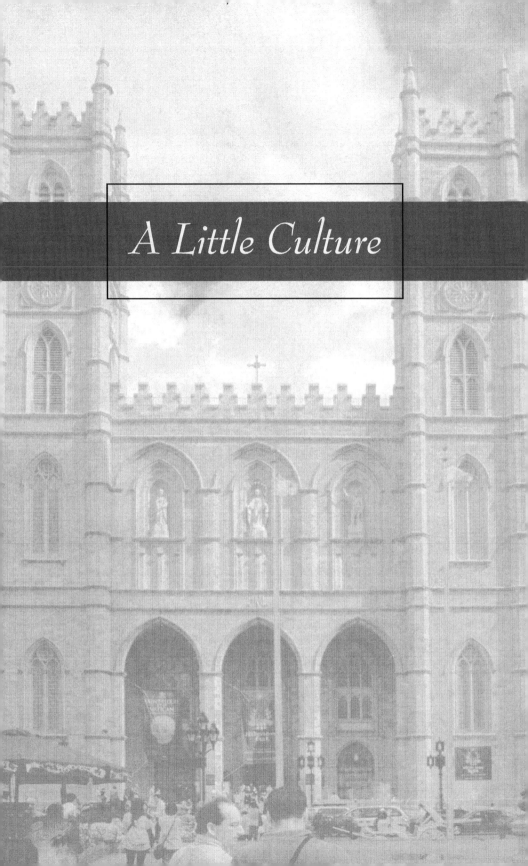

A Little Culture

A PIECE OF GREECE IN FLORIDA

S
ome people think you really haven't traveled unless you've had your passport stamped at least five or six times on one trip. Others like the allure of exotic destinations but just prefer to stay closer to home these days. So what's a traveler to do? Can you really have it all? Happily, the answer is a resounding "yes." So, if the mere thought of foreign travel conjures up images of long flights, surly customs agents and endless lines, then consider soaking up a dose of foreign culture a little closer to home. And Tarpon Springs, Florida, is the perfect place to do just that.

Located just 30 miles northwest of St. Petersburg, Tarpon Springs is known as the sponge capital of the world. Large numbers of Greek sponge divers immigrated to this small community near the turn of the century to work the bountiful sponge beds in the Gulf of Mexico. Today their descendants continue this old-world trade, along with the customs and traditions of their ancestral homeland. In short, Tarpon Springs is a little piece of Greece on Florida's Gulf Coast. And, it's also nicely accessible.

Your first stop in town should be the Tarpon Springs Cultural Center, located at 101 S. Pinellas Avenue. You can't miss it; if you're traveling north, it's on your right as you roll into town. You'll find accessible parking and the barrier-free entrance in Federal Plaza around the back of the building.

The Cultural Center offers tourist information and showcases the work of local artists. There is elevator access to the second floor and level access to the theater. A *National Geographic* film, which chronicles the history of the local sponge industry, is shown throughout the day. It's a good place to get a feel for the history of this unique community.

Just down the street from the Cultural Center you'll find the historic St. Nicholas Church. A ramped entrance is located on the left side of the building. St. Nicholas is the patron saint of the Tarpon Springs sponge-diving community. Pop in and have a look at the beautiful rotunda patterned after Istanbul's St. Sophia. The church also features Grecian marble that was originally part of the Greek pavilion at the 1939 New York World's Fair. It's quite beautiful.

And when you get hungry, authentic Greek cuisine is just a short roll away. Try the dolmades (stuffed grape leaves) or pastitso (Greek style lasagna) at Mama's, located just a block from the docks at 735 Dodecanese Boulevard. Mama's has a ramped entrance, accessible restrooms and an extensive menu of Greek specialties.

Mama's is located just a block from the waterfront in an area of town that's really alive with Greek culture. You'll see strings of sponges swaying in the breeze and smell the tempting aromas coming from the bakeries that border the waterfront. Access is good in this area, with wide sidewalks, curb cuts and level access to most of the shops.

Of course, the sponge dock area is the real heart and soul of Tarpon Springs. This is where it all happens, from sponge harvests to the weekly wholesale sponge auctions. Stop and see the sponge diver's suit (complete with lead booties) on display in front of the Billiris sponge market. The whole sponge dock area is nicely accessible, as it's flat and there's plenty of room to roll around.

For a closer look at the sponge industry, take a tour with St. Nicholas Boat Line, located right in back of Billiris sponge market. To board the boat, you have to be able to negotiate two steps, but there is plenty of room for a wheelchair aboard this authentic 50-foot Greek sponge-diving boat. The half-hour tour includes a brief history of the sponge-diving industry in Tarpon Springs, plus a demonstration of sponge harvesting by a diver in the traditional helmet and diving suit. It's quite interesting.

To be honest, anytime is a good time to visit Tarpon Springs, but, if you want the full dose of Greek culture, be sure and visit during the feast of Epiphany. Held annually on January 6, this massive celebration marks the most sacred day on the Greek Orthodox calendar. The festivities begin at St. Nicholas Church and then move on to nearby Spring Bayou, where young Greek men dive for a cross that has been blessed and thrown into the water. This day-long festival also features the blessing of the fleet and lots of entertainment, dancing and food.

Tarpon Springs truly is the best of both worlds — it's a little piece of Greece not very far from home. So, stop in next time you're in the neighborhood.

- IF YOU GO
  - Tarpon Springs Cultural Center, (727) 942-5605
  - Mama's, (727) 944-2888

· ·

Ali the sponge diver, in his diving suit, next to the mural in Tarpon Springs.

- St. Nicholas Boat Line, (727) 942-6425
- Tarpon Spring Chamber of Commerce, www.tarponsprings.com

AND WHAT'S WRONG WITH GRACELAND?

Let's face it, when you think of Memphis, you just can't help but think about Elvis. After all, The King was a big part of the musical history of the area. But what if you're not a huge Elvis fan? Can you still find happiness in Memphis? Gladly the answer is a resounding yes because, although Graceland is just the tip of the Memphis musical iceberg, you don't really have to be a huge Elvis fan to enjoy it. That goes for the rest of the city as well. Truth be told, Memphis is all about music, and if you like music — any kind of music — chances are you'll love Memphis.

Located about 25 minutes from the downtown area, Graceland deserves a full day on any Memphis itinerary. Although the mansion was built in 1939, access features have been added over the years, so today it's an excellent choice for wheelchair users and slow walkers. The access starts in the huge parking lot, which features a bevy of accessible parking spaces near the Sincerely Elvis Museum. There is level access from the parking lot to Graceland Plaza, where visitors board shuttle buses to the mansion. Lift-equipped shuttle buses are available, but there may be a slight wait.

The mansion features ramp access to the front door and good pathway access on the first floor. The second floor, which was considered Elvis' private sanctuary, is closed to visitors. The basement is only accessible by a flight of stairs, but a video of the area is available. A self-guided audio tour is included in the admission price, so you can tour the site at your own pace.

There's much more to see at Graceland besides the mansion, including the beautiful grounds, the Sincerely Elvis Museum, the Automobile Museum (which houses the pink Cadillac) and Elvis' grave. There are also several places to eat and, of course, a gift shop. There is barrier-free access to all areas of Graceland, except Elvis' jets, and it's just a fun place to spend the day.

Sun Studio, which is billed as the birthplace of rock and roll, is another Memphis must-see. It's the place where Elvis launched his career

Sun Studio tour guide sits at Marion Keisker's desk as she talks about the history of the studio.

when he recorded *That's All Right Mama*. He was in very good company, as Johnny Cash, Charlie Rich, Roy Orbison, Carl Perkins and Jerry Lee Lewis also cut some big hits at Sun Studio. By night, this historic location is still a working recording studio, but during the day it's open for tours.

Actually Sun Studio consists of two buildings, the studio and the adjacent soda shop. The first level of the soda shop and the studio both have level access, but the second-floor museum is only accessible by a flight of stairs. To be honest, the tour is still worth doing even without the museum, as the tour guides really offer some great insight about Sun Studio's heyday.

The tour includes outtakes from sessions and stories about those early days of rock and roll. And in the end, you can even stand on the spot where Elvis recorded his first hit and pose with the microphone he used.

For a different perspective on the Memphis music scene, visit the Memphis Rock "n" Soul Museum. Located just a block from Beale Street, this Smithsonian affiliate focuses on music as a catalyst for social change. The museum tells the story about the evolution of the Memphis sound and illustrates how this unique music style influenced culture and lifestyles around the world.

Exhibits range from hand-written lyrics and vintage juke boxes to more personal items such as Ike Turner's piano and Dick Clark's American

Bandstand podium. The well-done audio tour features clips from memorable recording sessions and allows visitors to listen to as many old tunes as they like. There is level access to the museum and barrier-free access throughout the spacious galleries. Indeed, real music buffs could spend a good chunk of the day there.

Another Memphis favorite, and a true music hot-spot, is historic Beale Street. Known as a blues venue for more than 50 years, Beale Street experienced a rebirth in the 1980s when the city purchased the property and developed the Beale Street Entertainment District. Today it's a major tourist draw with a multitude of clubs, restaurants, shops and bars. It's *the* place to listen to music in Memphis.

The street itself is closed to vehicles on the weekends to accommodate the influx of pedestrians. Access is good along the street with wide sidewalks and plenty of curb cuts. Approximately 50% of the buildings feature a level entry, whereas the rest have one or two steps. Even with the limited access, there are still lots of dining and entertainment choices. Although this party street can get pretty crowded, it's lots of fun. Indeed, it's part of the total Memphis experience and a must-see on any Memphis musical tour.

- IF YOU GO
  - Graceland, (901) 332-3322, www.elvis.com/graceland
  - Sun Studio, www.sunstudio.com
  - Memphis Rock "n" Soul Museum, (901) 205-2533, www.memphisrocknsoul.org
  - Memphis Convention & Visitors Bureau, 901-543-5333, www.memphistravel.com

BEYOND THE FAIRWAY

Known as a golfing Mecca by duffers around the world, the Phoenix and Scottsdale area is also an ideal winter holiday choice for nongolfers. The winter temperatures are mild, wheelchair-access is excellent and the area is awash with a wide variety of cultural diversions. And quite frankly it's just an excellent place to relax, unwind and enjoy the natural beauty of the Arizona desert.

Located on 40 acres of pristine Sonorian desert, the Four Seasons Scottsdale makes a perfect home base for a multiday Phoenix-Scottsdale getaway. Built in 1999, this low-rise resort features 188 oversized guest rooms and 22 suites, all with a patio or a balcony. The resort has seven accessible casita guest rooms, two accessible one-bedroom suites, and one accessible two-bedroom suite.

The accessible guest rooms feature wide doorways, excellent pathway access and a bathroom with a roll-in shower and a hand-held showerhead. Other access amenities include grab bars in the shower and around the toilet, a plastic shower chair and a full five-foot turning radius. Access throughout the complex is excellent, too, with wide paved pathways and golf cart transportation to and from the lobby. And in true Four Seasons style, you'll never want for anything.

Art and architecture buffs are in luck in Scottsdale, as there's no shortage of interesting sites to visit. At the top of the list is Frank Lloyd Wright's Taliesin West. Originally developed as a winter camp by the famous architect, today Taliesin West is the international headquarters for the Frank Lloyd Wright Foundation, the site of the Frank Lloyd Wright Archives, and the winter campus for the Frank Lloyd Wright School of Architecture.

This architectural masterpiece is also open for tours, and although the original structure was not built to be accessible, portable ramps have been added to improve the access.

There is ramp access to the gift shop and a barrier-free route on all the house tours. There are also many places to sit down along the way. Content-wise it's an excellent tour, even if you're not a huge Frank Lloyd Wright fan. It's also a rare opportunity for wheelchair users to tour a Frank Lloyd Wright structure.

Another site worth a visit is Cosanti, the sculpture studio of architect Paolo Soleri. Originally drawn to the Sonoran desert in 1956, Soleri designed an experimental community in the mountains but established his own home and studio near Taliesin West. Today the Cosanti Foundation helps fund Soleri's continued work on experimental communities through the sale of his trademark sculptured windbells.

Designated as an Arizona historic site, Cosanti offers visitors a close-up look at Soleri's innovative construction techniques. Admission is free and there is level access throughout most areas; however a few places are too narrow or bumpy for wheelchairs. Still you can get a good feel for the site without accessing all areas. It's a little bit offbeat but definitely worth a look.

Of course you can't go to Scottsdale without a visit to neighboring Phoenix. That's the beauty of Scottsdale; it's a little removed from the hustle and bustle of the big city but still close enough so that visitors can take in the major attractions. Although there are a number of top-drawer cultural attractions in the capital city, The Pueblo Grande Museum and Archaeological Park is one of the more unique sites. This combination museum and archeological dig takes an in-depth look at the Hohokam Indians, who once thrived in the area and then mysteriously vanished.

There is barrier-free access to all of the interpretive exhibits inside the museum and a wide paved trail through the outside archeological site. The archeological site also includes a ballcourt and reproductions of some Hohokam homes. Your best bet is to hit this site early in the day to beat the heat.

Finally, don't miss my hands-down favorite Phoenix attraction, the Desert Botanical Garden. Located on 1,450 acres near the Phoenix Zoo, this Phoenix mainstay features more than 50,000 plants, a butterfly pavilion and five themed interpretive trails. Access is good throughout the complex, with level access on most of the trails. Not only is it a great place to see native plants in their natural settings, but the arid desert landscape is also a sure-fire cure for those pesky wintertime blues. In short, the Desert Botanical Garden is just what the doctor ordered, and it's *the* perfect way to top off any Scottsdale-Phoenix getaway.

- IF YOU GO
  - Four Seasons Scottsdale, (480) 515-5700, www.fourseasons.com/scottsdale
  - Taliesin West, (480) 860-2700 ext. 494/495, www.franklloydwright.org
  - Cosanti, (480) 948-6145, www.cosanti.com
  - Pueblo Grande Museum, (602) 495-0901, www.pueblogrande.com
  - Desert Botanical Garden, (480) 941-1225, www.dbg.org

HAIL TO THE CHIEFS
. . . .

Museums by their very nature are for the most part pretty accessible. That goes double for presidential museums, which are administered by the National Archives and Records Administration. As a federal agency, the National Archives and Records Administration must make these facilities

Jimmy Carter Library & Museum in Atlanta, Georgia.

accessible; however since these museums also serve as a very visible face of former presidents, they most go beyond the letter of the law. After all, what political figure would want to exclude someone with a disability?

The official presidential museum system consists of 12 presidential museums; however, when President Bush leaves office, construction will most likely begin on number 13. In most cases, the museums are funded by private foundations and donations, and they are located in the former presidents' home state or in a state where he had close ties or spent the majority of his life. The museums are also connected to presidential libraries, which contain an archive of presidential documents and photographs. And that's where the similarities end, as each presidential museum has its own distinct personality.

As an interesting aside, you don't have to be a fan of a particular president to enjoy his presidential museum. Take the Gerald R. Ford Presidential Museum for example. Located in Grand Rapids, Michigan, it's one of the best presidential museums I've even visited. No matter what your political party affiliation, if you lived through the Watergate years, you'll love this museum. That's because the former president wanted the museum to be more about history and less about him.

There is level access to the front entrance of the museum, elevator access to all floors and ample room to wheel around in all of the galleries. Part of the museum focuses on the 38th President's career, family and military life; however the bulk of it is dedicated to events that occurred just prior to and during his presidency or those that were influenced by his presidency. Must-sees include the tools used in the Watergate break-in and a fascinating exhibit about the Nixon pardon.

Interestingly enough, across the country in Yorba Linda, California, the Richard Nixon Presidential Library and Museum tends to play down the whole Watergate period and instead focuses on Mr. Nixon's long political career. Along with the requisite replica of the Oval Office and a sampling of state gifts, there's an interesting exhibit of items collected by Vietnam POWs. Outside, there's the Richard Nixon birthplace and the presidential helicopter, which was used by presidents Kennedy, Johnson, Nixon and Ford.

Access is good throughout the museum, with plenty of accessible parking, ramped access to the front entrance and barrier-free access throughout all the galleries. Outside there is an accessible path from the museum to the birthplace and a ramped entrance at the back door of the birthplace. There are several steps up to the helicopter; however there is a wide level space around it, with plenty of room to navigate a wheelchair.

Not to be outdone, former president Ronald Regan also made sure to include a presidential aircraft in his museum in Simi Valley, California, Air Force One to be specific. There is elevator access down to the hangar level in the Air Force One Pavilion and, although there is lift access up to the plane, there's only 28 inches of clearance in the tightest spaces on board. Upon inquiry, I discovered that the lift was installed so wheelers could get their photographs taken (for an extra charge) in front of Air Force One. Still it's doable for slow walkers and highly recommended if you can manage it. If you can't manage the whole plane, at least you'll be able to peek inside thanks to the stair lift.

Down in Abilene, Kansas, the Dwight D. Eisenhower Presidential Library is more of a traditional presidential museum, with nary an aircraft in sight. The museum complex consists of the Visitors Center, the Place of Meditation, Ike's boyhood home, the museum and the library. There is level access to the Visitors Center, where you can pick up a free loaner wheelchair. Just to the left of the Visitors Center, you'll find Ike's boyhood home. Although there are three steps at the front, there is also a wheelchair lift on the side. The first floor of the house is open to the public and it features original furnishings, photographs and personal items of the Eisenhower family.

The museum itself is just a short walk from the home and it features barrier-free access and a wheelchair lift at the front entrance. It contains exhibits that chronicle the life and political career of President Eisenhower and the major events that occurred during his presidency. This museum is really a must-see for anyone interested in World War II history, as an excellent D-Day exhibit is featured in the military gallery.

The newest addition to the presidential library system–the William J. Clinton Presidential Library–is located in Little Rock, Arkansas. Perched on the banks of the Arkansas River, this massive structure features a whopping 20,000 square feet of exhibition space. Access features include barrier-free access to all galleries, sleek wood floors, accessible restrooms, level access to the front entrance and wheelchairs available for loan at the front desk. It's also one of the most architecturally striking presidential museums, so take some time to admire the structure before you move inside.

Inside, you'll find a large collection of exhibits that chronicle the Clinton presidency, items from Bill's childhood, and a hilarious collection of *Saturday Night Live* clips of Clinton impersonations. There's also a wing that features the splendor of the White House during the holidays, which shows how the Clinton's gave the presidential residence some personal touches to really make it their home. Plan to spend the whole day at this museum, as it's massive.

Last but not least, don't miss the Jimmy Carter Library and Museum down in Atlanta, Georgia. Highlights of this museum include a replica of the Oval Office and photographs and memorabilia from the Carter presidency. Access is excellent throughout the museum, with barrier-free access to all of the galleries and wide level pathways to most of the outdoor areas. As an added bonus, this is the presidential museum where you're most likely to spot a member of the former first family, as Mr. Carter and his wife, Rosalynn, spend a good part of each month on site managing their foundation. Former first daughter Amy also lives nearby and it's not unusual to spot Jimmy fishing with his grandson in one of the lakes out back. And that's quite an unexpected treat!

- IF YOU GO
  - Presidential Libraries, www.archives.gov/presidential-libraries
  - Gerald R. Ford Presidential Library and Museum, (616) 254-0400, www.fordlibrarymuseum.gov
  - Richard Nixon Presidential Library and Museum, (714) 572-9679, www.nixonlibrary.org

- Ronald Reagan Presidential Library and Museum, (805) 577-4000, www.reaganlibrary.com
- Dwight D. Eisenhower Presidential Library and Museum, (785) 263-6700, www.eisenhower.archives.gov
- Jimmy Carter Library and Museum, (404) 865-7100, www.jimmycarterlibrary.gov
- William J. Clinton Presidential Library, (501) 374-4242, www.clintonpresidentialcenter.org

MONTREAL: THE OTHER PARIS

Visiting Montreal is like visiting Paris in many respects. First off there's the language; however the similarity goes well beyond the language issue. True, you will probably hear French spoken more often than English in Montreal; however the city itself also exudes a distinctly French personality. From the architecture to the people to the cultural attractions, visiting Montreal is almost like visiting Paris.

Of course there are a few differences too. Not only is Montreal more affordable than the City of Lights, but it's also closer to the US. And closer translates into less time and money spent on actually getting there. And let's not forget about access. Again Montreal stands head and shoulders above Paris in that category too. Thanks to the efforts of Kéroul, a local disability organization, Montreal has a fairly high level of physical access. Additionally, because of Kéroul's high profile and diligent work over the past 25 years, most local tourism providers also have an above-average awareness of access issues.

Keroul is also a good resource for accessible lodging, as their excellent access guide to Quebec (*Le Quebec Accessible*) features access information on hotels throughout the province. The book is written in French; however, because of the use of pictograms and short descriptive phrases, only a minimal fluency is required. Alternatively, the lodging information is translated into English on the Kéroul website.

My top Montreal lodging pick, the Le Centre Sheraton, remains a personal favorite not only for their good physical access, but also because of their progressive attitude about access issues. In fact, Kéroul's founder,

The Notre-Dame Basilica in Old Montreal.

Andre Leclerc, worked closely with the Le Centre Sheraton staff to design a fully accessible club-level suite. The suite is appropriately named the Andre Leclerc Suite, and it features a bathroom with a roll-in shower. This two-room suite is very nicely done, and great attention was paid to even the smallest access details, such as lowered hooks and clothing rods.

Accessible ground transportation is also available in Montreal. Says Isabelle Duchesnay of Kéroul, "Renting an accessible van is probably the best transportation choice for visitors, as it's the most convenient." Location Jean Legare rents lowered-floor Ford Windstar vans by the day or the week. Each van can accommodate up to seven people, including three wheelchairs. Alternatively, accessible taxi service is available through Taxi Boisjoly and Taxi Para-Adapté. Despite the fact that these companies operate 44 accessible vans between them, it's best to book trips at least 24 hours in advance due to the high demand. Although not a good solution for spur-of-the-moment trips, accessible taxis are perfect for airport transfers.

There's certainly no shortage of cultural attractions in Montreal, and the massive Montreal Museum of Fine Arts tops my museum must-see list. It's so large that it takes up two buildings, right across the street from one another. There's barrier-free access throughout both buildings, and, although there are stairs up to the front entrance of the historic wing, there is an accessible entrance on the side.

The McCord Museum of Canadian History, which is located just down the street, is also worth a visit. This three-story building offers a comprehensive look at Canadian history and includes many interactive exhibits. Again, you'll find the accessible entrance on the side.

Old Montreal also has its share of cultural attractions, including the Notre-Dame Basilica. There is ramp access to this historic building, wide doorways on the far left and plenty of room to navigate inside. Quite simply, the inside of the basilica is gorgeous. Don't miss it.

The Montreal Museum of Archaeology and History is also highly recommended. This unusual in-situ museum is built around the ruins of the Royal Insurance Building. Don't miss the basement, where you can get a look at the foundation and the cistern of the old building. Access is excellent throughout the building, including lift access down to cistern level. It's fascinating, and very convenient for cruise ship passengers, as it's located right across from the cruise ship terminal.

Finally, for a combination indoor-outdoor attraction, visit the Montreal Biodome, which features realistic re-creations of some of the most beautiful and diverse ecosystems in the Americas. Access is good throughout the biodome, with level pathways and boardwalks, wheelchair-height viewing platforms and access to all areas. It's a great place to spend the day, and it's an excellent all-weather attraction.

- IF YOU GO
  - Tourisme Montreal, (877) 266-5687, tourisme-montreal.org
  - Kéroul, (514) 252-3104, www.keroul.qc.ca
  - Le Centre Sheraton, (514) 878-2000, www.sheraton.com/lecentre
  - Location Jean Legare, (514) 522-6466, www.locationlegare.com
  - Taxi Boisjoly, (514) 255-2815
  - Taxi Para-Adapté, (514) 821-3355
  - Montreal Museum of Fine Arts, (514) 285-2000, www.mmfa.qc.ca
  - McCord Museum of Canadian History, (514) 398-7100, www.mccord-museum.qc.ca
  - Notre-Dame Basilica, (514) 842-2925, www.basiliquenddm.org
  - Montreal Museum of Archaeology and History, (514) 872-9150, www.pacmuseum.qc.ca
  - Montreal Biodome, (514) 868-3000, www.biodome.qc.ca

MUSEUM HOPPING IN ST. PETERSBURG

Although Florida is well known as a great beach destination, many cities throughout the state also offer a wide range of cultural attractions. Such is the case with St. Petersburg. The good news is, this coastal community goes one step further; as not only does it boast a bevy of accessible cultural attractions, but it also features wheelchair-accessible transportation. The lift-equipped Looper Trolley runs a circular route through downtown St. Petersburg and stops at all of the major museums. And, at just 50 cents a ride, it's also a very affordable choice.

Museum hopping is a popular pastime in St. Petersburg, and, since all of the major museums feature good access with level entries and plenty of room to maneuver a wheelchair, it's also a very accessible choice. Your best bet is to begin your museum hopping day at The Pier, as it's the first stop on the Looper Trolley route.

The Looper Trolley stop at The Pier is well marked, and the trolley schedule is posted at the stop. And if you have some time between trolleys, there are plenty of shops inside to pass the time. The trolley drivers are very helpful and most offer a pretty good narrative tour of the city, so don't be afraid to ask them questions or request assistance. Most go well above and beyond their job descriptions.

The St. Petersburg Museum of History is the first stop after The Pier. This museum features interactive exhibits of the chronology of St. Petersburg's history. Significant artifacts include a canoe of the Tocobaga Indians from the 1500s, a replica of the world's first commercial airliner and a 3,500-year-old mummy.

Located just one block north of The Pier, the Museum of Fine Arts is the next museum on the Looper Trolley route. Opened in 1965 as St. Petersburg's first art museum, the Museum of Fine Arts features works of the masters, plus special touring pieces. Wheelchairs are available for free loan at the front desk.

Bay Walk, the next stop on the Looper Trolley, is a good spot to stop for a lunch break. This Mediterranean-themed complex is known as the "Soul of St. Petersburg" and includes restaurants such as Dish and Dan Marino's Town Tavern.

The accessible Looper Trolley at the St. Petersburg Pier.

Dish is particularly unique. It's best described as a stir-fry buffet. You pick your veggies, mix your sauce, select your meat and then have the chef throw them on the circular grill in the center of the restaurant. It's very tasty and lots of fun! Dish is located on the second floor of Bay Walk and is accessible by elevator or escalator. It has accessible restrooms and good pathway access.

After lunch, you can either walk down to the Florida International Museum or hop back on the Looper Trolley. The Florida International Museum features the world's largest private collection of John F. Kennedy memorabilia. The exhibition includes a re-creation of Kennedy's Oval Office, PT 109 and a Jackie Kennedy gallery plus two theater presentations.

Next stop is the Florida Holocaust Museum, the third largest Holocaust Museum in the United States and the only Holocaust museum in the United States, which features Holocaust art exhibits. The centerpiece exhibit is a box car from the Poland death camps. Although there are no graphic images portrayed in the museum, it's not recommended for children younger than 10 years old. Wheelchairs are available for free loan at the front desk.

The Salvador Dali Museum is the final museum stop on the Looper route. All of Dali's periods are represented in this comprehensive collection, including pieces from the artist's early and transitional periods. Dali is well known for his surrealist pieces and masterworks, which are both well represented in this collection. Dali considered a masterwork any piece that took more than a year to complete and measures at least five feet in any one direction. All in all, it's really an impressive collection, which offers some interesting insights into the artist's body of work.

Of course it's impossible to see all these great museums in one day, so set aside a few days for museum hopping in St. Petersburg. And don't forget about the Looper Trolley because, at 50 cents a trip, it's St. Petersburg's best bargain.

- IF YOU GO
  - Looper Trolley, (727) 821-5166
  - St. Petersburg Museum of History, (727) 894-1052, www.stpetemuseumofhistory.org
  - Museum of Fine Arts, (727) 896-2667, www.fine-arts.org
  - Florida International Museum, (727) 822-3693, www.floridamuseum.org
  - Florida Holocaust Museum, (727) 820-0100, www.flholocaustmuseum.org
  - Salvador Dali Museum, (727) 823-3767, www.salvadordalimuseum.org
  - St. Petersburg Clearwater Convention & Visitors Bureau, (727) 464-7200, www.floridasbeach.com

PUERTO RICO SAMPLER

San Juan is a city with two distinctly different faces, from the high-rise hotels and casinos that line the shores of beautiful Condado Beach to the historic buildings and cobblestone streets that lie behind the city walls of Old San Juan. Indeed, it's entirely possible to go to Puerto Rico and go no further than the casinos and Condado Beach, if that's your preference; however, if you want to see the colorful and cultural side of the city, a visit to Old San Juan is a must.

The best place to begin your tour of Old San Juan is at the Plaza de Marina. Located just west of the cruise ship piers, this plaza is a gathering place for locals and a great place to people watch. You'll find this area of Old San Juan especially wheelchair friendly, perhaps because of its proximity to the cruise ship piers. The wide sidewalks and curb cuts make this one of the more accessible areas of Old San Juan. The only drawback is that here, as in the rest of the old city, the streets are made of bricks, which makes for a bumpy ride.

To the west of the plaza lies the Paseo de la Princesa, one of San Juan's showcase promenades. This wide tree-lined promenade continues past the old prison to the Raices fountain, where you'll find spectacular views of the sea as well as the walls that surround much of Old San Juan.

Although Old San Juan contains a number of historic sights, the fort of El Morro is perhaps the most magnificent and, fortunately, also the most accessible. Built in 1539, this Spanish stronghold helped defend Puerto Rico from attacks by the British, French and Dutch. Converted to a US Army installation in 1898, El Morro continued to weather the test of time. The lighthouse, which is the most recent addition to El Morro, was constructed by the US Army in 1908.

The views from El Morro are spectacular, and the lower levels of the fort are completely accessible. The upper level has a ramp with a rather steep incline, and manual wheelchair users may require some assistance here. El Morro is far more accessible than San Cristobal, (its sister fort on the other side of town), as the entrance to San Cristobal is located on the second level at the top of a very steep ramp.

The real flavor of Old San Juan, along with the best shopping and food, is found along the streets of Calle Fortaleza, Calle del Cristo and Calle San Francisco. Getting around the old part of the city can prove a challenge. The curbs are high and the streets are paved with bricks. In fact, when you see the blue bricks, you will know you are in the oldest part of the city, as these bricks were used as ballast in Spanish ships.

Driving is not recommended in Old San Juan, as parking can be a problem. If you do drive, rent the smallest car possible, as negotiating the narrow streets and high curbs can be difficult in a large vehicle. Finally, there are some hefty uphill grades in the old city. All of this aside, the heart of the city is a great experience if you can possibly manage it. The best Old San Juan travel tip comes from a veteran traveler and manual wheelchair user, "Stick to the less traveled streets and wheel down the center. And get in shape before you go," he advises.

Alternatively, you can book a tour with Wheelchair Transportation and Tours. This local operator provides city and island tours in wheelchair-accessible vans. Rafael, the company owner, has been providing accessible tours on the island for many years, and he's happy to work with visitors to design individually tailored tours to meet specific needs and interests.

If you'd like to add a little mix of the countryside to your city tour, consider a day trip to the El Yunque rainforest, with a stop at Luquillo Beach. Although the trails in El Yunque are not accessible, you can still enjoy the beauty of the rainforest from the boardwalks at El Portal Visitors Center. Don't, however, expect full accessibility on the park trails, as many of them are very rocky and steep. Additionally, even in the dry season, there are muddy and swampy sections along the trails. The drive through the forest however is very scenic, with many accessible places to stop along the way.

If you'd like to hit the beach, be sure and stop at Luquillo Beach, located about six miles east of the El Portal Visitors Center. Accessible beachside facilities include changing rooms, restrooms, a picnic area and a playground. The beach is nicely accessible as well, with hard-packed sand and ramp access into the water. It's known as the sea without barriers throughout Puerto Rico, and it was constructed especially for people with mobility disabilities. It's not only one of the most beautiful beaches in the Caribbean, but it's also the most accessible. And it's a great place to enjoy the natural side of Puerto Rico.

- IF YOU GO
  - Wheelchair Transportation and Tours, (800) 868-8028

SANTA FE CULTURE CLASH

S anta Fe is an eclectic mix of old and new, and if you enjoy art, culture and history, that's a very good thing. Diversity is the key word in this historic city, as three cultures — Indian, Hispanic and Anglo — exist side by side. Actually they do more than exist, they thrive.

And nowhere is this cultural diversity more apparent than in the downtown Plaza area. Indeed, this cultural heart of the city is the perfect place to base yourself, as everything you need is well within walking distance. And despite the historic nature of the area, it's still pretty accessible.

Curb cuts are plentiful even in the oldest areas of town, and most of the historic buildings now have at least one accessible entrance. The new museums were constructed to be accessible, and most gallery owners have

Front entrance to the Museum of Fine Arts in Santa Fe.

also made efforts to accommodate all visitors. Of course you'll want to take it slow until you get acclimated to the 7,000-foot elevation, but just go at your own pace and drink plenty of water. All in all, it's pretty easy to get around and enjoy the cultural side of Santa Fe.

Museum hopping is a favorite activity in Santa Fe, as the city boasts a bevy of world-class cultural institutions. Several of the city's major museums are located in the Plaza area within easy walking distance of one another. At the top of the list is the Palace of the Governors located just across the street from the Plaza.

Originally constructed as the regional headquarters for the Spanish government, the Palace of the Governors dates back to the 17th Century. Although it no longer houses political offices, the historic architecture of the building is quite interesting and it makes a perfect venue for the state history museum. Exhibits focus on New Mexico history, from early Spanish colonization to the present. Even though this museum is housed in a historic building, access is good, with a level entrance and barrier-free pathways throughout the complex.

Next door to the Palace of the Governors, The Museum of Fine Arts is also housed in a historic building. Although not as old as her neighbor, it is the oldest contemporary art museum in the United States. Constructed in 1917, the museum showcases local talent and contains traditional as well as contemporary pieces. Don't miss the WPA murals in the courtyard.

There is ramp access to the museum and good pathway access throughout the galleries. Although stairs lead to the second floor, a freight elevator is available for wheelchair users. Ask the guard for assistance. There are also two wheelchairs available for loan at the front desk.

The Georgia O'Keeffe Museum is another must-see in the Plaza Area. This museum is dedicated to the art of O'Keefe and to the study of American Modernism, and it boasts the largest collection of O'Keeffe's paintings, drawings and sculptures in the world.

Special exhibitions supplement the permanent collection, and the museum is closed during installations between special exhibitions. Access is excellent throughout the single-level gallery, and free loaner wheelchairs are available at the front desk. Docent-led tours are also conducted at 10:30 every morning.

If you still haven't had your fill of museums, head up to Museum Hill to explore a few more. Convenient transportation is available from the Plaza area to Museum Hill on the accessible M Line Bus. The bus stops on Sheridan Street, just around the corner from the Museum of Fine Arts. The bus drivers are very helpful and they just love chatting with tourists, so it's really the ideal way to get up to Museum Hill.

Up on Museum Hill, the M Line stops in front of Milner Plaza, where you'll find the Museum of International Folk Art, the Museum Cafe and the Museum of Indian Arts & Culture. There is elevator access up to the plaza level, and all of the museums offer barrier-free access.

If you are going by car, or if you don't mind a short walk, then check out the Wheelright Museum of the American Indian and the Museum of Spanish Colonial Art. They both feature good access, but they are located next door and across the street from Milner Plaza. Indeed, you could spend several days exploring Museum Hill and discovering the diverse culture of Santa Fe.

- IF YOU GO
  - Santa Fe Convention & Visitors Bureau, (505) 955-6200, www.santafe.org
  - Palace of the Governors, (505) 476-5100, www.palaceofthegovernors.org
  - Museum of Fine Arts, (505) 476-5072, www.mfasantafe.org
  - Georgia O'Keeffe Museum, (505) 946-1000, www.okeeffemuseum.org

- Museum of International Folk Art, (505) 476-1200,
  www.internationalfolkart.org
- Museum of Indian Arts & Culture, (505) 476-1250, www.miaclab.org
- Wheelright Museum of the American Indian, (505) 982-4636,
  www.wheelwright.org
- Museum of Spanish Colonial Art, (505) 982-2226, www.spanishcolonial.org

SEDUCTIVE SEDONA

There's a certain seductive allure to Sedona. Some folks come for the mystical experience, some come for the galleries and some just come for the spectacular scenery. No matter what your attraction to this northern Arizona artistic enclave, you won't be disappointed. It's truly a magical place, a place to get away from it all and enjoy nature, browse through some galleries and learn about the mystery that surrounds the famous Sedona vortices. And if you like to people watch, then Sedona is definitely the place for you.

The best way to get your bearings in Sedona is to stop by the Visitors Center in Tequa Plaza in the Village of Oak Creek. Located just south of Sedona, where the magnificent red rock formations begin, the Visitors Center features level access with plenty of accessible parking in front. Even better, the volunteers who staff this office are very knowledgeable about the accessible sites and venues in the area. I was quite impressed with the volunteer who assisted me, as she didn't even bat an eye when I inquired about wheelchair access, and then she matter of factly got out the map and pointed out several accessible sites. I'm assuming from her very informed response that they get a lot of inquiries of this nature.

Just up the road from the Visitors Center, you'll find Bell Rock on the right. You can't miss it, as it's shaped like, well, a bell. Bell Rock is one of Sedona's four vortices, which are sites believed to have a high concentration of psychic energy. The other vortex sites are Cathedral Rock, Boynton Canyon and the Airport Mesa, and, regardless of their metaphysical qualities, they're all still worth a visit for their scenic value. Bell Rock is one of the more accessible red rock areas, as the upper part of Bell Rock Trail is

Cathedral Rock, one of Sedona's vortex sites.

wide, level and made of hard-packed dirt. It's doable for most wheelchair users, however you can also get a great view of Bell Rock from the parking lot overlook.

One of the most popular things to do in Sedona is to take a jeep tour. Indeed you'll see jeeps packed full of tourists just about everywhere. Although there's no shortage of jeep tour companies in Sedona, Red Rock Jeep Tours is the most accommodating as far as access goes. Granted, jeeps are not accessible by their very nature, but if you are willing to transfer to the front seat, then the folks at Red Rock Jeep Tours are happy to assist you. The drawback is that you must leave your wheelchair at the tour office, so you won't be able to get out of the jeep during the tour. Still, you can get some great views of the red rock canyons from the jeep, so you don't have to get out of the vehicle to fully enjoy the tour.

And although Red Rock Jeep Tours offers a lot of off-road tours, some are gentler than others, so be sure to inquire about how much off-roading is involved before you sign up for a tour. If you want to take an off-road tour, you need to be able to hang on, as the ride gets very rough at times. Alternatively, you can opt for the on-road Easy on the Asphalt tour, which visits some of Sedona's most magnificent overlooks.

Another popular activity in Sedona is gallery hopping; however galleries are a real mixed bag as far as access goes. A good place to find a wide variety of accessible galleries is at the Tlaquepaque Arts and Crafts Village. Located on Highway 179 near the junction of Highway 89A (known as the "Y" to the locals), this retail center is patterned after the Mexican village of the same name. There is level access to most of the shops, plenty of accessible parking and lots of room to wheel around the peaceful courtyards. It's a fun place to spend the day, do a little shopping, visit with the artists and get a bite eat.

There are a number of interesting sites located just outside of Sedona too, so save at least one day to explore the outlying area. Montezuma Castle, which is just three miles off Highway 17 near exit 268, is perhaps one of the most interesting and accessible archeologic finds in the state. This five-level cliff dwelling was constructed by the Sinagua Indians more than 600 years ago, and today it's considered one of the best-preserved cliff dwellings in North America.

There is level access to the Visitors Center and a paved level pathway out back to a good viewing spot. To preserve the ruins, visitors are not allowed to climb up them, so all viewing is done from the trails in the back of the Visitors Center. The accessible part of the trail is about a quarter-mile loop, but after that, it gets a bit steep for wheelers. Still, it's definitely worth a visit and, since it's a National Park Service site, admission is free to America the Beautiful – National Parks and Federal Recreational Lands Pass – Access Pass holders.

Finally, no visit to the red rock area is complete without an excursion on the Verde Canyon Railroad, located just west of Sedona in Clarkdale. Billed as Arizona's other Grand Canyon, Verde Canyon is well known for its red rock pinnacles. The four-hour train trip winds through a 680-foot tunnel, passes over towering trestles and chugs past Indian ruins.

There is lift access to the train and wheelchair users can opt to stay in their own wheelchairs or transfer to a seat for the ride. The lift has some width limitations, but loaner wheelchairs are available if your equipment exceeds the 25-inch maximum width. Additionally, the lift cannot accommodate loads heavier than 300 pounds, so sometimes power wheelchair batteries must be removed; however the staff is very accommodating and they are wiling to work with wheelchair users so that everyone can enjoy this scenic ride. It's a great day trip and probably the most accessible way to enjoy the beautiful red rock formations that surround Sedona.

- IF YOU GO

  - Sedona Visitor Information, (928) 282-7722 , www.visitsedona.com
  - Red Rock Jeep Tours, (800) 848-7728, www.redrockjeep.com
  - Tlaquepaque, (928).282.4838, www.tlaq.com
  - Montezuma Castle, (928) 567-3322, www.nps.gov/moca
  - Verde Canyon Railroad, 800-320-0718, www.verdecanyonrr.com

THE OTHER HOLLAND

When thoughts of wooden shoes, Delftware and tulips entice you to plan a trip across the Big Pond, remember that the country bordered by Belgium, Germany and the North Sea is not your only Holland option. In fact, you can experience Holland without even leaving North America. Just head north to Chicago, make a hard right at the lake and follow the shoreline. Three hours later you'll be in Holland, the other Holland, that is.

And there's no better time to visit Holland, Michigan, than during the annual Tulip Time Festival. Held annually in May, this festive event is a celebration of Dutch culture and tradition. The city is awash with color during the festival, as tulips, costumed dancers, parades and craft shows fill the streets. Admission is free to most events, and access is excellent throughout downtown Holland.

Be sure and stop in at the Holland Area Convention and Visitors Bureau at 76 E. 8th Street for tourist information, lodging suggestions and maps of the area. I highly recommend the *Statues of Holland* brochure, which presents a short walking tour of the public art in the downtown area. It's just a very pleasant area to roll or stroll.

Just around the corner on 10th Street, you'll find the excellent Holland Museum, which features a ramped side entrance and barrier-free access throughout the building. Inside you'll find exhibits about the local history, gifts form the Netherlands and even a display from the 1939 Golden Gate International Exposition. And don't miss the new Dutch gallery, which features 55 Dutch paintings from the 17th to 19th century and more than 150 cultural objects, from fine furniture and Delftware to silver and original Dutch costumes.

*Delftware at DeKlomp Delftware Factory; the only blue and white
Delftware factory in the US.*

For a real taste of mother Holland, head on over to Windmill Island,
located on 7th and Lincoln Streets. This 30-acre park features a miniature
Dutch village, interpretive exhibits, a variety of shops, a tropical greenhouse,
a Dutch carousel, an Amsterdam street organ and of course the windmill.
Access is good throughout the park, with level access to all the shops and
buildings. Be sure and stop in at the Posthouse Museum first and see the
orientation film, browse through the exhibits and learn a little bit about the
history of the windmill.

The windmill, which is named De Zwaan, is a short walk from the
Posthouse Museum over on the island. Wheelchair users should use the flat
bridge, which is located just to the right of the draw bridge, as the draw bridge
has several access obstacles.

The 240-year-old De Zwann windmill is not only America's only
authentic Dutch windmill, but also a working windmill. It was disassembled
and shipped from Zaandam to Holland in 1965. Today it serves as a reminder
of this Michigan city's Dutch roots. And it's absolutely gorgeous in the spring,
with millions of tulips surrounding it.

There is level access to the bottom floor of the windmill, but the upper
levels can only be accessed by stairs. Still, it's all very interesting and there

is a photo album of the upstairs areas. And don't miss the old-time Dutch dancers, complete with folk costumes and wooden shoes. They perform frequently at the windmill, so be sure and check at the Posthouse Museum for the performance times.

Another Holland must-see is the DeKlomp Wooden Shoe and Delftware Factory, located just four miles north of downtown Holland on Quincy Avenue. And yes, this is where the Dutch dancers buy their wooden shoes. It's also the only blue and white Delftware factory in the US. There is level access to the factory and store, where you can watch artists carve wooden shoes and paint Delftware. There is an excellent selection of Delftware available for purchase, but, if you don't see exactly what you want, they will make it for you and ship it.

Of course the highlight of a spring visit to Holland is a stroll through Veldheer Tulip Gardens, located next door to DeKlomp's. The grass-covered garden area is level, and most wheelchair users won't have any problems rolling around on dry days. And with more than five million bulbs in bloom each spring, it's really hard to believe you're in Michigan. It's simply gorgeous.

- **IF YOU GO**
  - Tulip Time Festival, (616) 396-4221, www.tuliptime.com
  - Holland Area Convention and Visitors Bureau, (616) 394-0000, www.holland.org
  - Holland Museum, (616) 392.9084, www.hollandmuseum.org
  - Windmill Island, (616) 355-1030, www.windmillisland.org
  - DeKlomp Wooden Shoe and Delftware Factory, Veldheer Tulip Gardens, (616) 399-1900

WINTER CARNIVAL IN QUEBEC

People deal with winter in a variety of different ways. Some choose to quietly hibernate, whereas others are much more vocal about the falling temperatures and frigid conditions. And then you have your snow birds, who just pack their bags and move on to greener (warmer) pastures. The people of Quebec City

Old city walls still guard Quebec City.

take a different approach to it all, as not only do they embrace winter, but they also celebrate it with their annual winter carnival. Billed as "Carnival in Rio northern style," Carnaval de Quebec is the world's largest winter carnival. As the locals say, "It's samba dressed up in a flannel shirt."

This two-week celebration of winter attracts more than 1 million people to Quebec City every winter. Carnival activities include a variety of daily diversions topped off by two spectacular night parades and a fireworks display. Dogsleds race through the snowy streets of Old Quebec while canoe racers compete on the ice-covered St. Lawrence River. And don't miss the ice sculpture competition. You can check out the life-size entries in this unusual contest on the Les Desjardins on the Plains of Abraham throughout the run of the carnival.

And 2008 will be a special year for Carnival, as Quebec City will be celebrating its 400th anniversary that year. A huge program will be designed by cultural institutions, major Quebec event organizers and regional organizations. The theme of Quebec City's 2008 Carnival will be "The Meeting Place," to highlight the historic and present-day role of Quebec City as a place for exchanges between peoples and cultures.

Of course there are also a number of inside attractions in Quebec City. If the winter chill gets to you, spend a day or two exploring the museums. The Musee de la Civilisation is located near the port on Dalhousie Street. It's completely accessible, with a level entrance, wide doorways and accessible toilets. The Musee de Quebec is located near the Plains of Abraham Battlefield and features a good collection of contemporary art. Perhaps the most unique thing about this museum is its space. The museum is housed in three buildings, including a former women's prison. An old, brick, cell block remains intact, among the galleries of contemporary artwork. All buildings are accessible, except the turret in the old prison.

No visit to Quebec is complete without a visit to the old city. Take the accessible funicular (located in front of the Chateau Frontenac) down to the old city and browse along Champlain Street. Here you'll find a collection of quaint shops, galleries and pubs. This is also the most level part of the old city. Some people may be able to negotiate the steep street of Sous-le-Fort, which leads down to the historic Place Royal section of the old town. Most people however should approach this section of town from the port area rather than from the funicular area.

Take the funicular back to the top, and stroll along the boardwalk in front of the Chateau Frontenac for some spectacular views of the St. Lawrence River. When you've had enough of the cold, stop in the Chateau Frontenac for a hot drink and browse through the attached (and heated) shopping mall.

Of course there are a few things to consider about the accessibility of Quebec. Although many of the attractions are accessible, Quebec is a hilly city. The hills generally prevent wheelers from rolling from one area of town to another. Your best bet is to plan ahead and cover a different area of town each day.

The second problem is the lack of accessible public transportation. There are no taxis with roll-on wheelchair access, but some cabs can carry a folding wheelchair in the trunk. Since only some cabs can provide this service, you must make arrangements by phone. Still, if you choose your hotel wisely, you won't have to go far to enjoy the winter carnival festivities.

All in all, the winter carnival is a great experience, and, with a little advance planning, you can get around the access obstacles. Indeed, some areas of Quebec are very nicely accessible. So, when the winter weather gets you down, make your way to Quebec, embrace the winter and celebrate at the Carnaval de Quebec.

- IF YOU GO
    - Future Carnival Dates, February 1-17, 2008,
      January 30 - February 15, 2009, January 29 - February 14, 2010
    - Carnaval de Quebec, www.carnaval.qc.ca
    - Quebec City Tourism, (418) 641-6654, www.quebecregion.com

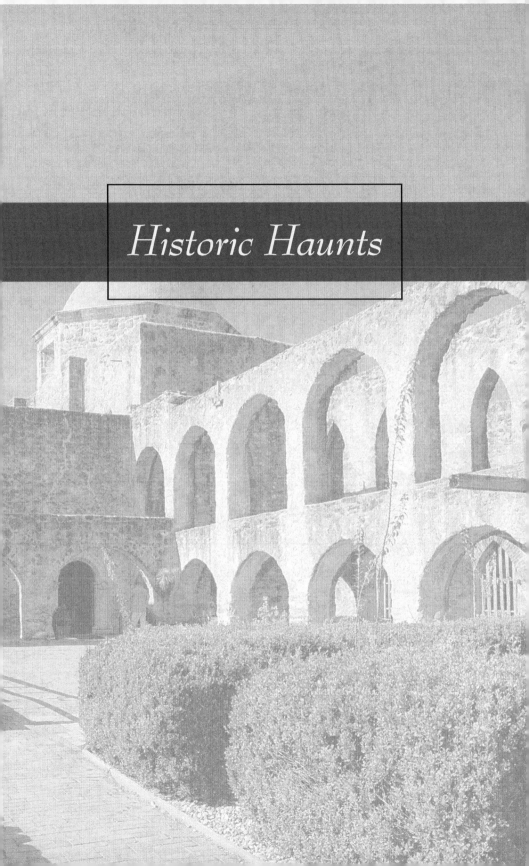

Historic Haunts

HISTORIC PHILADELPHIA

There's no better place to get a real feel for colonial history than the home of the Liberty Bell, Independence Hall and the Philly cheese steak — Philadelphia. And although historic and accessible can be mutually exclusive terms, gladly that's not the case in the City of Brotherly Love. Most of the historic buildings in Independence Square have wheelchair access to at least one floor. Granted, this access is sometimes by portable ramps so as to not alter the facades of the historic buildings, but at least the effort has been made. Additionally, because of the proximity of the Independence Hall sites, it's a great place to explore on foot, so you don't have to worry about accessible transportation.

The best place to begin your historic Philadelphia tour is at the Independence Visitors Center, located at 6th and Market Streets. There is level access to the building and barrier-free access to all of the exhibits. Accessible public restrooms are also located in this building. This is the place to get your maps, brochures and tour tickets for Independence Hall. Although the timed tickets are free, they are issued on a first-come basis to control the crowds. Your best bet is pick up your tickets first thing in the morning, then plan the rest of your visit around your tour.

If you have some time before your Independence Hall tour, then head over to the Liberty Bell Center, located across Market Street from the Independence Visitors Center. There is level access to the main entrance of this new building and plenty of room to maneuver a wheelchair inside. The Liberty Bell Center features a number of interpretive exhibits about the Liberty Bell, a video presentation and of course the bell itself. Visitors line up and pass by the Liberty Bell, which is housed in a glass chamber, with Independence Hall visible in the background. It's very nicely done.

Across Chestnut Street from the Liberty Bell Center, you'll find the historic buildings of Independence Square. Independence Hall is in the center, Old City Hall is on the east side and Congress Hall is on the west side.

Independence Hall tours begin in the East Wing, which is accessible by a ramp from Independence Square. Constructed between 1732 and 1756 as the Pennsylvania State House, Independence Hall was the meeting place for the Second Continental Congress and the site where the Declaration

of Independence was signed. The tour covers both wings of the building; however the second floor is only accessible by a stairway. Alternatively, there are photo albums available of the second floor. The West Wing also features the Great Essentials Exhibit, which includes surviving copies of the Declaration of Independence and the US Constitution, along with the silver inkstand that was used to sign these documents.

Next door, in Congress Hall, visitors are admitted on a first-come basis. There is ramp access to the first floor, but the second floor is only accessible by a stairway. There is a photo album available of the second floor, for visitors who cannot manage the stairs. Originally constructed as the Philadelphia County Courthouse, Congress Hall served as the meeting place for the US Congress from 1790 to 1800. The House of Representatives met on the main floor while the Senate met upstairs. A short ranger-led tour is available of the building throughout the day.

Old City Hall is also open to the public on a first-come basis. There is ramp access on the east side of the building. Originally constructed as the City Hall of Philadelphia, the building was later used by the US Supreme Court until 1800, when the federal government was moved to Washington, DC. A ranger-led presentation about the history of the Supreme Court and a short tour of the building are offered throughout the day.

Another historic building worth a look is the Second Bank of the United States, located just a half block east of Independence Hall. Although steps grace the front of this building, there is an accessible entrance on the west side. Inside you'll find a stunning portrait gallery, which contains 185 paintings of Colonial and Federal leaders, military officers, explorers and scientists. The building itself is also a real gem, as it's considered to be one of the finest examples of Greek Revival architecture in the United States.

And for a real architectural treat, be sure and stop by the Bourse, just across the street from the Liberty Bell Center. The accessible entrance is located on 5th Street. Constructed in 1895, the Bourse served as the first commodity exchange in the US. Today, it's home to a food court and mall, and it makes a great stop for a quick lunch or a nice place to take a break and get a cool drink. If you enjoy old architecture, the inside of the Bourse is a must-see.

. . . .

Independence Hall in historic Philadelphia.

- IF YOU GO
  - Independence Hall National Historical Park, (215) 965-2305, www.nps.gov/inde
  - The Bourse, (215) 625-0300, www.bourse-pa.com

HISTORY AND CULTURE IN THE BIG PEACH

Known by a variety of nicknames, from The ATL to Dogwood City, Atlanta just oozes history. After all, it's the city where *Gone with the Wind* was written and Coca-Cola was invented. And thanks to the 1996 Olympic and Paralympic Games, it's also a very accessible city with a wide selection of accessible lodging options and excellent access to even the most historic attractions.

The Atlanta History Center is a good place to get your feet wet history-wise. Located on 33 wooded acres, it's one of the Southeast's largest history museums, and it features two historic homes and the Swan Coach House restaurant. Accessible parking is available in front of the main building, and there is level access to the museum and barrier-free pathways throughout all of the galleries. Inside you'll find everything from an excellent Civil War exhibition to an interactive exhibition on the Centennial Olympic Games.

Outside, access is variable, but a tour of the Swan House is highly recommended. If you have a car, it's best to drive up to the Swan Coach House and park there. If you're on foot, ask the person at the front desk to map out the most accessible route for you. There is an accessible pathway up to the Swan House; however, be sure you have the right directions, as it's easy to get lost and end up on one of the inaccessible pathways.

The excellent docent-led tour of the 1926 Swan House is most definitely worth the price of admission. There is level access to the main floor and you'll get a good look at the foyer, dining room, sitting area, library, porch, living room, butler's pantry and kitchen on the tour. The second floor is only accessible by stairs, however only a bedroom and bathroom are open upstairs, so the bulk of the tour is accessible.

The Swan House at the Atlanta History Center.

The other historic home, the Tullie Smith Farm, has eight steps at the entrance, so the house tour is not doable for wheelchair users. Alternatively you can get a good overview of this typical 1850s rural southern home by just rolling around the grounds, looking in the barn and checking out the outbuildings.

And don't forget to save some time for a leisurely lunch at the Swan Coach House. Originally the coach house and servant's quarters for the Swan House, this teahouse-style restaurant serves up a scrumptious lunch Monday through Saturday. There is ramp access to the front door and valet parking is available. Menu items range from their signature chicken salad to curried chicken, sandwiches, salads and even crab cakes. Be forewarned that it's a favorite spot for ladies group lunches, so it might not be the ideal choice for all men. If you find it a bit too feminine, then just grab a Chick-fil-A sandwich at the Coca-Cola Cafe in the main museum building.

Another fun yet historic lunch venue is Mary Mac's Tea Room, located in the downtown area. There is accessible parking in front of the restaurant, level access at the front entrance and ample room for a wheelchair inside. Bear in mind, this is not your traditional ladies-only prim-and-proper tea room, as the crowd is mixed, the atmosphere is casual and the portions are very generous.

This Atlanta mainstay opened its doors in 1945, when Mary McKinsey decided to use her southern cooking skills to make some money. In those days restaurant management was a man's business, so Mary called her place a tea room for it to gain acceptance in the community. Over the years it's expanded and changed hands a few times, but the emphasis remains on fresh ingredients, rib-sticking southern cooking and homemade breads and desserts. And their made-from-scratch peach cobbler is to die for.

Another historic Atlanta must-see is the Margaret Mitchell House and Museum, which features a small Visitors Center, the apartment where Margaret Mitchell lived when she penned *Gone with the Wind* and the Gone with the Wind Movie Museum. Accessible parking is available in the lot across the street from the apartment, next to the Gone with the Wind Movie Museum; however it's at bit of a walk over to the Visitors Center on the next block. The good news is, if you call ahead, they will open the locked apartment gate so you can shortcut through the apartment courtyard to the Visitor Center.

Access throughout the complex is good, with level access to the Visitors Center and the Gone with the Wind Museum and ramp access to the apartment building. There is elevator access to the second floor of the apartment building, where the historic apartment is located. In most cases wheelchair users can use the front entrance to the apartment; however if the space is too tight, the more accessible back entrance will need to be used. The docents are very good about meeting access needs and happy to make modifications to their tour route so that everyone can see all parts of the apartment. It's a great tour and a fun look at the place where literary history was made.

- IF YOU GO
    - Atlanta History Center, (404) 814-4000, www.atlantahistorycenter.com
    - Swan Coach House, (404) 261-0636, www.swancoachhouse.com
    - Mary Mac's Tea Room, (404) 876-1800, www.marymacs.com
    - Margaret Mitchell House and Museum, (404) 249-7015, www.gwtw.org
    - Atlanta Convention & Visitors Bureau, (404) 521-6600, www.atlanta.net

MUST-SEES IN DC

Y ou just can't talk about historic destinations without mentioning Washington, DC. Truly you can spend a whole month visiting all the museums, monuments and historic attractions in our nation's capital. Of course most folks don't have a month to spare, so choices need to be made. In the end, a cursory amount of pretrip research is essential, no matter what sites you decide to visit, Although most of the attractions are free, some require advance tickets, others require special arrangements and still others have limited days and hours of operation. And then of course, there are the access issues. Truly it's a mixed bag, and knowing where to go, how to get there and what kind of tickets you need will help you have a more enjoyable visit.

One of the best ways to get around and see the sights in Washington, DC, is on the Tourmobile. The Tourmobile stops at most of the top attractions in the District and offers a driving tour through Arlington National Cemetery. Visitors can get on and off as they choose and then just board the next Tourmobile bus when they are ready to move along. Buses run every 15 to 20 minutes.

If you can manage a few steps and sit in a traditional bus seat, then you can ride in the standard Tourmobile vehicle, which also has space for wheelchair storage. If you are unable to transfer or need a lift-equipped vehicle, Tourmobile provides an on-call service. If you opt for this choice, the driver will drop you off and then either wait for you or come back and pick you up at an appointed time. It's a great way to see the sights, and the on-call service is almost like a personal tour. No advance reservations are required for the on-call service; however they are recommended, especially during peak travel times.

One of the best accessibility resources in Washington, DC, is the Congressional Special Services Office, which is located in the crypt of the US Capitol Building. Not only does this office arrange accessible tours of the Capitol, but it also publishes two excellent access guides; *The Congressional Special Services Brochure* and *Washington Highlights: Tour Information for Visitors with Disabilities*. The former contains information about access at the Capitol, whereas the latter features access information about other Washington, DC, tourist sites.

Statues of President Franklin D. Roosevelt and his dog, Fala, at the FDR Memorial in Washington, DC.

All public tours of the Capitol are accessible; however individuals with disabilities may opt for an adapted tour provided by the Congressional Special Services Office. These tours last approximately one hour and they can be arranged in advance through your Congressional Representative. Accessible tours are also available on a walk-in basis as staffing permits, but it's really best to arrange things in advance. The Congressional Special Services Office also provides loaner wheelchairs for slow walkers.

The White House tour is also a popular ticket for visitors; however, with increased security measures, it's not exactly easy to arrange these days. In days of yore, wheelchair users could show up at the White House without a ticket and get fast-tracked to the front of the line. These days, public tours are only available for groups of 10 or more, and they must be arranged through a member of the Senate or House, well in advance. The suggested lead time for reservations is a whopping six months, so, suffice it to say, advance planning is a must. The good news is, the tours are accessible.

Alternatively you can visit the White House Visitor Center, located on Pennsylvania Avenue between 14th and 15th Streets. There is level access to the building, which includes a variety of interpretive exhibits and a video presentation about the White House. It's actually a nice substitute, as the exhibits are very well done.

Although there's certainly no shortage of monuments and memorials in Washington, DC, one of the more accessible choices is the FDR Memorial. No tickets are required and it's very nicely done access wise, with lots of open space, fountains and a tactile exhibit. The path around the Tidal Basin is also accessible and makes for a very pleasant stroll.

The United States Holocaust Memorial Museum is another DC hot ticket. The permanent exhibition of this excellent museum traces the story of Jewish persecution under Nazi rule from 1933 to 1945. The museum features barrier-free access to all exhibits and everybody must queue up for the daily distribution of timed entry passes. Doors open at 10 AM and the tickets are usually gone by noon. Alternatively you can purchase advance tickets at tickets.com. The on-line tickets are free, but there is a small per-ticket service charge; however, it's well worth the money, as it saves a lot of time waiting in line.

Of course no visit to Washington,, DC is complete without a visit to at least one of the Smithsonian museums. Of course you could spend a week alone at the Smithsonian, but, if you only have a day, check out the National Air and Space Museum. Admission is free, you don't need a ticket and access is excellent. Highlights include the original Wright 1903 Flyer, the Spirit of St. Louis, the Apollo 11 command module and a lunar rock sample you can actually touch. There's a reason why this is the world's most visited museum — in a word, it's great.

- IF YOU GO
  - Tourmobile, (703) 979-0690, www.tourmobile.com
  - White House Visitor Center, (202) 208-1631, www.whitehouse.gov
  - Congressional Special Services Office, (202) 224-4048
  - United States Holocaust Memorial Museum, (202) 488-0400, www.ushmm.org
  - Smithsonian National Air and Space Museum, (202) 633-2494, www.nasm.si.edu

MYSTIC GETAWAY

People go to Mystic to escape. Indeed this Connecticut coastal town boasts all the requisite ingredients for a first-rate weekend getaway. Located just 100 miles southwest of Boston, it's well within weekend driving distance for many New Englanders. As an added bonus, Mystic is just conducive to relaxation. You can kick back and do nothing at all or opt to explore some of the historic attractions in the area. And despite the historic nature of the town, many of the local attractions feature good access.

Mystic Seaport is the anchor attraction in town and a required stop for anyone with an interest in maritime history. This 19-acre open-air museum contains shipyard exhibits, historic vessels and maritime galleries, all built around a replica of a 19th century seafaring village.

Access varies throughout the park, but most of the inside exhibits feature ramped or level access. On the other hand, access in the village is more difficult, as there are uneven dirt streets that make for rough wheeling in wet weather.

On the positive side, there is ramped access to the Visitors Center, and loaner wheelchairs are available at the front desk.

As far as inside exhibits go, the figureheads exhibit in the Wendell building is a must-see. There is level access to the front entrance and plenty of room inside the spacious gallery. This unusual collection contains figureheads that once adorned sailing vessels, and it includes carvings in a wide range of subjects, from supernatural beasts to patriotic figures.

Next door, *Voyages: Stories of America and the Sea*, fills all three floors of the Stillman Building. There is ramped access at the entrance and elevator access to all floors. This signature exhibit focuses on how Americans have been and are connected to the sea. It features interpretive exhibits and interactive displays that share the seagoing experiences of everyone, from the early explorers and ocean traders to fisherman and even modern-day vacationers. It's very well done.

For a slightly different take on maritime history, head on over to the Mystic Aquarium, where you'll find everything from Beluga whales to relics from the *Titanic*. Access at the aquarium is good, with accessible pathways, level entrances and wide doorways throughout the complex. And although

African Black-footed penguins at the Mystic Aquarium

it's hard to pass up the Beluga whales or the ever-so-cute African black-footed penguins, save some time for two excellent historic exhibits: *Collision with History* and *Return to the Titanic.*

Both exhibits focus on the work of Dr. Robert Ballard and his oceanographic expeditions. *Collision with History* chronicles Dr. Ballard's search for John F. Kennedy's PT-109, whereas *Return to the Titanic* marks Ballard's third *Titanic* expedition.

Highlights of *Collision with History* include footage of the expedition and artifacts recovered from the wreck, whereas the *Titanic* exhibit features a 25-foot replica of the ships bow, a reproduction of the Marconi radio room and an interactive exhibit that allows visitors to search the ocean floor for *Titanic* artifacts. Both exhibits are excellent, as they offer visitors a decidedly different slant on ocean exploration.

If you're interested in Native American history, then take a drive up to the Mashantucket Pequot Museum, just seven miles north of Mystic. Although this museum focuses primarily on the history of the Mashantucket Pequot tribe, it also includes exhibits and information on other tribes and on the natural history of the area. The museum features barrier-free pathways and excellent access; in fact, I'd say it's the poster child of universal design. It's a beautiful building, one that by its very design encourages integration rather than segregation.

The museum features more than 85,000-square-feet of permanent exhibit space, and it includes interpretive exhibits, historic artifacts, photographs and dioramas that illustrate the history of the tribe. Highlights of the museum include a recreated 16th century coastal Pequot village and a very sobering video presentation about the massacre of 1637.

Outside the museum, there is also a pleasant natural area, where you can walk around and enjoy the scenery. As with everything else in the museum, this area features level access and barrier-free pathways. And if you are looking for jewelry, then don't miss the gift shop, as it features some beautiful pieces with excellent craftsmanship at reasonable prices.

And if you're looking for a historic, yet accessible, place to stay in Mystic, then look no further than the Inn at Mystic. The 67-room property sits on 15 acres of prime hillside real estate and features great views of Mystic Harbor and Long Island Sound.

The most accessible guest room (204) is located in the Main Building. Accessible parking is available right outside the room, with ramp access to the sidewalk and level threshold access to the guest room. Access features include wide doorways, good pathway access and a bathroom with a tub/shower combination, a hand-held showerhead, grab bars in the shower and around the toilet and a roll-under sink. There are two double beds in the guest room, both of which are the appropriate height for a wheelchair transfer. This room also has a very convenient location, right next door to the office and just across the parking lot from the Flood Tide Restaurant.

As an added bonus, the inn pretty much just oozes with romance; after all, it's where Bogie and Bacall honeymooned. What better place for a quiet weekend getaway?

- IF YOU GO
  - Mystic Seaport, (860) 572-5315, www.mysticseaport.org
  - Mystic Aquarium, (860) 572-5955, www.mysticaquarium.org
  - Mashantucket Pequot Museum, (800) 411-9671, www.pequotmuseum.org
  - Inn at Mystic, (860) 536-9604, www.innatmystic.com
  - Mystic Chamber of Commerce, (860) 572-9578, mysticchamber.org

REMEMBER SAN ANTONIO

S
an Antonio is a marvelous mix of old and new. You can stay in a sleek new property overlooking the historic RiverWalk, visit the surrounding missions, remember the Alamo and end your day in a modern eatery enjoying a hearty helping of anything from pasta to enchiladas. In truth, San Antonio is the best of both worlds, with a gaggle of historic sites surrounded by the creature comforts that modern travelers demand. Let's face it; it's great to see how Davey Crockett and Jim Bowie lived but even greater to come back to an air-conditioned hotel room with indoor plumbing.

Billed as one of the most visited places in Texas, the 2.5-mile RiverWalk is one of San Antonio's signature attractions. Constructed in 1933, this pedestrian-friendly riverside greenbelt is home to some of San Antonio's most spectacular hotels and a wide variety of restaurants, bars, clubs and shops. And although the RiverWalk was built at a time when wheelchair access was seldom included in community projects, access has greatly improved over the years. Today, approximately 75% of the RiverWalk is accessible.

Although the RiverWalk has a few access obstacles, such as footbridges with stairs, these inaccessible places are clearly noted on the RiverWalk Access Map, which is posted in prominent places along the River Walk. Researched by the City of San Antonio Disability Access Office, this excellent resource not only shows the access points (elevators and ramps), but also denotes the inaccessible portions of the RiverWalk. In the end, with a little planning and the RiverWalk access map, it is possible to enjoy the flagstone paths on both sides of the river.

As far as local historic attractions go, the hands-down favorite is of course the Alamo. Originally named Mission San Antonio de Valero, the Alamo is a true Texas landmark. Not only is it a tribute to the men who perished defending San Antonio from Santa Anna's army, but it's also a symbol of determination, honor and courage. The Daughters of the Republic of Texas maintain this historic site, and they've done a great job with access.

Most of the site is outside. There are level flagstone paths around the complex and over to the long barracks. The shrine, formerly the church, is the most recognizable facade. It features ramped access in the front and three steps in the back. Inside, visitors are routed past the artillery positions of

Jim Bowie and Davey Crockett. This is perhaps the most popular attraction of the site. The line moves pretty slowly and it can get crowded in the afternoon, so it's best to visit this well-touristed site early in the day.

The Alamo is not the only San Antonio mission. Indeed there are four others along the Mission Trail, two of which have fairly good access. The Mission Trail starts at Highway 410 and Villamain Road and winds along the San Antonio River and past the four missions. It's a very scenic drive and a great way to spend the day.

Mission San Jose y San Miguel de Aguayo is the most accessible mission. There is barrier-free access to the Visitors Center and level access to most of the mission grounds by a hard-packed dirt path. There is ramp access to the church in good weather; however the portable ramp is removed when the doors are closed in the winter.

Mission Conception is also worth a stop, as it's one of the most scenic missions. It features level access to most areas, including the church and museum. Some doorways are a bit tight, but you can still see most of the mission.

Although not a mission, another church worth a visit is the San Fernando Cathedral. Located a few blocks from the RiverWalk across from the Main Plaza, the cathedral was constructed in 1738. Don't let the three steps at the front of the cathedral dissuade you, as there is a ramped entrance on the left near the back. From there you can access the whole sanctuary, including the marble coffin, which reportedly contains the remains of some of the defenders of the Alamo. The chapel itself is well worth a visit, as it's comparable to some of the spectacular churches in Mexico and South America.

And if you'd like to check out an offbeat historic attraction, then stop by the Buckhorn Saloon and Museum, located just two blocks from the Alamo. The museum got its start in 1881 when saloon owner Albert Friedrich offered a shot of whisky to anyone who brought in some deer antlers. Suffice it to say that more than a few people took him up on his offer. Today the bar still serves whiskey, but the museum now also includes fins, feathers, taxidermy, a wax museum and an interesting collection of beer bottles. There is level access to the bar, restaurant and the first floor of the museum and elevator access to the second floor. It's one of those "only in Texas" experiences and truly one of the oddest museums I've ever visited. Don't miss it.

· ·

Mission San Jose y San Miguel de Aguayo, along the Mission Trail outside San Antonio.

- IF YOU GO
  - The Alamo, (210) 225-1391, www.thealamo.org
  - San Fernando Cathedral, (210) 227-1297, www.sfcathedral.org
  - Buckhorn Saloon and Museum, (210) 247-4000, www.buckhornmuseum.com
  - San Antonio Convention & Visitors Bureau, (210) 207-6700, www.SanAntonioVisit.com

THE BIG EASY, POST-KATRINA

Although New Orleans suffered immeasurable damage in the aftermath of Hurricane Katrina, the good news is, most of the tourist infrastructure has been rebuilt or repaired and reopened. That's good news because tourism is big business in the Crescent City, and quite frankly, the locals need the tourist crowds to survive. Of course some attractions are still open only sporadically, so it's best to check before you venture out; for the most part, however, the Big Easy is once again open for business. As far as access goes, well, it's a mixed bag. Some things have been rebuilt to be more accessible, whereas others were a permanent loss in the storm. Still, with a little planning, you can have a very fun, festive and accessible New Orleans visit.

The French Quarter is the cultural heart of New Orleans, and fortunately it was one of the least damaged areas of the city. The result is, it's still a great place to roll around, explore the sights, watch the street musicians and just take in the ambiance. To be honest, the French Quarter was not built for wheelchair access, but access improvements have been added over the years. The most accessible street in the French Quarter is Decatur Street, which runs parallel to the Mississippi River and is adjacent to the accessible Woldenburg Riverfront.

The Historic French Market Inn, located on the corner of Decatur and St. Louis Streets, is a good place to base yourself. It's just a short roll away from most of the French Quarter attractions, and it features an accessible guest room with a tub/shower combination, a hand-held showerhead, grab bars in the shower and around the toilet, a roll-under sink and a plastic

The Blues Man plays on the corner of Toulouse and Royal Streets in the historic French Quarter.

shower bench. There is level access to the public areas, including the private courtyard. Additionally, there's plenty of accessible parking (a hard-to-find commodity in this area) right across the street in the public parking lot.

The Historic French Market Inn is just two blocks away from Jackson Square, where you can stop in at the Visitors Center and pick up your free *French Quarter Self-Guided Walking Tour* map. There is ramp access to the entrance and, the volunteers inside are very knowledgeable about everything in town, including wheelchair access. You can do the self-guided walking tour at your own pace or choose an alternate route if you encounter any access obstacles.

If you'd prefer a more organized walking tour, then go next door and sign up for the Friends of the Cabildo Walking Tour. Tours are held twice a day on Tuesday through Sunday, and the volunteer tour guides are excellent. The two-hour tour covers 12 to 20 blocks, depending on the guide. The tours can be made wheelchair accessible upon request; however, since the tour runs through the historic part of the city, the ride can still be a little bumpy. Each guide adds his or her own personal touch to the tour, so you can take the same tour over and over, yet have a totally different experience each time.

Right behind Jackson Square, you'll find The Presbytere. This historic building formerly served as the clergy residence for neighboring St. Louis Cathedral, and today it's part of the Louisiana State Museum. New ramps grace the front of this historic building and there is barrier-free access to all of the galleries. Inside you'll find a semipermanent exhibit on the Mardi Gras.

Next door, you'll find the Cabildo, the site of the Louisiana Purchase Transfer. There is level access to the building, elevator access to all floors and barrier-free access to all exhibits. A loaner wheelchair is also available at the front desk. The Cabildo features exhibits that focus on the history of Louisiana; however the building itself is an architectural treasure.

Of course, you can't visit the French Quarter without the obligatory stop at Cafe Du Monde, located across the street from Jackson Square. There is level access to this 24-hour open-air cafe, and it's a nice place to linger over your cafe au lait and beignets and enjoy the street musicians. Before Hurricane Katrina, the morning crowds were overwhelming, but these days they are a thing of the past, and many days there are even empty seats.

Another French Quarter staple is the French Market, which is located just a few blocks from Cafe Du Monde. There is level access to the entrance, and, although there a few steps inside, most merchants are happy to assist customers by handing items to them.

The biggest access change to the French Quarter in post-Katrina times is the elimination of the accessible streetcar line along the riverfront. Unfortunately, all of the accessible cars were destroyed in the storm, so they have been replaced with the older inaccessible models from the St. Charles line. Hopefully at some time in the future, new accessible cars will be purchased.

If you'd prefer a guided tour, check out Gray Line Tours. Lift-equipped coaches are available on their city tour, with 48 hours notice. The city tour includes the French Quarter, the Garden District and a stop at St. Louis Cemetery #3. Access is doable at the cemetery, but there are patches of uneven ground. Still, it's a fun and interesting tour.

And if you'd like a ghostly night tour of the French Quarter, then wander down to Flanigan's Pub and sign up for the very popular New Orleans Ghost Tour. In a word, it's excellent. There is one step up into the pub, but the folks inside are very friendly and they will gladly bring your tickets out or serve you a brew on the sidewalk.

There are two tours each night, one at 7 and one at 8:30 and the distance covered is less than a mile. The tour route is based on the abilities of the participants and if there are wheelchair-users on the tour, the guide will find an accessible route. Company owner, Lisa Huber, is very proactive about making her tours accessible. Says Lisa, "Accessibility is very important to me as I broke my back a few years ago and had a very small personal experience with difficulty getting around."

Alternatively, you can see New Orleans by boat aboard the steamboat Natchez. There is ramped access to the boat but only stairway access between the decks. The food and entertainment are located on the second deck, so if you board on the second deck, it's pretty accessible. The nightly jazz cruise is pretty lively and it's just fun to cruise along the river.

All in all, New Orleans still has plenty of accessible and historic offerings, and of course she'll never, ever loose her spirit.

- IF YOU GO
  - Historic French Market Inn, (504) 561-5621, www.frenchmarketinn.com
  - Friends of the Cabildo Walking Tour, (504) 523-3939, www.friendsofthecabildo.org
  - The Presbytere & The Cabildo, (504) 568-6968
  - Cafe Du Monde, (504) 525-4544, www.cafedumonde.com
  - Gray Line Tours, (504) 569-1401, www.graylineneworleans.com
  - Steamboat Natchez, (504) 586-8777, www.steamboatnatchez.com
  - New Orleans Metropolitan Convention Bureau, (800) 672-6124, www.neworleanscvb.com
  - New Orleans Ghost Tour, (504) 628-1722, www.neworleansghosttour.com

THE FUN SIDE OF THE POTOMAC

Billed as the "fun side of the Potomac," Alexandria, Virginia, is a good choice for a variety of travelers. It's a fun destination in itself, especially if you enjoy history, art and architecture; however, because of the availability of accessible public transportation to the nation's capitol, it's also the ideal home base for Washington, DC, visitors. Whatever your preference, you won't be disappointed with the access, ambiance or variety in Alexandria.

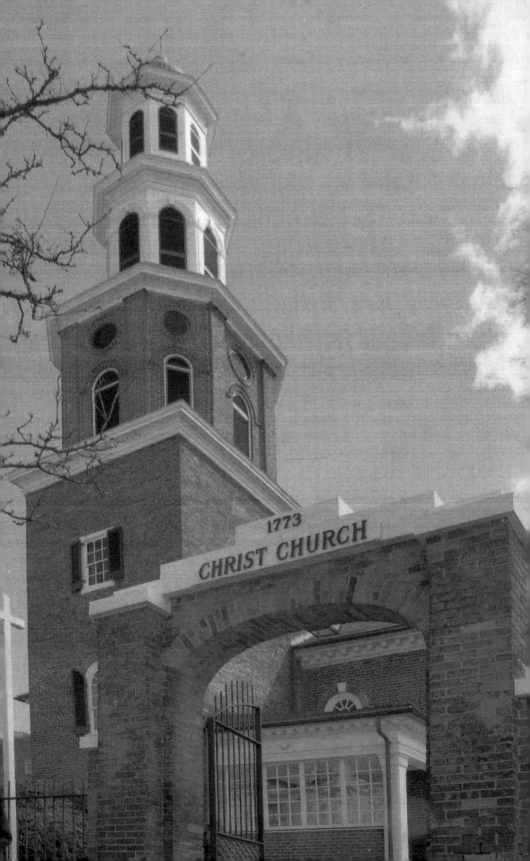

In contrast to hectic Washington, DC, Alexandria is a fairly laid-back town. The best way to see Old Town Alexandria is to wander through the streets and enjoy the ambiance. The main thoroughfare of Old Town is King Street, and you'll find a bevy of shops, restaurants, bars and galleries along this main drag. You'll also find the Visitors Center at the corner of King and Fairfax Streets. Stop in and pick up a free Visitors Guide and a map of Old Town before you hit the streets.

Getting around in Old Town Alexandria is pretty easy. The brick sidewalks on the main streets are well maintained and fairly smooth. Parking is limited, so get there early for the best selection. Accessible spaces are located on the street, but, again, the early bird gets the worm. Additionally, don't forget to pick up your free all-day visitors parking pass at the Visitors Center.

If you'd like to visit the nation's capitol, the accessible DASH bus provides service from Old Town to the King Street Metro station. From there you can take the train to Washington, DC, or Reagan National Airport. The Metro features roll-on access and wheelchair spaces on all cars. It's an easy and convenient way to get around.

As far as Alexandria historic sites go, Gadsby's Tavern Museum tops the list, as it's one of the few remaining 18th century taverns in the US. During colonial times, this tavern was the center of Alexandria's political, business and social life. Prominent local patrons included George Washington, John Adams, Thomas Jefferson and James Madison. Today the museum depicts a working tavern of the 1700s. The accessible entrance is on the left and there is barrier-free access throughout the first floor. The second floor, which includes the tavern sleeping accommodations, is only accessible by stairs; however, a video is available for folks who can't manage the stairs.

No visit to Alexandria is complete without a stop at Christ Church, better known as "George Washington's Church." Washington purchased a pew during the construction of the church, and today that pew is the only one preserved in the original three-sided seating or box configuration. Although there are steps at the main entrance, there is an accessible entrance located on Columbia Street. Docents are available to give visitors a brief overview of the history of the church. Save some time to wheel around the adjacent graveyard for an insightful glimpse into Alexandria's past.

• •

Christ Church in Alexandria, Virginia.

For a different view of Alexandria, visit the revitalized waterfront area near Union and King Streets. Here you'll find the Torpedo Factory Art Center and The Alexandria Archeology Museum. The Torpedo Factory Art Center is home to more than 160 working artists in 83 studios. The accessible entrance is located on the waterfront side of the building, and there is elevator access to all floors.

The Alexandria Archeological Museum is located on the third floor. There is no admission to this working museum, which includes a solid collection of local artifacts. Outside the Torpedo Factory, you'll find a wide selection of accessible dining options along the waterfront promenade. Stop in for a quick snack at the food court, or enjoy a more leisurely meal at the Chart House Restaurant, both of which have level access.

And finally, if you'd like to see our nation's capital by water, then book a lunch or dinner cruise on the very accessible *Nina's Dandy*. Docked in Alexandria, *Nina's Dandy* cruises past popular Washington, DC, monuments and through Georgetown before returning home. The boat features roll-on access, barrier-free pathways throughout the vessel and an accessible restroom. Not only is it a very accessible dining vessel, but it's also a very pleasant way to enjoy Washington, DC.

- IF YOU GO
  - DASH Bus (Alexandria Transit), (703) 370-3274, www.dashbus.com
  - Gadsby's Tavern Museum, (703) 838-4242, www.gadsbystavern.org
  - Christ Church, (703) 549-1450, www.HistoricChristChurch.org
  - Torpedo Factory Art Center, (703) 838-4565, www.torpedofactory.org
  - Alexandria Archeological Museum, (703) 838-4399, www.alexandriaarchaeology.org
  - *Nina's Dandy*, (703) 683-6076, www.dandydinnerboat.com
  - Alexandria Convention & Visitors Association, (703) 838-4200, www.FunSide.com

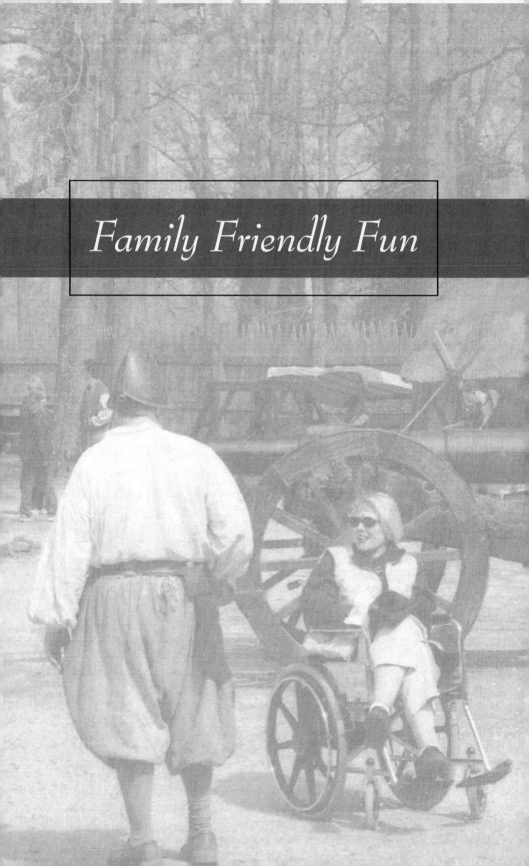

Family Friendly Fun

DISCOVER FLORIDA'S SPACE COAST

Located just 35 miles east of Orlando, Florida's Space Coast is an excellent multigenerational destination. This diverse coastline stretches from Titusville in the north to well past Melbourne in the south and is well within driving distance of the Miami area airports. Best of all, access is excellent along the Space Coast, where you'll find everything from wildlife and warbirds to moon rocks and manatees.

First stop on any Space Coast visit should be the Kennedy Space Center, the anchor attraction of the area. Access is excellent throughout the complex, with level walkways, wide doorways, accessible restrooms and ample space to maneuver in all the exhibition areas. An access brochure is also available at the ticket booth.

The best plan is to arrive early and take the first bus over to Launch Complex 39 and the Apollo/Saturn V Center. The bus tour is included in the admission price, and all buses have wheelchair lifts and tie-downs. Back at the main visitors complex, you'll find a number of other diversions to round out your day. Make sure and catch the 3-D presentation at the IMAX theater, and save some time to walk (or roll) aboard the Space Shuttle Explorer. And don't miss the famous Rocket Garden, where you can get a close-up look at eight historic rockets.

Kennedy Space Center shares its property with Merritt Island National Wildlife Reserve, a 35-mile long barrier island populated with an abundance of wildlife. So pack a picnic lunch, take your binoculars and spend a day exploring the area.

Your first stop should be the Visitors Center, which is located on State Route 402 approximately five miles from the refuge entrance. A .25-mile accessible boardwalk trail winds behind the Visitors Center and allows wheelers an unobstructed view of the surrounding salt marsh. Just up the road, the Black Point Wildlife Drive is also a must-see, with several viewing platforms and turnouts along the road.

And of course, don't leave the reserve without getting a glimpse of the playful manatees. The best place to view them is at the manatee observation deck near Haulover Canal, approximately 10 miles from the Visitors Center. There is ramp access to this boardwalk deck, which overlooks a popular manatee feeding area.

Manatee observation area on the Haulover Canal.

The Space Coast's newest attraction features "wildlife" of a different kind — warbirds. Located west of Kennedy Space Center at the Space Center Executive Airport in Titusville, the Valiant Air Command Warbird Museum includes a comprehensive display of military aircraft dating back to WWI. Access is good throughout the museum, with accessible parking near the entrance and level access to the main building and the restoration shed. It's a must-see for aircraft buffs.

And, for a little star gazing, head on over to the Astronaut Memorial Planetarium & Observatory, located on the campus of Brevard Community College. There's no admission charge to the rooftop observatory, which is accessible by elevator. Be forewarned though, the observatory is only open on Friday and Saturday nights, so plan ahead.

Last but not least, don't miss Lori Wilson Park in Cocoa Beach. Located next to the Holiday Inn on Atlantic Avenue, this beachside park includes a 1,000-foot beach boardwalk, the Johnnie Johnson Nature Center and an excellent marine hammock boardwalk trail. There is ramped access to the nature center, which contains a number of interpretive exhibits about local wildlife and marine ecology. Accessible parking is available near the nature center, and the beach boardwalk is just around the corner.

The highlight of the park is the Marine Hammock Trail. This 3,155-foot interpretive trail is 6 feet wide and has level access from the nature center. The boardwalk is not entirely flat – undulating would be a better description – but it's shaded and there are lots of spots to stop and take a break. It's hard to believe such a diverse ecosystem exists literally in the backyard of the Holiday Inn, but it does. If you like nature, then this is definitely the place for you, and it's a great way to top off your Space Coast vacation.

- **IF YOU GO**
  - Kennedy Space Center, (321) 449-4444, www.KennedySpaceCenter.com
  - Merritt Island National Wildlife Reserve, (321) 861-0667
  - Valiant Air Command Warbird Museum, (321) 268-1941, www.vacwarbirds.org
  - Astronaut Memorial Planetarium & Observatory, (321) 433-7373, www.brevardcc.edu/planet
  - Lori Wilson Park, (321) 868-1123, www.brevardparks.com
  - Space Coast Office of Tourism, (800) 872-1969, www.space-coast.com

EXPERIENCE LIVING HISTORY IN WILLIAMSBURG

I f you have kids, a visit to Williamsburg is probably on your must-do list. And that's a very good thing because there's no better place to learn about colonial history than in America's historic triangle. Located in the Hampton Roads region of southeastern Virginia, the area features a large collection of interpretive exhibits at three main sites: Williamsburg, Jamestown and Yorktown. And, although some buildings have steps and there's some uneven terrain here and there, all of the venues feature at least some wheelchair-accessible options.

Colonial Williamsburg is probably the most well-known attraction in the area. This open-air living history museum features 301 acres filled with historic buildings, gardens and public greens and staffed by costumed docents who interact with visitors. The docents are especially good with kids, and they even make learning about colonial history fun.

Living history at the Jamestown Settlement.

There is level access to the Visitors Center, where you can buy tickets, pick up maps and find out about the accessibility of Colonial Williamsburg. An on-line access guide is also available; however the most updated access information is available from the Visitors Center employees. A limited number of wheelchairs are also available for rent at the Visitors Center. They are available on a first-come basis for $7 per day.

Although most of Colonial Williamsburg is fairly level, some of the uneven brick sidewalks make for a rough ride. Your best bet is to just roll down the middle of the street, which is fairly safe because no vehicle traffic is permitted in the park.

Access to the buildings in Colonial Williamsburg varies greatly. The capitol building has a unique concealed lift, whereas the gunsmith's shop has a standard ramp. Some buildings, such as the Governor's Palace, the Raleigh Tavern and the Randolph House, have lift or ramp access to the first floor but only stair access to the top floors. Photo albums of the top floors are available for visitors who are unable to navigate the stairs. And if you'd like to sit down for a tasty lunch or dinner, try the Shields Tavern, which has ramp access around the back.

Just down the road from Colonial Williamsburg, you'll find Jamestown, the first permanent English settlement in the US. This site features two attractions: Historic Jamestowne and the Jamestown Settlement.

Operated by Colonial National Historical Park, Historic Jamestowne is the original site of the Jamestown colony. It contains archeologic ruins, reconstructed buildings, a glasshouse, an interpretive center and a scenic auto loop drive. Access to most of the site is by level dirt paths covered with oyster shells; however the trails leading to the glasshouse have steep grades and some visitors may require assistance on these. There is level access to the Visitors Center, which is where the accessible restrooms are located. Wheelchairs are available for free loan on a first-come basis at the Visitors Center. Additionally, the Memorial Church is accessible by a ramp on the south side.

Although Historic Jamestowne provides visitors with a good historic interpretation of the Jamestown colony; Jamestown Settlement, which is located next door, is usually the preference of the younger generation. Like Colonial Williamsburg, the Jamestown Settlement presents an excellent living history program with costumed docents. The re-created Powhatan Indian Village and James Fort are very popular with kids. And it's just a fun place for kids to explore, as access is excellent throughout the settlement with wide level pathways and wheelchair access to most buildings.

The last point on America's historic triangle is Yorktown, where the final battle of the American Revolutionary War was fought in 1781. The Yorktown Victory Center features the battlefield, Visitors Center and an auto driving loop. There is level access to the Visitors Center, and, although the area of the battlefield right outside has a few dirt walking trails, wheelers may require assistance on the steep sections. Still, it's interesting to see, as there's an outdoor living history Continental Army encampment, which is usually a big hit with kids. If you find the terrain too rough to navigate, pick up the free Battlefield Driving Audio Tour in the Visitors Center. It's a very accessible way to enjoy the site and a great idea for when the kids get tired.

- **IF YOU GO**
  - Colonial Williamsburg, (757) 229-1000, www.history.org
  - Jamestown Settlement, Yorktown Victory Center, (757) 253-4838, www.historyisfun.org.
  - Historic Jamestowne, (804) 648-1889, www.historicjamestowne.org

FAMILY FUN IN SAN DIEGO

I t's hard to beat San Diego for accessibility. Thanks to the efforts of local advocacy groups, this southern California community remains at the forefront of advances in accessible tourism. In addition to a large inventory of accessible hotel rooms, an excellent access guide and a local population that's aware of access issues, San Diego also boasts a bevy of family-friendly attractions, many of which are wheelchair accessible. Add to that mix, a mild year-round climate, and you can understand why San Diego gets top billing as an accessible family-friendly vacation destination.

The best way to get acquainted with San Diego is to take a tour on the Old Town Trolley. This narrated tour stops at a number of tourist attractions throughout San Diego, including Old Town, the Gaslamp Quarter, Balboa Park and Coronado Island. You can start the tour at any trolley stop and hop on and off as you please. There is lift access to the trolley, so wheelchair users don't have to transfer in order to ride. It's a fun tour and you can do as little or as much of it as you like. Although reservations are not required, it's best to call ahead for maximum accessibility.

Another fun way to see San Diego is to take a Seal Tour, a unique land and water adventure. This 90-minute narrated tour departs from Seaport Village and focuses on the military history of the area. The majority of the tour is conducted on land; however the Hydra Terra tour vehicle splashes into San Diego Bay for the last 20 minutes of the tour. It's a fun tour for all ages, and there is lift access to the tour vehicle for wheelchair users.

Although there's no shortage of tourist attractions in the area, you just can't visit San Diego without a stop at the world famous San Diego Zoo. The best way to get a good overview of this massive attraction is to take the 40-minute bus tour, which winds through the canyons and mesas of the compound. Wheelchair users must transfer to a bus seat in the wheelchair area of the bus. There is space to stow folding wheelchairs on board, and rigid (nonfolding) wheelchairs can be stored at the boarding terminal and picked up at the end of the tour.

After the tour, you can decide which areas of the Zoo to visit on your own. Although there are a number of steep areas in the zoo, a free shuttle service for disabled visitors is available. There are also several moving walkways

The San Diego waterfront.

in the zoo; however, these are best suited for slow walkers, as wheelchairs are not permitted on them.

Another way to enjoy the zoo is to hop on the Skyfari, a sky ride that crisscrosses the zoo compound. Park employees can stop the ride for slow walkers and wheelchair users. All guests must transfer to the Skyfari gondola, however employees are available to offer assistance. Guests who use a folding wheelchair can have the wheelchair transported in the gondola ahead of them, so it's available in the opposite terminal when they arrive, whereas those folks in rigid wheelchairs can leave their chair at the departing terminal and take a round-trip ride.

A detailed map showing the accessible restrooms and the areas of the park that have steeper grades is available at the zoo entrance. And, if you have any access-related questions or need assistance during your visit, just ask any zoo employee.

Another animal attraction worth a visit is the San Diego Wild Animal Park, which, like the zoo, is operated by the San Diego Zoological Society. The Wild Animal Park is actually located outside of town, 30 miles northeast of downtown San Diego to be specific. If you are traveling by car, consider visiting the Wild Animal Park on your way to or from San Diego to minimize your driving time.

Like the zoo, the Wild Animal Park has some rugged terrain within its boundaries; however the park publishes an accessibility map that highlights the most accessible routes through the park. A courtesy shuttle is also available to the Heart of Africa and Condor Ridge exhibits.

Most of the restaurants and shops feature barrier-free access, and one amphitheater is wheelchair accessible. Wheelchairs are also available for rent near the entrance.

The highlight of the Wild Animal Park is the new Journey into Africa tour, which takes visitors into some of the field exhibits and allows folks to an up-close-and-personal look at the African residents. The brightly colored safari vehicles have one wheelchair-accessible space, so wheelchair users don't have to transfer to take the tour. Preboarding privileges are also offered to anybody with a mobility disability who can transfer into a seat on the tour vehicle. It's a fun and educational tour and a great way to get a close look at the rhinos, giraffes, ostriches and other compound inhabitants.

Another San Diego family favorite is Sea World. Indeed you can spend a whole day at this marine park. There's plenty of accessible parking up front, and wheelchairs and scooters are available for rent at the main entrance. Access is excellent throughout most of the park, including barrier-free access to restaurants, shows, gift shops and restrooms.

Portions of the Shark Encounter and Penguin Encounter exhibits have moving walkways, and although these work well for some slow walkers, they are not recommended for wheelchair users. Wheelers can avoid these walkways by using the upper viewing area in the Penguin Encounter and by doubling back and using the entrance as an exit in the Shark Encounter.

As far as the rides go, most of them require that you transfer to a seat and have good upper body strength and the ability to hang on tightly. The exception is the Skytower, which is fully accessible. There is room for one wheelchair on each cabin level, so you don't have to be able to transfer to ride this ride. The gentle ride takes visitors up the 265-foot Skytower for a panoramic view of the area. On a clear day, you can see up to 100 miles in every direction and get a breathtaking view of the San Diego skyline. Although it's a pretty tame ride, most kids enjoy it. When in Sea World, you have to see Shamu and you have to ride the Skytower.

Finally, don't forget to contact Accessible San Diego to get your *Access in San Diego* guide. Published yearly, this great resource is available for $5 and contains information on accessible properties, attractions, transportation and restaurants throughout the San Diego area. Additionally this nonprofit organization provides access information by telephone, so don't be afraid to give them a call should you have any access questions. They're the local access experts and they have the latest and greatest San Diego access information.

- IF YOU GO
  - Old Town Trolley Tours, (619) 298-8687, www.oldtowntrolley.com
  - Seal Tours, (619) 298-8687, www.sealtours.com
  - San Diego Zoo, (619) 234-3153, www.sandiegozoo.org
  - San Diego Wild Animal Park, (760) 747-8702, www.wildanimalpark.org
  - Sea World, (619) 226-3901, www.seaworld.com
  - Accessible San Diego, (858) 279-0704, www.accessandiego.com
  - San Diego Convention & Visitors Bureau, (619) 236-1212, www.sandiego.org

JUST CALL ME SKIPPER

Houseboating is fast becoming a popular family vacation choice. And although boat ownership is a pricey proposition, you don't have to actually own your own houseboat to enjoy a yearly holiday on the lake. Even better, you don't really have to know anything about boating to participate. Houseboat rentals, which are available at many marinas across the US, offer a hassle-free and affordable way for folks to enjoy a family houseboating vacation.

Forever Houseboats, which manages a number of marinas throughout the country, also rents houseboats; the good news is, many of their locations offer accessible houseboats. Such is the case with Moccasin Point Marina, perched on the northern shore of Lake Don Pedro. Located approximately 45 miles southeast of Stockton, California, it's the perfect place to begin your family houseboating vacation.

The marina features accessible parking near the entrance and level access to the snack bar, store and office. Accessible public restrooms are located in the back of the marina. Additionally, there is level access to all areas of the dock, so there is roll-on dockside access to all boats.

Cruising Lake Don Pedro aboard the Millennium houseboat.

Forever Resorts offers two accessible rental choices: the 59-foot Deluxe XT and the 70-foot Millennium. Both vessels are billed as "wheelchair accessible with assistance," and the major difference between the two is the sleeping capacity. The Deluxe XT sleeps 10, whereas the larger Millennium sleeps 12.

Access features on both vessels are identical. They include a wide side boarding gate, a threshold ramp at the front sliding glass door and good pathway access throughout the living room, kitchen and dining room on the main deck. The forward bathroom features a wide door-way, grab bars by the toilet and a roll-under sink. The low-step shower is actually better suited for somebody who can walk at least one step. There is an 11-inch step up to the shower, and it would be difficult to safely transfer to the built-in seat in the back of the shower without taking at least one step.

Access is limited to the forward section of the main deck, as a 24-inch hallway leads to the sleeping quarters in the aft section. The sofas in the living room convert to beds, and this is the most accessible sleeping option. The sundeck (on top) is only accessible by a narrow flight of stairs, however the lower front deck features roll-on access. It's a nice place to relax, enjoy the scenery or even fish.

And the houseboat is very easy to drive. The folks at Forever Resorts give all customers a 45-minute orientation, which covers the basics of operation, before they take out the boat. Additionally, the staff will pull the boat in and out of the dock for you, which is actually the most difficult part of piloting the vessel. After that, it's all smooth sailing.

The minimum rental period is three days, however most folks rent for a week. All pots, pans, utensil and linens are furnished, and customers receive a video detailing the features of the boat after their reservation is confirmed.

All in all, it's a fun family vacation boat. It's also worth noting that these rental vessels are manufactured by Forever Resorts, so access is consistent at all Forever Resort locations. In other words, you'll find the same accessible features on a Millennium at Moccasin Point Marina as you will on a Millennium at Callville Bay Marina on Lake Mead. Now you, too, can be the captain of your own accessible houseboat.

- IF YOU GO
  - Moccasin Point Marina, (209) 989-2206, www.moccasinpointmarina.com
  - Forever Resorts, (800) 255-5561, www.foreverresorts.com

MEET ME IN ST. LOUIS

Meet Me in St. Louis was the popular 1904 song that helped draw people from around the world to the St. Louis World's Fair. And apparently it was a very effective draw, as an average of 86,000 visitors passed through the gates every day. People came from all over to see new innovations, learn about far-away places, ride the world's largest Ferris wheel and just have fun. And although the World's Fair has long since closed its doors, people still come to St. Louis to have fun.

And there's no better place to have fun than at the St. Louis Zoo, where the slogan is, "You're not at the zoo, you're in it." Located in Forest Park,

the zoo was established shortly after the 1904 World's Fair, largely due to the popularity of the World's Fair Flight Cage. Today this walk-through free-flight aviary is part of the zoo; in fact, it's a top zoo attraction.

Other must-sees at the zoo include the Monsanto Insectarium and the Children's Zoo, where you'll find plenty of hands-on activities for kids. And when you get tired, hop on the Zooline Railroad for a good overview of the 79-acre property. Each Zooline train features one ramp-equipped car, with adjacent companion seating.

Most of the attractions at the zoo offer barrier-free access, including the restaurants, exhibits and the gift shop. An access map is also available at the entrance. And don't forget to take a gander at Phil the Gorilla (a former zoo resident) in the gift shop on your way out. Phil is a big hit with kids.

For more fun, head on over to the City Museum. Housed in a former shoe warehouse, this quirky funhouse is built from salvaged and recycled materials. This interactive museum features lots of spaces to crawl, roll or climb. There are plenty of staff on hand to assist visitors, and their motto is, "We're all here, because we're not all there." Access features include a level entry, cement floors and elevator access to all levels.

Among other things, the City Museum includes a working tide pool, a shoelace factory and a wheelchair-accessible cave. Must-sees are the world's largest pair of men's underwear, the collection of recycled art and the re-creation of a 1950s-era shoe store. And just in case you're wondering, the City Museum isn't just for kids. Plenty of adults can also be found there — crawling, jumping, running and of having fun.

Another great attraction, with plenty of room to roam is the Museum of Transportation. Admittedly the name doesn't exactly ooze fun; however what kid can resist an attraction that has more than four miles of railroad track and 70 locomotives? Located on 150 acres at Barton Station, the museum illustrates the ever-changing nature of transportation and also features cars, buses and trolleys dating back to the turn of the century.

Inside the 10 exhibition halls you'll find everything from Bobby Darin's dream car and a horse-drawn streetcar to a portion of the old Coral Court Motel. The outside exhibition area houses a large collection of steam and diesel locomotives and even an airplane and a riverboat.

There is barrier-free access to all of the indoor exhibits and a well-marked accessible route along asphalt paths in the outdoor exhibition area. Additionally,

. . . .

The St. Louis Arch.

the Roberts Building contains accessible platforms that allow visitors to peer inside select rail cars, including restored Pullman sleepers, dining cars and even a railroad president's private office car. It's a fun place for kids of all ages.

Another fun place, especially for animal lovers, is Grant's Farm. President Ulysses S. Grant farmed a portion of this land in the 1850s, before it became the ancestral home of the Anheuser-Busch family. In keeping with their commitment to animal conservation, the Busch family later converted the land to a wildlife preserve and opened it to the public.

Today, visitors can board a tram and tour the 281-acre deer park, home to a large variety of deer, antelope, zebras, elk and bison. The first car of the tram features ramp access with room for two wheelchairs. The tram stops at the Tier Garden and the Bauerhof before it returns to the main entrance.

Visitors can visit the Tier Garden to feed the animals or stop by the Bauerhof to see the carriage collection. There are a few steep grades along the asphalt paths in the Tier Garden, but wheelchair users can still get an up-close-and-personal look at most of the animals. Guests can also enjoy a free sample of their favorite Anheuser-Busch adult beverage. And the really good news is, Grant's Farm is not only fun, but it's also free.

- IF YOU GO
  - St. Louis Zoo, (314) 781-0900, www.stlzoo.org
  - City Museum, (314) 231-2489, www.citymuseum.org
  - Museum of Transportation, (314) 965-7998, www.museumoftransport.org
  - Grant's Farm, (314) 843-1700, www.grantsfarm.com
  - St. Louis Convention & Visitors Commission, (800) 916-0040, www.explorestlouis.com

ROCKET CITY, USA

Located in northern Alabama, Huntsville earned the nickname of Rocket City, USA, when Dr. Wernher von Braun jumpstarted a fledgling US Space program by developing the rocket technology that would one day put a man on the moon. His work at Redstone Arsenal began in the 1950s and, by the

Rocket Garden at the US Space and Rocket Center.

end of the decade, a von Braun rocket carried the first American into space. These days, the space program still plays a vital role in the local economy; however today that role is largely tourism related.

The US Space and Rocket Center is of course a must-see while in Huntsville. More commonly known as the home to Space Camp, the center also houses a museum with exhibits ranging from the Saturn V rocket and the Apollo 16 Command Module to a historic display of Dr. von Braun's work. Basically, if it's space related, it's there. Top it all off with a stroll through rocket garden and an IMAX show and you have a pretty full day.

The museum features a ramped entry, accessible restrooms and level pathways to most of the inside exhibits and the outside rocket garden. If you encounter a few steps, just ask an employee to point out the accessible pathway. They are very knowledgeable and happy to help.

If you'd like to give your kids a deeper exposure to the space program, then consider enrolling them in Space Camp. Actually there are three levels of Space Camp, segregated by age. Space Camp is for kids from 9 to 11 years of age, Space Academy is for 12- to 14 year-olds and the Advanced Space Academy is for students from 15 to 18 years old. All programs work on age-appropriate space-themed activities and simulations that build confidence, encourage teamwork and improve communication skills. Access needs are accommodated on an individual basis at Space Camp, but because the accessible US Space and Rocket Center is the campus, most of the activities can be easily adapted. Advance arrangements are required, but the staff works hard to make the whole experience as accessible and integrated as possible.

Billed as the South's largest hands-on history museum, the Early Works Children's Museum is another fun kids' attraction. Children can hear stories from a talking tree, play a tune on giant-sized instruments or try building a house in the interactive architecture exhibit. There's something to suit just about every interest. Access is excellent throughout the museum, including roll-on access to a 46-foot keelboat.

Just around the corner you'll find the equally accessible Constitution Village. This re-created 1819 village is billed as the birthplace of Alabama, as it's located on the site where the Alabama Territory leaders met to petition congress for statehood. This living history museum features costumed docents who interpret the early 1800s history. You'll find the docents throughout the village doing a variety of chores, from spinning wool and making baskets to tending the garden and even doing the laundry (the old-fashioned way).

There is ramp or level access to most buildings and wide level pathways around the village. A few of the buildings have narrow doorways or a few steps, but you can still see inside them. All in all, it's a great glimpse into the past.

As for getting around Huntsville, it's a snap, thanks to the Tourist Trolley. The fare is a reasonable $1, or just $2 for an all-day pass (disabled passengers get 50% off). Although this is a fixed-route system, you can call for a pick-up from most major hotels, even if they aren't regular stops. As the name indicates, it's a very tourist-friendly service, and the lift-equipped vehicles deliver passengers to the front door of attractions, shopping centers, and hotels, so there's no need to worry about parking. It's the easy way to get around Huntsville.

Finally, save one day for a road trip to the Unclaimed Baggage Center, located approximately 46 miles east of Huntsville in Scottsboro. Yes, this is where most of that lost luggage ultimately ends up. And from the looks of the 40,000-square-foot store, the airlines are doing a healthy business misdirecting our belongings.

Still if you don't think too hard about it, it's a fun place. There is level access to the store, with accessible restrooms located near the main entrance. The whole store is nicely laid out, with wide aisles and plenty of room to navigate between the racks.

Depending on when you go (merchandise turns over quickly), you'll find a wide selection, from clothing and jewelry to sports equipment and camera accessories. My most unusual find was a pink sequined Mardi Gras costume (compete with a feathered boa) whereas my most practical find was a network cable for my laptop. Best buys include sunglasses, books, CDs and DVDs. Even if you don't purchase anything, it's a fun place to browse, even if you aren't a shopper.

- **IF YOU GO**
  - US Space and Rocket Center, (256) 837-3400, www.spacecamp.com/museum
  - Space Camp, (256) 837-3400, www.spacecamp.com
  - Early Works Children's Museum, Constitution Village, (256) 564-8100, www.earlyworks.com
  - Tourist Trolley, (256) 427-6811
  - Unclaimed Baggage Center, (256) 259-1525, www.unclaimedbaggage.com
  - Huntsville CVB, (256) 551-2230, www.huntsville.org

SPRING BREAK, FAMILY STYLE

Years ago Daytona Beach was a popular spring beak destination for the college crowd; however, these days Florida spring breakers tend to favor Key West and Panama City. What once was party time at Daytona Beach has evolved into family time at Daytona Beach. Sure, college kids still come to Daytona Beach; however, they are coming in smaller numbers and their activities are pretty much confined to a distinct party district. For the most part, the drunken parties, bikini contests and *Girls Gone Wild* film crews have relocated to greener pastures. They have however been replaced by a new breed of spring breaker. Today, spring breakers of yesteryear are returning to Daytona Beach with their own families for a different kind of spring break experience, one that includes lots of kid-friendly activities, family fun and of course the beach.

Known as the birthplace of speed, Daytona Beach is also home to Daytona USA, a must-see for kids of all ages. Billed as the official attraction

The Ponce Inlet Lighthouse.

of NASCAR, Daytona USA offers interactive exhibits, historic displays and multimedia presentations that trace the history of the NASCAR. As an added bonus, visitors can tour the speedway, see the infield, visit Victory Lane and (if there's not a race in progress) even ride on the track.

There is barrier-free access to all of the inside areas of Daytona USA and ramp access to the open-air tour tram. There are tie-downs on the tram, so you can stay in your wheelchair for the duration of the tour. The tour stops once, so folks can stroll down Victory Lane, but there is level access from the tram stop through the paved fan area to Victory Lane. All in all it's a very accessible experience. Don't miss the winning car from the Daytona 500, which is put on display (complete with confetti and champagne stains) for a year following the victory.

Of course, a trip or two to the beach is always on the itinerary at Daytona Beach. The great thing about the local beaches is that they are made of hard-packed sand, which makes wheeling a lot easier. You can even drive on many of the beaches; in fact, years ago they used to race motorcycles and even cars on the beach. That's how racing got its start in Daytona Beach. Today, just look for the well-marked vehicle access points and hit the beach.

There is a $5 charge for vehicle access, but if you have a disabled placard or plate, that fee is waived.

Beach wheelchairs are also available for free loan at beaches in Ormond Beach, Daytona Beach, Daytona Beach Shores, Ponce Inlet, New Smyrna Beach and Ormond-by-the-Sea. Contact Volusia County Beach Management for the exact locations.

If you'd like to park your car for the day, then just hop on the A1A Trolley, which runs up and down Atlantic Avenue and stops at the major attractions and beach hot spots along the way. Fares are just $1.25 and there is lift access to all vehicles. It's the easy way to get around Daytona Beach.

Another fun kids' attraction is the Museum of Arts & Sciences. Located on the Tuscawilla Nature Preserve, the museum complex features an accessible boardwalk behind the main museum building; however the Root Family Gallery is the big attractions for kids. Suffice it to say, the Roots were collectors of everything, and the gallery houses part of their massive collection.

From a 1948 Lincoln Continental and cars that raced on the Indianapolis Speedway to a bevy of Teddy bears and the second largest collection of Coca-Cola memorabilia in the world, the Root Family Gallery is somewhat overwhelming. In fact, it makes you want to go home and clean out your garage. Top it off with the Root family railcars, which are parked out back, and it's just hard to imagine where they kept all this stuff before the museum was built.

There is excellent access to all areas of the museum, including ramp access to the railcar platform. Although the railcar doors are too narrow for wheelchair access, you can still look into them from the platform. All in all it's a fun place. And don't miss the 13-foot skeleton of a giant ground sloth in the Center for Florida History section of the museum. It's a real kid favorite.

Another family-friendly attraction is the Ponce Inlet Lighthouse, located just south of Daytona Beach. Built in 1887, the lighthouse and the surrounding buildings have been lovingly preserved. Today, costumed docents offer tours and give visitors a glimpse into the past of Florida's tallest lighthouse.

There is level access from the parking area to the gift shop (just follow the signs) and ramped access to all of the outbuildings. And although the lighthouse itself is not wheelchair accessible, there are plenty of other accessible exhibits to enjoy if part of your party wants to climb the 175-foot tower. Don't miss the lens museum, which houses the original Fresnel lens or the historic boats in back of the keepers' quarters. Not only are there enough displays to entertain even the most inquisitive kids, but it's also just a fun place to visit.

- IF YOU GO
  - Daytona USA, (386) 947-6530, www.daytonausa.com
  - A1A Beachside Trolley, (386) 761-7700, www.volusia.org/votran/trolley.htm
  - Volusia County Beach Management, (386) 239-7873
  - Museum of Arts & Sciences, (386) 255-0285, www.moas.org
  - Ponce Inlet Lighthouse, (386) 761-1821, www.ponceinlet.org
  - Daytona Beach Convention & Visitors Bureau, (800) 854-1234, www.daytonabeach.com

Off the Beaten Path

AMERICA'S ACCESSIBLE CARIBBEAN

As the most developed US Virgin Island, St. Thomas remains a top choice for accessible Caribbean fun. That said, it's also important to remember that access in the Caribbean is still in its infancy and even St. Thomas has a good number of physical barriers. On the positive side, access is improving, and the island now boasts accessible hotels, transportation, tours and tourist sights. In short, with a little advance planning, St. Thomas is a good place to enjoy an accessible slice of Caribbean life.

One of the most popular attractions on St. Thomas is Coral World Marine Park and Undersea Observatory. Located just 20 minutes from the Charlotte Amalie harbor, Coral World offers visitors an intimate look at local marine life, with hands-on touch pools and aquariums filled with indigenous sea creatures.

Says Coral World General Manager, Trudie J. Prior, "As part of the reconstruction following Hurricane Marilyn, we redesigned the park to provide accessibility to as many exhibits as possible. We created wheelchair-accessible walkways to the major exhibits and removed many physical barriers."

The park now features level pathways and barrier-free access to most buildings. The Undersea Observatory is only accessible by stairs; however a video of the underwater activity is available on the top level of the Observatory Tower. A map of the park, with the accessible routes depicted, is available at the entrance. Plan to spend the day at Coral World, have some lunch, visit the shark tank and then feed the resident iguanas. They just love lettuce!

If you'd like an even closer look at the local marine life, then visit Carl Moore at Aqua Action Dive Center. Located right on the beach at the accessible Secret Harbor Beach Resort, Aqua Action offers Handicapped Scuba Association-certified instruction, equipment rentals and shore and boat dives. Secret Harbor is a good place to get your feet wet if you're new to snorkeling or scuba, and Carl is more than willing to help beginners.

For a more historic look at St. Thomas, stop by Fort Christian in downtown Charlotte Amalie. Built in 1672, the fort now houses the Virgin Islands Museum. There is ramp access to the fort, and many of the galleries and exhibits are accessible. Some exhibits have one step at the entry, but you can still view them from the courtyard.

Accessible pathways at Coral World.

Don't miss the vendors' plaza, located right next door to Fort Christian. This open-air market is filled with local vendors, and it's as much fun to browse as it is to buy. There is curb-cut access to the plaza; however it gets a bit crowded when cruise ships are in port.

And for getting around the island, St. Thomas Dial-A-Ride provides accessible transportation in lift-equipped vans. Visitors pay a one-time registration fee of $25, which includes a round-trip transfer to any St. Thomas property. After that, St. Thomas Dial-A-Ride fares are equivalent to local taxi fares. St. Thomas Dial-A-Ride also offers accessible day tours of the island. Tours must be booked one month in advance, and transportation arrangements must be made at least 24 hours in advance.

As far as lodging goes, there are a number of accessible choices on St. Thomas; however my favorite is Secret Harbor Beach Resort. I like it because of its low-key atmosphere and its proximity to Aqua Action. This all-suite beachfront resort has four accessible rooms, including one with a roll-in shower. There is level access to the entire resort, including the restaurant, bar and gift shop. Approximately 85% of Secret Harbor's guests are repeat visitors. Says the resident manager, "We consider our visitors more than just guests; we think of them as part of the family."

All in all, St. Thomas gets pretty good marks for access. Again, it's not the same access you'll find on the US mainland, but it's not bad for the Caribbean.

- IF YOU GO
  - Coral World Marine Park, (340) 775-1555, www.coralworldvi.com
  - Aqua Action Dive Center, (340) 775-6285, www.aadivers.com
  - St. Thomas Dial-A-Ride, (340) 776-1277
  - Secret Harbor Beach Resort, (340) 775-6550, www.secretharbourvi.com
  - US Virgin Islands Tourism, (800) 372-8784, www.usvitourism.vi

CATALINA TODAY

During its heyday, Catalina Island played host to a bevy of Hollywood celebrities, including Marilyn Monroe, Natalie Wood and Laurel & Hardy. It was the playground of Hollywood's rich and famous and even the filming location for a few movies. Today some kitschy remnants of the past remain, such as the buffalo that roam the island, offspring of the herd used in the 1920s movie, *The Vanishing American*. The big difference is now, for the most part, Catalina is a pretty mainstream destination. And as far as access goes, that's great, as getting there and getting around is much easier these days.

Located 22 miles southwest of Los Angeles, Catalina makes a great southern California daytrip. The most accessible way to get there is on the Catalina Express, a high-speed catamaran ferry that offers daily service from Long Beach and San Pedro. There is accessible parking at both locations and barrier-free access to the terminals. Advance reservations are advised; however walk-ins can be accommodated on a space-available basis.

All of the Catalina Express boats have one accessible restroom; however it's only a one-hour trip, so it's a good idea to plan ahead in case the seas are rough. There is ramp access to the boat, but because of slippery conditions and fluctuating tides, wheelchair users may need some boarding assistance. Not to worry though, as the crew is happy to assist. Once aboard, wheelers can transfer to a seat or stay in their own wheelchair for the short trip.

Avalon's Art Deco Casino Theatre.

Additionally, Catalina is a port of call for several cruise ships; however it should be noted that it is a tender port. The cruise ships drop anchor in the harbor and passengers are ferried to the dock on small tender boats. Tender accessibility varies depending on the ship, but, generally, power wheelchairs cannot be tendered. Check with your cruise line for updated information on tender accessibility. Your best bet is to bring along a manual wheelchair for shore access at tendered ports like Catalina.

Once ashore, getting around Catalina is pretty easy, partly because it's so small, and partly because golf carts are the major mode of transportation on the island. From the Avalon dock it's just a short distance to the center of town. Most people can walk or roll their way along the brick promenade, however it may be a bumpy ride for some folks. The alternative is to roll along the street. Don't worry, as there isn't a lot of car traffic. The good news is, once you get into town, curb cuts are plentiful and the sidewalks are pretty accessible.

Catalina Transportation Services operates the taxi and trolley service on the island. Accessible taxis are available, and the best way to get one is to call and order one or stop by the taxi stand on the corner of Crescent and Metropole Avenues. Some of the trolley cars are wheelchair accessible, but it's best to check with the folks at the taxi stand to find out which routes have accessible vehicles, as they rotate form day to day. In the end, the trolley is your best deal, as a day pass is priced at a very affordable $6.

Many people come to Catalina for the scenery, and, in that respect, Wrigley Memorial Garden is the best choice for wheelers and slow walkers. It's easy to get to, as it's a stop on both trolley lines. There is barrier-free access to the Visitors Center, but the garden itself is accessed by a series of dirt paths with loose rocks, bumps and gravel here and there. Still, it is doable and the staff promises assistance if you call in advance. It's not your typical lush garden but is very interesting, as it focuses on plants that grow naturally on Catalina.

The Wrigley Memorial, which is located right above the garden, is not wheelchair accessible, as there are about 50 steps leading up to it. Since there's no alternative barrier-free access route, you'll have to enjoy it from below. Still, the garden is well worth the visit.

Another way to enjoy the scenery is to take an island tour. Unfortunately, none of the bus tours are wheelchair accessible, so a private tour with Catalina Transportation Service is your most accessible guided tour option. Alternatively, you can rent a golf cart at several places in town, so, if you can transfer to a seat, consider taking a self-drive golf-cart tour along scenic Skyline Drive.

And although you can easily see Catalina in a day, the best way to really experience it is to spend the night. The recently remodeled Pavilion Lodge, which is located in the heart of Avalon, is a top accessible lodging choice. It's located just steps from the ocean, and it has accessible rooms with roll-in showers — a hard commodity to find on the island. It's a little pricey, but it's worth the splurge, as Catalina takes on a different character after the day trippers depart on the last ferry. It's a beautiful place to enjoy the sunset with someone you love.

- IF YOU GO
  - Catalina Express, (800) 481-3470, www.catalinaexpress.com
  - Catalina Transportation Service, (310) 510-0025, www.catalinatransportationservices.com
  - Wrigley Botanical Garden, (310) 510-2288, Pavilion Lodge, (800) 626-1496
  - Catalina Island Chamber of Commerce & Visitors Bureau, (310) 510-1520, www.catalinachamber.com

CRUSH TIME IN CALAVERAS COUNTY

. . . .

Although there's no shortage of wineries in California, some are just more accessible than others. So where can you go to enjoy a little wine tasting if you use a wheelchair, a walker or a cane? Head for the hills, the foothills that is — Calaveras County to be exact. And fall is the perfect time for a Calaveras County wine-tasting weekend.

Located 133 miles east of San Francisco in the heart of California Gold Country, Calaveras County is perhaps best known as the home of Mark Twain's famous "jumping frog." But the county has evolved over the years, and today it's also a great off-the-beaten-path wine-tasting destination. Truth be told, not only is Calaveras County a more relaxed pick than Napa and Sonoma counties, but it's also the more affordable choice.

With nearly 20 wineries throughout the county, there's certainly no shortage of tasting opportunities; however, if you'd like to sample selections from a number of wineries in one location, then check out some of the accessible tasting rooms in downtown Murphys.

Domaine Becquet and Newsome Harlow are located on Main Street, just a few doors down from one another. Both tasting rooms offer level access through a courtyard entrance, and, although Domaine Becquet has a small one-inch threshold at the door, it's still doable for most folks. Domaine Becquet is the place to go for port, whereas Newsome Harlow produces an excellent Meritage.

The massive Twisted Oak complex — complete with a tasting room, a gorgeous garden and an ample supply of picnic tables — is located just across the street. It's a nice place to linger and enjoy a picnic lunch or a glass of wine. Accessible parking (which is in short supply in Murphys) is available near the back (Church Street) entrance, and there is level access to the tasting room and barrier-free access throughout the grounds. Twisted Oak specializes in hand-crafted wines from varietals native to the Rhone Valley.

And don't miss Malvadino Vineyards, located on Algiers Street, just a half block off Main Street. Your best bet is to park in the accessible space next to Murphys Park, as it's the closest accessible parking. The tasting room has

Wine tasting at Domaine Becquet in Murphys.

a level entry and barrier-free access. This winery features wines made from zinfandel, syrah, chardonnay and nebbiolo grapes.

It should be noted that some of the tasting rooms are closed on Mondays and Tuesdays, so check with the winery or the Calaveras Winegrape Alliance before making travel plans.

As noted earlier, parking in Murphys is somewhat limited and street parking is the norm. Accessible parking is available in the public lot on Church Street and in the lot behind the Victoria Inn. There is also an accessible street space on Main Street in front of the Native Sons of the Golden West building. Accessible public restrooms are located in Murphys Park. And although sidewalks are not standard issue throughout town, most of the pavement is level and wheelable in dry weather. Additionally, some businesses have a step or two at the entrance, but many others have level access.

And for a place to spend the night, check out the Victoria Inn, located just steps from Main Street. This 12-room inn features a ramped entry, barrier-free access to the public areas and a first-floor accessible guestroom (Mae's Room). This spacious room has wide doorways, lever handles, lowered controls and a lowered closet rod. Access features in the bathroom include a roll-in shower with a hand-held showerhead and a fold-down shower seat, grab bars in the shower and around the toilet, and a full five-foot turning radius. It's all very nicely done.

Save some time to explore the surrounding countryside, as Sheep Ranch Road (located just off Main Street) makes for a very scenic fall drive. And for that total wine-tasting experience, visit a few of the tasting rooms outside of town. Two of my favorites, for both access and ambiance, are Ironstone Vineyards and Irish Vineyards.

With more than 5,000 acres devoted to winemaking grapes, Ironstone Vineyards is billed as both a winery and an entertainment complex. It includes a tasting room, a lakeside park, the Heritage Museum and an amphitheater. Access is good in most areas of the winery, with plenty of accessible parking, elevator access to all floors and level access to the Heritage Museum, tasting room and gardens.

Free tours of the facility (including the wine-aging caverns) are offered three times a day, and most of the areas on the tour feature level access. Although this walking tour covers a large area, golf-cart transportation is available for slow walkers. Highlights of the complex include the 44-pound gold nugget in the Heritage Museum, the 1,200-pipe organ in the Alhambra Music Room and the spectacular seasonal flower gardens.

Although Irish Vineyards pales in size compared with Ironstone, it offers visitors a refreshingly intimate tasting experience. Located just outside of Murphys in Vallecito, this family-owned operation features accessible parking, level access to the tasting room, a lowered wine bar for wheelchair users and an accessible restroom. Of course the real bonus of visiting a small vineyard is the opportunity to chat with the winemaker. And Russell Irish won't disappoint you in that respect, as he's rarely at a loss for words as he pours his award-winning wines.

Russell is happy to chat about winemaking techniques or even regale visitors with the tale of how this former Turlock hatchery employee pulled up stakes and moved to the foothills to pursue his lifelong dream of opening a winery. Alternatively, you can sit outside and enjoy a bottle of wine on the patio or nosh on a picnic lunch under the trees. The nicely landscaped grounds include picnic tables and wheelchair access to most areas.

And for a quick overview of all the Calaveras County wineries, don't miss the Calaveras Grape Stomp and Gold Rush Street Faire. Held on the first Saturday of October in Murphys, this annual event is sponsored by the Calaveras Winegrape Alliance. It includes a grape-stomp competition (Lucy and Ethel style), musical entertainment, a silent auction, a BBQ and wine tasting from all the Calaveras County wineries. It's great fun and the perfect way to celebrate the fall crush.

- IF YOU GO
  - Calaveras County Visitors Bureau, (209) 736-0049, www.gocalaveras.com
  - Calaveras Winegrape Alliance, (209) 736-6722, www.CalaverasWines.org
  - Victoria Inn, (209) 728-8933, www.victoriainn-murphys.com
  - Ironstone Vineyards, (209) 728-1251, www.ironstonevineyards.com
  - Irish Vineyards, (209) 736-1299, www.irishvineyard.com

COON DOGS, CORNBREAD AND COUNTRY MUSIC

Billed as being within a day's drive from any place in the mid-South, northwest Alabama is filled with surprises. Take the Key Underwood Coon Dog Memorial Graveyard, for example. Not your average tourist attraction by any stretch of the imagination, it got its start when Key Underwood's faithful coon dog, Troop, went to coon dog heaven.

Now Troop wasn't just your average coon dog; in fact, he was known throughout northwest Alabama as one of the best. Troop had what they call a cold nose, which means that he could follow even cold coon tracks. And that's a very good thing if you are a coon hunter. Those who remember Troop claim that he never left the trail until he treed the coon.

And when his coon-dog hunting days were over, Troop was laid to rest at his favorite hunting camp on September 4, 1937. Today, more then 185 coon dogs are buried at what's now known as the Key Underwood Coon Dog Memorial Graveyard. Truth be told, it's just one of the many

W.C. Handy's childhood home.

off-the beaten-path gems you'll stumble across in northwest Alabama. But, just so you stumble in the right direction, let me also add that it's located about 30 miles from Tuscumbia, on Alabama Highway 247, just 12 miles south of US Highway 72. Watch for the signs.

And, the coon dog graveyard is well worth the drive. There is a small gravel parking area, and although there are no formal paths through the graveyard, the terrain is fairly level, and in dry weather it's doable for most wheelers. You'll see a little bit of everything at the graveyard, from marble monuments and wooden headstones to dog collars and even a plastic raccoon grave marker. There is also a picnic shelter with a grill, so it's the ideal place for a secluded lunch stop.

Now don't get me wrong, just because northwest Alabama boasts a bevy of off-the-beaten-path gems, doesn't mean it lacks luxury properties. Nothing could be further from the truth; in fact, the new four-star Marriott Shoals Hotel & Spa boasts the best of all worlds, as it's affordable, accessible and very luxurious.

Located in Florence on the banks of the Tennessee River, this 200-room property features six accessible rooms, including two with roll-in showers. The accessible rooms all have wide doorways, lowered closet rods, spacious sleeping areas and a full five-foot turning radius in the oversized bathrooms. Each accessible bathroom includes grab bars by the toilet and in the shower, a roll-under sink, a hand-held showerhead and either a tub/shower combination or a roll-in shower with a fold-down shower seat.

All rooms have a private balcony with a great view of the pool area and the Tennessee River. There is barrier-free pathway access to all of the public areas, including the restaurant, outdoor pool area and the cocktail lounge. As an added bonus, the pool features a sloped entry for easy access.

A lot of famous folks hail from northwest Alabama, including W.C. Handy, otherwise known as the Father of the Blues. Born in a log cabin on the banks of the Tennessee River, Mr. Handy went on to write many blues classics, such as *Memphis Blues* and *Saint Louis Blues*, before he founded his own music-publishing company in New York City. He died in 1958, but his spirit lives on in his hometown, at the W.C. Handy Home, Museum and Library in Florence.

Opened on June 1, 2004, the museum features a collection of personal papers, photographs and artifacts that chronicle W.C. Handy's life. Also included in the collection are several pages of hand-written sheet music, his trumpet and his piano. As an added treat, visitors who have the inclination (and presumably the musical talent) are invited to play the piano.

There is level access to the museum, a free wheelchair available for loan at the front desk and good pathway access throughout the property, including the two-room log cabin where W.C. Handy grew up. The cabin was disassembled, moved to its present location log by log and then reassembled. It's now furnished as it would have been at the time of Mr. Handy's birth in 1873.

And if you're in the area during the last week of July, don't miss the annual W.C. Handy Music Festival. The week-long musical celebration kicks off with a New Orleans-style parade and features more than 200 musical events at venues throughout the county. And the best news is, many of the events are free.

A good number of other talented musicians also have Alabama roots, and the Alabama Music Hall of Fame celebrates that local connection. Located in Tuscumbia, this combination museum and gallery honors music achievers who have some connection to Alabama. Some honorees, such as

Hank Williams and Sam Phillips, are natives, whereas others have lived in Alabama or had some other connection to the state.

There is level access to the building, with good pathway access to most of the exhibits. The one exception is the Alabama tour bus, which has several steps at the entrance. Throughout the museum, you'll find guitars, clothing, records, cars, personal items, photographs and other memorabilia from some of the biggest names in the music industry. All styles of music are represented, as are all music-related professions. It's a fun attraction, and it truly has something for everyone, including a studio where you can record your own song. Who knows, you could be the next Elvis.

- **IF YOU GO**
  - Key Underwood Coon Dog, Memorial Graveyard, www.coondogcemetery.com
  - Marriott Shoals Hotel & Spa, (256) 246-3600, www.marriottshoals.com
  - W.C Handy Home, Museum and Library, (256) 760-6434
  - Alabama Music Hall of Fame, (256) 381-4417, www.alamhof.org
  - Colbert County Tourism & Convention Bureau, (256) 383-0783, www.colbertcountytourism.org
  - Florence Tourism, (256) 740-4141, www.flo-tour.org

POLK COUNTY MEMORIES

Billed as "the best of Florida, not far from the rest of Florida," Polk County lies smack in the center of the state, about halfway between the tourist meccas of Orlando and Tampa. As you can imagine, the neighboring theme parks draw the bulk of the tourist throngs, but that's actually good news for visitors to Polk County. People come to Polk County to slow down, relax and get away from the hustle and bustle of life. In short, if you want to bypass the crowds, avoid the lines, enjoy off-the-beaten-path sights, save money on lodging and just meander through your holiday, then Polk County is for you.

For a historic look at the area, make the Polk County Historical Museum in Bartow your first stop. Housed in the former courthouse at

Vintage aircraft at Fantasy of Flight in Polk City.

100 E. Main Street, this small-town museum offers something for everybody. It features interpretive exhibits about the early Indian inhabitants, pioneers, political history and early town life.

There is a great collection of arrowheads downstairs, along with a general store and a children's discovery room. Upstairs you'll find the rotating exhibits, including the very popular community Christmas trees during the holiday months.

There is ramped access to the museum through the Genealogical Library and wheelchairs are available for loan at the front desk. Volunteer docents are usually on hand to answer questions about the history of the area. The museum is closed on Sunday and Monday and there is no admission charge.

And although the county is pretty small, it still boasts a top-notch aviation museum — Fantasy of Flight — located in Polk City. The brainchild of Kermit Weeks, this unique museum features interpretive exhibits that illustrate the history of flight, a large collection of vintage aircraft and real-time flight simulators. The exhibits chronicle the history of flight through film clips and interpretive displays from the Wright brothers adventures at Kitty Hawk to the WWII B-17 Flying Fortress.

Access features at Fantasy of Flight include accessible parking and restrooms, a level entry and ramped access to most exhibit areas. Although the inside of the B-17 bomber is not accessible, wheelchair users can roll around the aircraft and get a close-up look at this beauty. Access to the B-17 is by a narrow stairway, and there are steps inside the plane and it has a very narrow cockpit door.

The highlight of Fantasy of Flight is the vintage aircraft collection, which includes more than 40 aircraft from the 1900s to the 1950s. The collection is displayed in a large hangar with cement floors and level access. There is a viewing platform above the hangar, but it is only accessible by stairs. Still, you can get a great view from ground level.

Last but not least, don't miss the flight simulators. One simulator is wheelchair accessible. You can roll right into the modified Corsair cockpit and participate in a mock battle over the Pacific Ocean. It's great fun, and a must for aviation buffs.

Certainly there's no lack of greenery in Polk County, so save time to visit some of the lovely area gardens. One of better-known choices, Bok Tower Gardens, is located in Lake Wales. This 200-acre garden site features an Olmstead-designed woodland garden, a centerpiece bell tower with a carillon and numerous nature trails.

Although Bok Tower Gardens is very scenic, the path to the carillon has a steady incline and it's really better suited for power wheelchair users and strong manual wheelchair users. Adult strollers (which look more like heavy-duty manual wheelchairs) are available for free loan at the entrance. Alternatively, you can rent a heavy-duty scooter at the gift shop. They are available on a first-come basis.

Another nice garden to visit is Hollis Gardens in Lakeland. This 1.2-acre formal garden is located within Lake Mirror Park and features more than 10,000 flowers and ornamental shrubs. Hollis Garden chronicles Florida's history, from the wild beginnings of the state's agrarian period to the modern era in which horticulture is driven primarily by aesthetics.

There are six steps at the front entry; however there is level access from the promenade on the shores of Lake Mirror. Accessible parking is at the far end of the lot, near the Parks and Recreation building. There is good pathway access throughout the park and an accessible route to every plot. It's the undiscovered gem of Polk County and a great place to spend a quiet afternoon. And best of all, there's no admission charge.

• IF YOU GO

  • Polk County Historical Museum, (863) 534-4386
  • Fantasy of Flight, (863) 984-3500, www.fantasyofflight.com
  • Bok Tower Gardens, (863) 676-1408, www.boktowergardens.org
  • Hollis Gardens, (863) 834-6035
  • Central Florida Visitors and Convention Bureau, (863) 420-2586, www.sunsational.org

THE OTHER NEW MEXICO

Located just 20 miles from the Mexico border, Las Cruces is a bit off the main tourist track. And in my book, that's a very good thing. Truth be told, there's much more to Las Cruces than meets the eye; in fact, if you just drive through it, it's pretty unremarkable. But if you take some time to explore, you'll soon discover what this often-overlooked New Mexico city has to offer. Good access, friendly people, cultural diversity and very affordable prices abound in Las Cruces. And that's just the tip of the iceberg.

The best place to begin exploring Las Cruces is at the Branigan Cultural Center, located in the downtown mall on Water Street. Don't be fooled by the mall moniker though, as this shopping area is one of those good old-fashioned, single-story, outdoor malls.

The Branigan Cultural Center is located near the middle of the mall, with accessible parking available in the lot off Water Street. If you miss it the first time, just make the loop and catch it on your second trip; it only takes a few minutes. Housed in a Depression-era building that was once the home of the City Library, the Branigan Cultural Center serves a dual purpose, as it features permanent exhibits that provide insight into the past plus rotating exhibits that showcase local artists.

There is level access to the main entrance through a shaded courtyard and barrier-free access to all of the galleries. Several spacious galleries house historic objects, old photographs and artwork, with the largest gallery doubling as a performance hall for cultural events.

The Branigan Cultural Center.

While you're on the mall, don't miss the Museum of Art, located next door to the Branigan Cultural Center. This museum features level access to two galleries, which display contemporary work from local artists. And if you're in the market for a unique (and affordable) hand-crafted gift, be sure and stop in the gift shop.

And believe it or not, both of these cultural attractions are free.

If you are looking for real deals on locally crafted merchandise, then don't miss the twice weekly Farmers & Crafts Market in the downtown mall. Held on Wednesday and Saturday mornings from 8 AM until noon, this small-town market has something for just about everybody. The best plan of action is to hit the market in the morning and then spend the afternoon in the mall museums.

You'll find good deals on silver and turquoise jewelry at the market. The craftsmanship is excellent and the prices are a fraction of what you'll pay up in Santa Fe. Entertainment and food are also abundant, and there is level access to all of the stalls.

Two historic attractions near the downtown mall are also worth a visit. The Bicentennial Log Cabin is just across the street, and, to be honest, you really can't miss it. As the only log cabin in downtown Las Cruces, it definitely stands out. Built in the late 1800s, the cabin was originally located in the mountains northwest of Las Cruces. It was subsequently disassembled and relocated to Las Cruces to commemorate the Bicentennial.

During the annual Heritage Days festival in October, the Bicentennial Log Cabin serves as the backdrop for a variety of living-history demonstrations, from soap and candle making, to butter churning, quilting and paper making. During the rest of the year, visitors can tour the log cabin by appointment. There is no charge to tour the cabin, and a ramp has been added for wheelchair access. It's very accessible; in fact, one of the docents is a wheelchair user. Parking is very limited near the cabin, so it's best to use the accessible parking across the street in the downtown mall.

The New Mexico Railroad and Transportation Museum is located several blocks from the mall, on the corner of Mesilla Street and Las Cruces Avenue. Unless you are in a particularly energetic mood, it's best to drive over, as there is plenty of accessible parking at the museum.

Located in the old Santa Fe Depot, this newly remodeled museum features a number of exhibits that focus on the history of train travel in the area, including old train memorabilia, photographs, logs and a model freight train. There is level access to the depot and the exhibits and there's no admission charge. Plan ahead though, as this museum is staffed by volunteers and it has limited days and hours of operation.

Another must-see museum in Las Cruces is the New Mexico Farm & Ranch Heritage Museum. Access features at this 47-acre interactive museum include plenty of accessible parking, level access to the entrance, accessible restrooms and barrier-free access to all of the inside galleries. Loaner wheelchairs are also available at the front desk.

The galleries house a variety of exhibits, including Tools and Traditions, which presents an overview of local farming history and features old machinery, photographs and farm tools. Other exhibits include Generations, which uses the biographies of 33 people to tell the agricultural history of New Mexico, and Legends in Leather, which details the history and process of saddle making. And don't miss the kids' area (Adventure Corral), which includes a number of fun hands-on educational activities. Plan to spend the whole day at the museum, as there's really a lot to see at this excellent attraction.

- IF YOU GO
  - Branigan Cultural Center, (505) 541-2155
  - Museum of Art, (505) 541-2137
  - Bicentennial Log Cabin, (505) 541-2155

- New Mexico Railroad and Transportation Museum, (505) 647-4480
- New Mexico Farm & Ranch Heritage Museum, (505) 522-4100, www.frhm.org
- Las Cruces Convention & Visitors Bureau, (505) 541-2444, www.lascrucescvb.org

THE QUIET SIDE OF LAKE PONTCHARTRAIN

Thirty-nine miles makes a world of difference. Take St. Tammany Parish for example. It's just 39 miles from New Orleans, yet a world away from the hustle and bustle of the Big Easy's party-time atmosphere. In fact, the quiet north shore of Lake Pontchartrain offers visitors a different kind of wild life, one that requires binoculars and a field identification guide. Access hasn't been overlooked either, as paved trails, boardwalks and a local can-do attitude make St. Tammany an ideal choice for all nature lovers.

The best place to start your north shore adventure is at the St. Tammany Parish Visitors Center in Mandeville. Here you'll find brochures and information on all the area attractions, along with detailed road maps of the parish. Outside you'll find an accessible boardwalk, so take a few minutes to wheel around and enjoy the sights and sounds of the surrounding wetlands.

Mandeville is a good place to access the Tammany Trace, a 31-mile rails-to-trails conversion that runs from Covington to Slidell. Although many parts of the Tammany Trace were severely damaged by Hurricane Katrina, volunteers have repaired the damage, and the trail is once again open for business. This paved pedestrian trail follows the old Illinois Central Railroad corridor over the wetlands and woods of St. Tammany Parish. The Tammany Trace includes more than 30 bridges that traverse wetlands and swamps filled with wildlife. Take your binoculars, as it's a great birding area.

Just east of Mandeville, you'll find another great birding area, the Northlake Nature Center. This wildlife refuge includes 400 acres of ancient pines, hardwood forest, marshes and beaver ponds. Known locally as "St. Tammany's Secret Garden," the Northlake Nature Center is the

Boardwalk at the Northlake Nature Center in St. Tammany Parish.

headquarters for the Great Louisiana BirdFest. This annual event is held during the spring migration when many species travel north from Mexico and South America. A level boardwalk that winds out over the marsh also makes a great accessible alternative to a swamp tour. Just wheel out, watch and listen.

For a different kind of wildlife experience, head up to the Global Wildlife Center in Folsom. Technically, the Global Wildlife Center is a wild animal park; however, the animals are far from "wild." In fact, Global Wildlife encourages visitors to "get eye to eye with the wildlife." And believe me, it's a very intimate experience!

Guided tours of the compound are conducted in covered wagons pulled by tractors. The wagons are ramped for easy wheelchair access. Visitors are encouraged to feed the animals, and the animals recognize the wagons as their meal ticket. Camels, giraffes, bison, water buffalo and scores of other animals descend on the wagons as visitors feed, photograph and pet them. It's really a great experience! Don't forget to take plenty of film, as it's a prime photo opportunity.

And of course, you just can't leave St. Tammany without taking a swamp tour. To be honest, swamp tours by their very nature aren't really accessible; however Dr. Paul Wagner can accommodate some wheelchair users on his

Honey Island Swamp Tour. To take his swamp tour, you must transfer to the boat and leave your wheelchair at the dock. Dr. Wagner and his staff are happy to assist with transfers, and the seats in the boat provide a good level of back support.

The two-hour tour of the cypress swamp gives visitors an excellent opportunity to get an up-close-and-personal look at the native flora and fauna. Dr. Wagner is a wetland ecologist and he offers a good overview of the history, folklore and ecology of the swamp and its inhabitants. His in-depth tour is informative as well as entertaining, and it's a great finale for a St. Tammany visit.

- **IF YOU GO**
  - Tammany Trace, (985) 867-9490, www.tammanytrace.org
  - Northlake Nature Center, (985) 626-1238, www.northlakenature.org
  - Global Wildlife Center, (985) 796-3585, www.globalwildlife.com
  - Honey Island Swamp Tours, (985) 641-1769, www.honeyislandswamp.com
  - St. Tammany Parish Convention & Visitors Bureau, (800) 634-9443, www.neworleansnorthshore.com

UNDISCOVERED OHIO

Located an hour north of Columbus in the middle of Ohio farm country, Bucyrus is more than just a little off the beaten path. Truth be told, you won't find a lot of tourists there, or even a lot of tourist attractions. But don't let that deter you from visiting Bucyrus, as it's the perfect pick for a quiet country getaway. If you like scenic drives, early nights, and small-town charm, then pack the car and head to Bucyrus.

Cooper's Mill, located on the north end of the main drag, is a required stop on any Bucyrus itinerary. This upscale country store started out life as fruit stand but later expanded to include a jam and jelly factory. Today the busy factory supplies the country store with everything from dandelion jelly to onion relish. At first I was a little dismayed to find a step at the front entrance, but a little detective work revealed an unmarked accessible entrance around the back.

Shopping at Cooper's Mill in Bucyrus.

Free tours of the jam and jelly factory (which features level access) are offered Monday through Friday, and the employees just couldn't be nicer. I'm a little embarrassed to admit that we showed up on a Saturday, but when I expressed an interest in seeing the factory, Mary Lou immediately offered us a tour.

After you stock up on some picnic fixings, head on over to Lowe Volk Nature Center to enjoy your feast. Located just outside of Bucyrus, this under-publicized park features some nicely accessible outdoor spaces. Constructed in 2002, the Lowe Volk Nature Center features 17 interpretive exhibits plus an indoor bird-watching station. Access features include plenty of accessible parking, level access to the building and barrier-free access to all areas inside the nature center.

Outside, the 1.5 miles of unpaved, hard-packed dirt hiking trails are sporadically covered with redwood chips. There are some bumps and dips along the trail, but for the most part it's level. An accessible route winds around the pond, through the pine forest to the overlook deck. You can also wheel out on the bridge across Allen Run; however steps on the far side of the bridge end the accessible pathway. It's a nice park in dry weather, but the muddy trails can be tough going after the rain. There are also several picnic tables near the entrance, and it's a pleasant place to enjoy those picnic items you picked up at Cooper's Mill.

Of course you need appropriate lodging for your country getaway, and in that respect the HideAway Country Inn fills the bill nicely. Bordered by cornfields, the inn is surrounded by 400 acres of farm land just outside of Bucyrus. It's a true country inn in every sense of the definition. But don't equate country with spartan. Billed as a luxury inn, the HideAway Inn is also a popular wedding venue and a great choice for romantic weekend retreats. And as innkeeper Debbie Miller points out, "Nature lovers also enjoy our property because of the 22 acres of wooded hiking paths along our northern border."

The accessible Louis XIV Suite is located in HideAway Hall, behind the main building. Accessible parking is available in a paved lot between the main building and HideAway Hall. The Louis XIV Suite has a hallway entrance and a back patio entrance, both of which have wide doorways and level thresholds.

The suite is named for the massive Louis XIV-style canopy bed purchased from the Plaza Hotel in New York City. Debbie is quick to point out that the bed is functional as well as attractive. "This bed is unique, as the height is adjustable," she says. "You can raise or lower it for an easier transfer. Sometimes these kinds of beds are way to high for wheelchair users." The romantic ambiance of the suite is further enhanced by a three-sided glass fireplace and a (nonaccessible) Jacuzzi tub in the bedroom area.

There is good pathway access throughout the accessible suite. The bathroom has a roll-in shower with a fold-down shower seat, a hand-held showerhead, grab bars in the shower and around the toilet and a roll-under sink.

There is ramped access to the main house, where the dining room and meeting room are located. Breakfast is served in the dining room, or (with advance notice) it can be delivered to your room.

Comfort in the middle of a cornfield — that's what the HideAway Country Inn is all about. It's a great place to enjoy the peace and quiet in a relatively undiscovered slice of rural Ohio.

- IF YOU GO
    - Cooper's Mill, (419) 562-4215, www.coopersmill.net
    - Lowe Volk Nature Center, (419) 683-9000, www.crawfordparkdistrict.org/html/naturecenter.html
    - HideAway Country Inn, (419) 562-3013, www.hideawayinn.com
    - Bucyrus Visitors Bureau, (419) 562-0720, www.bucyrus.org

Candy's Picks

A ROCKY MOUNTAIN RAIL TOUR

Many years ago I took Amtrak from San Francisco to Chicago. I could have flown, but I chose to travel by train because I wanted to enjoy the beauty of the Rocky Mountains from the comfort of a club car. Like many of my ideas, it seemed like a good plan at the time. Unfortunately my plan hit a few snags when we were delayed in Sacramento and then again in Reno. In the end, we rolled through the Rockies at midnight — not very scenic at all, and definitely not what I had planned.

Last year I decided to give the Rockies another shot, but this time I chose the Canadian Rockies. Since I was older and (presumably) wiser, this time I searched for a rail trip that would allow me to enjoy the scenery, even in the event of unexpected delays. And of course access was also a top priority. In the end, Rocky Mountaineer rail tours filled the bill in all respects.

At Rocky Mountaineer rail tours, the focus is on the journey rather than the destination. In short, it's more than just a train ride. It's a multiday, all-daylight excursion that includes all on-board meals, ground transportation and lodging. Of course there are a myriad of itinerary choices, but since access was a top priority, I opted for the Vancouver to Calgary Kicking Horse route. Due to the availability of accessible services along this route, Rocky Mountaineer is able to work with local suppliers to create a very accessible travel experience.

My own experience began in Vancouver. After a welcome mimosa and a few toots of the horn, we were rolling along through the Fraser Valley. As I settled into the comfortable GoldLeaf domed rail car, I enjoyed an unobstructed view over the trees and the telegraph lines. Each GoldLeaf rail car seats 70 passengers on the upper level and 35 passengers on the lower dining level.

The physical access in the GoldLeaf cars is pretty good, considering they are bilevel rail cars. There is lift boarding at all stations. Wheelchair users must transfer to an aisle chair and then to their assigned seats for the journey. There is a spiral staircase to the upper level, but a small elevator (which can accommodate the aisle chair) is available for wheelchair users. An accessible bathroom, with a wide doorway and grab bars, is located downstairs.

As soon as we were on our way, we were invited downstairs for an elegant breakfast. The dining room is richly appointed, but the booths are

View from a Rocky Mountaineer Railtours GoldLeaf domed car as it travels along the Fraser River.

somewhat narrow. Unfortunately, this makes for a very difficult (if not impossible) transfer. If all this sounds a bit daunting access wise, don't worry. The Rocky Mountaineer staff will gladly serve your meals upstairs, white linen and all. In fact, eating at your seat is a much better deal, as you don't miss any of the great scenery.

By late afternoon we had passed through Avalanche Alley, then continued on through Hells Gate and over the Jaws of Death Gorge. As we neared Kamloops, we saw osprey nests (and osprey) at eye level on the telegraph poles alongside the tracks. What a sight! We rolled into Kamloops at about 5 PM.

Accessible ground transportation was available at the Kamloops station, and we were given our hotel keys before we even got off the train. Our luggage was transferred to the hotel separately, and it was waiting for us in our room when we arrived. This all made for a very quick and efficient hotel transfer. Accessible rooms with roll-in showers were available to passengers who had requested them in advance.

The next day we traveled through the heart of the Canadian Rockies. Along the way, the on-board attendants educated us on the wildlife and natural history of the area. We passed over Stony Creek Bridge, went through the spiral tunnels, crossed the Continental Divide and arrived in Banff by late afternoon.

After a brief stop in Banff, we traveled on to Calgary, our final destination. Along the way, we were treated to hors d'oeuvres and wine as we enjoyed a spectacular sunset. There was one last wildlife sighting, an elk with his harem beside the river. It was a fitting end to a very memorable trip.

All in all, my Rocky Mountaineer rail tour experience was great. I didn't miss a lick of the spectacular scenery, the access was good and the GoldLeaf service was excellent. It's a great way to see the Canadian Rockies.

- IF YOU GO
  - Rocky Mountaineer Rail Tours, (877) 460-3200, www.rockymountaineer.com

ABSOLUTELY VANCOUVER

Whenever I'm asked to name my favorite accessible vacation destinations, Vancouver consistently tops my list. Not only does this diverse city feature some very accessible attractions and a great public transportation system, but it's also relatively easy on the budget. Factor in some very mild fall temperatures to this winning equation and you can see why Vancouver continues to nab the top slot on my favorites list.

Stanley Park is my traditional first stop whenever I visit Vancouver. This 1,000-acre urban park is lined with hemlock trees and filled with wildlife, yet it's located just minutes from the downtown core. A 5.5-mile seawall provides an accessible promenade around the park; however the best way to get a good overview of the park is to take a carriage ride.

Gerry O'Neil operates AAA Horse & Carriage, and thanks to his ingenuity, wheelchair users can roll right onto his horse-drawn carriages. Says Gerry, "My father used a wheelchair in his later years, so I have an understanding of some of the barriers that must be overcome. For this reason, I designed and built our own carriages to provide real wheelchair accessibility."

AAA Horse and Carriage in Stanley Park.

And he did a great job, as his accessible carriages have ramp access and removable bench seats, so they can accommodate many wheelchair users at the same time. Of course, if you'd prefer to transfer to a bench seat, you can stow your folding wheelchair behind the last row of seats.

These one-hour carriage tours depart every 20 to 30 minutes from the kiosk near the Georgia Street entrance. AAA Horse & Carriage also operates a free lift-equipped shuttle bus from the downtown area. See their website for pickup locations and times.

And if you'd like to explore the park at your own pace, then hop on the free Stanley Park Trolley. Operated by the Vancouver Trolley Company, these lift-equipped shuttles operate from June through late September and stop at 15 popular places throughout the park.

Another must-see in Stanley Park is the top-rated Vancouver Aquarium Marine Science Center. Access at the aquarium is good, with a level entry, accessible parking, accessible bathrooms, elevator access to the upper floors and good pathway access throughout the complex.

Plan on spending the whole day at the aquarium and don't miss the Wild Coast exhibit. This outdoor exhibit features boardwalk access to the habitats of Stellar sea lions, Pacific white-sided dolphins, harbor seals and sea otters. And for an even closer look at these hams, sign up for a Wild Coast trainer tour. These behind-the-scenes tours are wheelchair accessible, although some of the ramps are a bit slick when they're wet. Still, it's doable with a little assistance, and I highly recommend it. Hand-feeding a 250-pound Stellar sea lion was truly the highlight of my day!

Shopping is a favorite pastime in Vancouver for visitors and locals alike. Be sure and check out trendy Robson Street between Hornby and Bute Streets for an eclectic collection of clothing stores, restaurants, gift shops, lingerie shops and hair salons. It's also a great place to window shop or people watch. Access is good throughout the neighborhood, with wide sidewalks, curb cuts and level access to most stores. Additionally, many of the restaurants offer sidewalk dining, which is a pleasant option in the early fall.

For a change of pace, take the Sea Bus (ferry) over to Lonsdale Quay in North Vancouver. The ferry offers roll-on access and it only takes a few minutes to cross the bay. Over at Lonsdale Quay, you'll find a multilevel shopping complex that is home to more than 90 shops and services, including a variety of boutiques, restaurants and even a fresh produce market. There is level access to the complex and elevator access to the upper level. I always manage to find the coolest earrings there, so it's definitely worth a stop.

And getting around Vancouver is a snap, thanks to a plethora of accessible public transportation options. Your best bet for an accessible airport transfer is to go to the Airporter bus booth at the airport. Since this bus service doesn't have any accessible vehicles, they will take you over to the taxi stand and get an accessible taxi for you, and you'll pay the Airporter bus fare for a taxi ride. Depending on the number of passengers, this could be more economical, as taxis charge about $30, whereas the Airporter bus charges $13 per passenger.

On the Lower Mainland, more than 50% of buses are equipped with wheelchair lifts or lowered floors. Each accessible bus can carry two wheelchairs or scooters. Additionally, all Sky Train stations, except Granville, have elevator access; however a free accessible taxi shuttle service is available between the Granville and Burrard stations courtesy of Vancouver Taxi.

If you'd prefer to drive yourself, accessible rental vans are available from the Canadian Paraplegic Association or from Freedom Rentals. And if you drive up to Vancouver, don't forget to pack your parking placard, as it's also valid in Canada.

- IF YOU GO
  - AAA Horse & Carriage, (604) 681-5115, www.stanleyparktours.com
  - Vancouver Aquarium Marine Science Center, (604) 659-3521, www.vanaqua.org
  - TransLink, (604) 953-3333, www.translink.bc.ca
  - Vancouver Taxi, (604) 255-5111
  - Freedom Rentals, (604) 952-4499, www.wheelchairvanrentals.com
  - Greater Vancouver Convention & Visitors Bureau, (604) 682-2222, www.tourismvancouver.com

CAMPUS ATTRACTIONS

Have you visited a college or university lately? Not to take a class or to visit your kids, but as part of your holiday itinerary? Seriously. That's right, I'm sending you to school for your vacation! To be fair, it's something I completely overlooked, too,, until one day when I was strolling across the University of Missouri campus in Columbia. Truth be told, it all started with an ice cream cone.

In my search for Bucks Ice Cream (a MU-operated ice cream parlor that serves the best ice cream in Columbia, if not in the state of Missouri), I happened across two incredible campus museums: the Museum of Anthropology and the Museum of Art & Archeology. Not only did both of these museums have excellent access, but there was not admission charge to either one. Suffice it to say my ice cream quest was delayed.

In retrospect, MU was just the tip of the iceberg, as I subsequently discovered that many colleges have top-drawer cultural attractions, unique summer programs and affordable lodging — all with good access. The key is just knowing where to look.

On my next university visit, I was a little savvier, so I located the campus visitor center on the on-line map and made that my first stop at the University of Arizona in Tucson. Many large campuses have a visitors center for prospective students, parents and the community. I have to say that the folks at the University of Arizona visitors center were very helpful, as they directed me to the Steward Observatory Public Evening Series, which included a very

The Robert Dole Institute of Politics at the University of Kansas.

interesting lecture followed by an opportunity to check out the night sky with a 21-inch telescope. And, as with most university offerings, there was no charge, the access was excellent and it was open to the public.

A lot of campuses offer walking tours — self-guided or hosted. Some are better than others, especially if the majority of campus buildings were designed by a famous architect. Such is the case at Florida Southern College in Lakeland, which features the largest one-site collection of Frank Lloyd Wright architecture in the world.

Start your self-guided walking tour at the Child of the Sun Visitor Center, where you can pick up a free map for the Frank Lloyd Wright Walking Tour. There is good pathway access throughout the campus, with wide sidewalks, curb cuts, accessible parking and ramped or level entrances to the buildings. Don't miss the Annie Pfeiffer Chapel (known affectionately as the bicycle rack in the sky), the William Danforth Chapel (which has some beautiful cypress woodwork), and the 1.5 miles of esplanades that line the west campus.

Another hidden gem, the Museum of Southeastern Photography, is located on the campus of Daytona Beach Community College in northeast Florida. Access is excellent to this museum, as it just moved into a new building in 2007. The museum emphasizes teaching and learning through the medium of photography and hosts a wide variety of exhibitions around unifying themes. Past exhibitions have included the excellent Henry Diltz "Kiss the Sky" exhibition as well "Coal Hollow" by photographer Ken Light. There is no admission charge to the museum, but check the website, as it's closed between exhibitions.

And don't overlook famous graduates when searching for campus attractions. A case in point is the University of Kansas in Lawrence, where Bob Dole spent some of his undergraduate time. Today it's the home to the very accessible Dole Institute, which features exhibits, photographs and video clips from Senator Dole's many years in public service.

As far as campus lodging goes, it's difficult but not impossible to find. The good news is, it's very reasonably priced and usually accessible. For example, a quick inquiry to the Southern Utah University housing office turned up two accessible dorm rooms in Juniper Hall with a shared community bathroom (with roll-in showers) for just $12 per person. If you're traveling with a larger group, the housing office also offers an accessible apartment with six twin beds, two bathrooms (no roll-in showers), a kitchen and a living room for $152 per night. Best of all, the campus is located just 63 miles from Zion National park, in the center of scenic southern Utah.

In addition to providing standard housing, some colleges offer summer programs or vacation packages. For example the University of California at Santa Barbara operates the on-campus Santa Barbara Family Vacation Center during the summer months. This unique program offers lodging, food, a kids' program, access to campus recreation facilities and some off-campus tourism offerings. Accessible lodging options (with roll-in showers) are available, and there is wheelchair access in the dining commons and the on-campus recreational facilities. Although not all of the kids' program activities are wheelchair accessible, the staff is willing to arrange the activities so all children can participate.

So, the next time you are planning a vacation, don't overlook the local college campuses. The campus visitors center and the housing office are both great resources, and often times they can direct you to some very accessible, affordable and unique offerings.

- IF YOU GO

  - University of Missouri Museum of Anthropology, (573) 882-3573,
    anthromuseum.missouri.edu
  - University of Missouri Museum of Art & Archaeology, (573) 882-3591,
    maa.missouri.edu
  - Steward Observatory, (520) 621-2288, www.as.arizona.edu
  - Child of the Sun Visitor Center, (863) 680-4110,
    www.flsouthern.edu/fllwctr
  - Southeast Museum of Photography, (386) 506-4475, www.smponline.org
  - Dole Institute, (785) 864-4900, www.doleinstitute.org
  - Southern Utah University Housing Office, (435) 586-7966,
    www.suu.edu/ss/housing
  - Santa Barbara Family Vacation Center, (805) 893-3123,
    www.familyvacationcenter.com

CANDY AND THE VOLCANO

I get a lot of questions about Hawaii, as it's a very popular destination. Even though it's just a tiny speck on the map, there's a lot to see there, so ultimately some choices have to be made when planning a one-week getaway. Personally, if I had only a week, I'd rather spend it on just one island. But which island? For me that choice is easy. The Big Island is my top pick — more specifically, Hawaii Volcanoes National Park on the Big Island of Hawaii.

Located 30 miles southwest of Hilo, Hawaii Volcanoes National Park is home to Kilauea, one of the world's most active volcanoes. It's a low-key destination, so if you are looking for luxury resorts, spa packages and cabanas on the beach, you won't find them here. But if you enjoy dramatic landscapes, the great outdoors and want to learn about Hawaiian heritage, then Hawaii Volcanoes National Park is the perfect place for you.

Accessible lodging is somewhat limited in the area around the park; however the Volcano Guest House offers several accessible choices. Billed as a "private village nestled on six acres of the native high-altitude rain forest," it's the perfect place to get away from it all. Innkeeper Bonnie Goodell is

The Earthquake Trail at Hawaii Volcanoes National Park.

friendly and welcoming, yet she keeps a low profile. She doesn't hover, but she's available if you need her, which makes for a very pleasant atmosphere. To be honest, we spent a week there and a few days we just hung out at the property. It was that pleasant.

There are three accessible rooms at the Volcano Guest House: Claudia's Place, Twin I and Twin II. Claudia's Place features ramped access from the paved driveway. There are no designated parking spaces, but there is plenty of room to park a van near the base of the ramp. The parking area is only 10 feet from Claudia's Place.

Claudia's Place shares a front porch with the main house and features a queen-sized bed in the bedroom and a twin bed in the living area. There is also a small kitchen in the unit. Access features include wide doorways, wooden floors and good pathway access. The bathroom has a low-step shower with a hand-held showerhead and grab bars in the shower. There are adjustable grab bars (which can be lifted up out of the way for transfers) on both sides of the toilet. A portable shower bench is available upon request.

Twin I and Twin II mirror one another and share a large covered porch. Each unit has a bedroom alcove with a queen-sized bed, a spacious living room with two twin beds, a kitchen area and a large bathroom. The Twins each have a low-step shower, a hand-held showerhead, grab bars in the shower and around the toilet and a portable shower bench. Parking is available directly in front of the Twins, but some people will need assistance navigating through the gravel.

Bonnie may also be able to provide special equipment (such as a hospital bed or a manual wheelchair) with advance notice. "We have a community lending closet here, which sometimes has medical equipment," says Bonnie. "Last week I was able to borrow a manual wheelchair for a guest. It all depends on what is available, but it never hurts to ask."

And best of all, the Volcano Guest House is just five minutes from Hawaii Volcanoes National Park.

Your first stop in the park should be the Kilauea Visitors Center, which includes a number of interpretive exhibits. There is level access to the visitors center and accessible restrooms inside. There is also a ranger on duty who can answer questions, give directions and dole out maps and brochures. Ranger-led walks, some of which are wheelchair accessible, depart from the visitors center, so check with the ranger on duty for the daily schedule.

The Volcano Art Center, located behind the visitors center, is also worth a visit. This gallery features ramp access and includes a variety of artistic treasures. The gallery is operated by a local nonprofit organization, the goal of which is to perpetuate the artistic and cultural heritage of Hawaii's people. It's located at Kilauea because that's the home of Pele, the Hawaiian goddess of the volcano. Pele is believed to have inspired many Hawaiian artists.

Of course the Kilauea crater is the big attraction in the park, and for a great view of it, cross the parking lot and take the level hard-packed dirt rail to the right of the hotel. The trail winds around behind the hotel and opens up to a spectacular overlook of the crater. There are some picnic tables at the overlook, but it tends to get crowded, so resist the temptation to take a lunch break just yet.

There is ramped access to the hotel, which has a buffet and a sandwich shop. These are the only food concessions in the park, but they are very crowded because all of the bus tours stop here for lunch. It's especially bad when cruise ships are in port. For a more secluded lunch break, pack a picnic lunch and head over to the Earthquake Trail, just to the left of the hotel. This wide paved trail was a vehicle road until a November 1983 eruption closed it to traffic. At the end of the trail, you'll find a few picnic tables along with a spectacular view of the crater.

Another way to get a great view of the diverse landscape of the volcano is to drive around Crater Rim Drive. This 11-mile road encircles the caldera and passes through a variety of landscapes. There are several scenic pullouts along the road, so just take your time and do it at your own pace. Be sure and stop at the Jagger Museum for another great view of the caldera. There is level access to the building, which houses a variety of interpretive exhibits, and ramped access to the viewing platform out back.

Save a day to explore the Chain of Craters Road, which descends 3,700 feet and abruptly ends where the 2003 lava flow crossed the road. Most of the overlooks along the way are not accessible due to rough terrain, but the drive is still worthwhile, as it's very scenic. Depending on the volcanic conditions, you may even see some active lava flows from the end of the road. Be sure and take food and water with you, as there are no concessions along this road.

And, finally, a word of warning — even though the Devastation Trail is rated as "accessible," steep grades, undulating terrain and sustained uphill stretches make it unusable for most wheelchair users. On the other hand, the Puu Puai Overlook, which is located next to the Devastation Trail, is accessible; however it's not noted as such in most park literature.

- IF YOU GO
  - Hawaii Volcanoes National Park, (808) 985-6000, www.nps.gov/havo
  - Volcano Guest House, (808) 967-7775, www.volcanoguesthouse.com

FACTORY TOURS

I just love factory tours. Let's face it; it's just fun to see how things are made. Plus they're a nice departure from the standard tourist fare. And the good news is, most factory tours are at least partially accessible, and many are fully accessible. A few may have an area or two with a step, but for the most part they need to be accessible for their employees. Of course you should definitely check on the access before you head off to the factory, but fortunately you have a lot of accessible choices these days.

A good resource for factory tours is *Watch it Made in the USA*, by Karen Axelrod and Bruce Brumberg. This guidebook lists more than 300 factory tours across the US. The tours are grouped by state, so it's easy to

The tasting room at Ben and Jerry's.

find them when you're on the road, and the book contains information on everything from tour costs to what kinds of freebies the tours dole out. The access section specifies if the tour is wheelchair accessible, and, if it's not fully accessible, the guide lists the inaccessible parts. All in all, it's a great resource with solid access information.

So, next time you hit the road, consider a factory tour. Here are a few of my favorites to get your started.

At the top of my list is the Gibson Guitar Factory in Memphis. Located one block off Beale Street, just across the street from the FedEx forum, this factory tour is one of those don't-miss Memphis experiences.

There is level access throughout this factory, where BB King's trademark Lucille guitars are produced. The tour offers an inside look at Gibson's meticulous craftsmanship process and sheds some light on the Memphis music scene. There is a $10 charge for the tour, which is offered throughout the day, except on Sundays. Advance reservations are recommended, as this excellent tour sells out fast.

One of my favorite brewery tours is located in Abita Springs, Louisiana, just across Lake Pontchartrain from New Orleans. Abita Springs is historically known for its healing spring waters, an essential ingredient in the beers crafted by the Abita Brewery.

The Abita Brewery offers tours on Saturday afternoons at 1:00 and 2:30 and on Sundays at 1:00. Of course, as with most brewery tours, the highlight is the tasting room; however this tour starts in the tasting room. The taps are self-serve, there's no limit and visitors are encouraged to grab a full cup before heading out on the tour. No smoking is allowed in the brewery, but apparently you can drink as much as you like. There is level access to the factory, except the bottling room, which has one step. Still you can get a good look at the bottling process without entering the bottling room. And believe it or not, the tours (including all the beer you care to taste) are free. And if you don't care for alcoholic beverages, they make a great root beer too.

Across the lake, you can get a behind-the-scenes look at how Mardi Gras floats are made at Blaine Kern's Mardi Gras World. Just take the free Canal Street ferry over to Algiers Point and then walk along the paved riverfront path until you see the brightly painted factory. You can't miss it. The ferry features roll-on access and it only takes about 10 minutes to cross the river.

Mardi Gras World provides free van transportation from the Algiers Point pier for folks who can't manage the half-mile walk. If you can transfer to a seat, they will carry your folding wheelchair, but they can't accommodate power wheelchairs. The tour starts out with a movie about Mardi Gras, a slice of king cake and the opportunity to dress up in some Mardi Gras costumes. After that, visitors take a self-guided walking tour through the float-storage area and the adjacent workshops. There is level or ramped access to all areas, and you can do the tour at your own pace. Tours operate on weekdays and are priced at $17. It's a fun way to see how the Mardi Gras magic is created.

And finally, I've saved the best for last. If you're ever in Vermont, you just have to stop by Waterbury and take the Ben & Jerry's factory tour. There is accessible parking in the lower lot and level access to the lobby, where the tours start. The entire tour is wheelchair accessible, with level access to all areas. A wheelchair is available for loan at the tour desk. The tour gives folks a look at the history of Ben & Jerry's and shows how the ice cream is made. And of course, there are free samples at the end of the tour.

Be sure and go during the week, as that's when they make the ice cream. If you go on the weekend, you just get to see a video of the process. The tour is priced at $3, but look for the free discount coupon books around town, as they have a ticket for free admission. The books can be found in many area lodgings. And pack a picnic lunch before you leave, or pick up a sandwich en route, as there's a nice picnic area at the factory. It's just a fun and very scenic way to spend the afternoon.

- **IF YOU GO**
  - Gibson Guitar Factory, (901) 544-7998 ex 4017, www.gibson.com
  - Abita Brewing Company, (800) 737-2311 ext. 2, www.abita.com
  - Blaine Kern's Mardi Gras World, (504) 361-7821, www.mardigrasworld.com
  - Ben & Jerry's, (866) 258-6877, www.benjerry.com

HI HO, HI HO, A CAVING WE WILL GO

. . . .

Let's face it, caves by their very design just aren't accessible. So does that mean wheelers and slow walkers should give up on the idea of ever seeing a stalactite or a stalagmite? Hardly. The good news is, a few popular caverns have made their sites accessible. Granted, you can't just drive up to any old cave and expect to roll right into it; however you can explore a few of these accessible caverns.

Known as the granddaddy of caves, Carlsbad Caverns has been a popular national park since the 1930s. Of course in the early days, wheelchair access was nonexistent and visitors had to enter the cave in guano-mining buckets. Today things are a lot different, and although the natural entrance is too steep for wheelers or slow walkers, anybody who can't make the descent can ride down to the Big Room in the elevator. A large section of the self-guided tour in the Big Room is wheelchair accessible. There are a few narrow spots along the way, but the accessible route is well marked, All in all, it's pretty easy to navigate around the spectacular rock formations in this massive cavern.

And if you visit in the summer months, don't miss the daily exodus of bats from the natural entrance. August and September are prime month for the bat flights, as the colony is at its peak just prior to the October migration. A park ranger presents a bat-flight talk before each flight, but the starting time varies depending on the sunset. Check with the park for the daily starting time.

Located just 12 miles south of Benson, Arizona, Kartchner Caverns is also worth a visit. Discovered in 1974, this massive limestone cave consists of two rooms as long as football fields. Remarkably, it's still in pristine condition. And, even better, it's billed as being barrier free.

There is level access to the Discovery Center, which houses interpretive exhibits about the cave. The Rotunda-Throne Room features wide cement pathways, and although it's billed as being barrier free, in this case, that means step free. There are a few steep patches of cement where some wheelers may require assistance. Still, for a cave, it's pretty good. The tour is a half-mile long and it's the only way to see the cavern. No walkers or wheelchairs over 30 inches wide are permitted on the tour.

Missouri, which is known as the cave state, has two accessible choices: Meramec Caverns and Fantastic Caverns. Meramec Caverns, which is located just outside St. Louis in Stanton, is believed to have been used as a hideout by outlaw Jesse James. As legend has it, a posse tracked James and his cohorts to the cavern entrance, only to find the gang's abandoned horses. They searched the caverns to no avail, as the gang had already escaped through an underground river passage. Years later, in 1933, the caverns were opened to the public by well-known caveologist, Lester B. Dill. Today, Meramec Caverns is billed as the "greatest show under the earth."

As far as caves go, Meramec Caverns offers fairly good access. There are paved walkways throughout the caverns, with plenty of room for wheelchairs to maneuver. The lower level of the caverns is fairly level; however, because of the very steep grade, most wheelers will have a tough time getting to the upper level. Additionally, once you make it to the upper level, there are 52 steps up to the natural theater.

Still, the lower cavern offers some spectacular formations, crystal clear streams and Mirror River, an 18-inch deep pool that reflects a great hollow overhead dome. Abbreviated tours are available for wheelchair users who can't access the upper level.

Fantastic Caverns, which is located just north of Springfield, has addressed the access problem in a very unique way. Visitors are transported through this ride-through cave on a jeep-drawn tram. There is ramp access to the tram and wheelers can stay in their own wheelchair for the duration of the 55-minute narrated tour.

The tram follows an ancient riverbed and gives visitors a great look at some of the magnificent stalactite and stalagmite formations in the cave. The gift shop and visitors center are also nicely accessible with tile floors, level entries, accessible bathrooms and plenty of room to maneuver. Clearly, this is the most accessible cave I've ever seen.

• •

Stalactites and stalagmites in Carlsbad Caverns.

- IF YOU GO
  - Carlsbad Caverns, (505) 785-2232 – visitor information,
    (505) 785-3012 – bat flight information, www.nps.gov/cave
  - Kartchner Caverns, (520) 586-2283,
    www.pr.state.az.us/Parks/parkhtml/kartchner.html
  - Meramec Caverns, (800) 676-6105, www.americascave.com
  - Fantastic Caverns, (417) 833-2010, www.fantasticcaverns.com

NEW ZEALAND'S NORTHLAND

New Zealand is the often-forgotten (and sometimes neglected) stepchild of the South Pacific. Many tourists flock to Australia, however the masses seem to completely overlook New Zealand. Some visitors do manage a cursory Kiwi side trip, but most don't realize that New Zealand is a destination in itself. In fact, you can spend weeks exploring just the North Island. That's exactly what I did, and, if you're looking for great scenery, budget accommodations and good accessibility, then I encourage you to do the same.

New Zealand is a driving destination, and, as far as transportation goes, you have two accessible choices on the North Island. Galaxy Motors rents adapted vans and cars equipped with hand controls, whereas Mobility Motorhomes rents accessible motorhomes. Both companies serve the Auckland Airport, and they each offer their customers very personalized service.

My North Island adventure started in Pahia, which is located about three hours northeast of Auckland. Now granted, you might want to overnight in Auckland after your long flight, but I was anxious to start exploring, so I hit the road as soon as I cleared customs.

Pahia offers a wide variety of accommodations, restaurants and shops, plus it's also the home port for cruises and sporting excursions around the Bay of Islands. One of the most popular cruise excursions is Fuller's Hole in the Rock Cruise, which journeys out past Cape Brett and then through the Hole in the Rock. There is level access to the Pahia wharf and roll-on access to the Fuller's boat. The crew is happy to assist with boarding, and the twin-hulled

The Treaty House on the Waitangi Treaty Grounds.

catamaran is very stable with ample room to maneuver a wheelchair. It's a fun experience and a must-do on any Bay of Islands itinerary.

Just up the road from Pahia, you'll find the Waitangi Treaty Grounds, New Zealand's most historic site. The British signed the Treaty of Waitangi with the native Maori people here in 1840. In addition to the Treaty House, which was formerly the former governor's residence, you will also find a pair of Maori war canoes and a Maori meeting house at this site. Additionally there are miles of beautiful gardens and a scenic coast to explore. You can wander through the site on your own or opt for a guided tour. The site is very accessible, with lots of hard-packed dirt paths, accessible boardwalks, and a well-marked accessible trail down to the canoes and meeting house. It's a great place to get a real feel for the culture of New Zealand.

The east coast of the Northland presents an entirely different perspective of New Zealand. This coast is called the Kuari Coast, and it's a forest coast rather than a beach coast. Beautiful Hokianga Harbour is surrounded by small settlements, including the town of Omapere, which is an excellent place to stay for a few days.

Located in the hills above Omapere, Globetrekkers Lodge offers accessible accommodations, great views, and the opportunity to mingle with other travelers — all at very affordable prices. Technically this property is classified as a "backpackers," which in New Zealand is something akin to hostel. Access is pretty good throughout the property, including the shared kitchen, common area and back patio. Family and dorm rooms are available, and the shared bathroom includes a nicely accessible roll-in shower. And since it's on high ground, guests have a fabulous view of beautiful Hokianga Harbour.

Omapere is just north of the Waipoua Forest, one of the last remaining stands of old-growth Kauri trees. It's a beautiful drive and there are accessible pathways to several of the larger Kauri trees. Be sure and stop at Te Matua Ngahere, the largest tree in the forest. There is an accessible boardwalk leading to this massive tree, and it's also close to the Four Sisters, a collection of four tall trees, and the Phantom Tree, which is believed to be the second largest tree in the forest.

The Kauri Museum in Whangarei is also worth a visit. There is good access throughout most of this unique attraction, which tells the story of the early Kauri loggers who settled in the area in 1862. The museum includes interpretive exhibits, photographs, old logging equipment and even some samples of Kauri wood. There's also a great gift shop on the premises, which features items made from Kauri trees.

Last but not least, don't miss the Kiwi House and native bird park in Otorohanga. There is wheelchair access to the Kiwi House, where you can get a look at the nocturnal kiwis. Outside there are paved level pathways throughout the park, which includes a variety of different habitats that house native birds. The park also carries out successful kiwi, waterfowl, tuatara and native reptile breeding programs. Billed as "New Zealand's original walk-through aviary," it's a must-see for bird and animal lovers. After all, you can't leave New Zealand without seeing at least one kiwi.

- IF YOU GO
  - Galaxy Motors, +64 274 954 590, www.galaxyautos.co.nz
  - Mobility Motorhomes, +64 9 827 2265, www.mobilitymotorhomes.co.nz
  - Fuller's Cruises, +64 9 402 7421, www.fboi.co.nz
  - Waitangi Treaty Grounds, +64 9 402 7437, www.waitangi.net.nz
  - Globetrekkers Lodge, +64 9 405 8183
  - The Kauri Museum, +64 9 431 7417, www.kauri-museum.com
  - Kiwihouse and Native Bird Park, +64 7 873 7391, www.kiwihouse.org.nz

THE TEXAS TROPICS

A s an avid birder and the chair of the 2005 Texas Tropics Nature Festival, Ron Smith is quick to sing the praises of the McAllen area. In fact, I had a hard time keeping up with him as he rattled off accessible birding sites, boardwalks, trails, blinds, and even a hawk-viewing tower in the area. Indeed, Ron is a true expert on local access, as he's been rolling along South Texas birding trails for many years.

But the Rio Grande Valley wasn't always as accessible as it is today. Enter the World Birding Center (WBC), a network of nine birding sites dotted along 120 miles of south Texas river road. As the sites were developed, accessible trails, viewing platforms, blinds, boardwalks, and interpretive centers were added. Today, as a result of this development, the Rio Grande Valley is an excellent vacation destination for wheelchair users and slow walkers who enjoy nature, wildlife and the great outdoors.

Because of its central location, McAllen makes an ideal home base for a south Texas birding tour. As the largest city in the area, it has the biggest airport and a wide variety of lodging options, plus it's just a short drive away from all of the WBC sites. McAllen is also home to Quinta Mazatlan, probably the most urban WBC site. The centerpiece of this veritable oasis is a 10,000 square foot hacienda, which has been lovingly restored to its former grandeur.

Built in 1935, the mansion features adobe walls, beamed ceilings and tile murals. Wide doorways and good pathway access made the building a good candidate for access retrofits, so, during the renovation, ramp access was added to the front entrance. The mansion is now used as a conference center, but the real charm of this WBC site lies in the 15 acres surrounding the estate. Level pathways lead around the property, where Black-bellied Whistling Ducks and Plain Chachalacas are frequent visitors and food and water stations work to attract more than 100 bird species.

The official headquarters for the WBC is located just seven miles northwest of McAllen at Bensten State Park. Private vehicles are not allowed in the park; however a wheelchair-accessible tram makes a loop through the park every half hour. The tram features ramp access in the back, and although there are no tie-downs, it can accommodate a large number of wheelchair users.

Ramped, 230-foot Hawk Observation Tower at Bensten State Park.

Highlights of the park include the Green Jay Blind (where you'll find javelinas at dusk) and the Hawk Observation Tower. The Green Jay Blind features ramp access with wheelchair-height viewing slots, whereas the 210-foot high Hawk Observation Tower has ramped access to the top, level areas every 30 feet and unobstructed wheelchair-height sight lines. They're both very nicely done.

For a look at a different type of habitat, head on over to Edinburg Scenic Wetlands, the first WBC to open its doors. The accessible interpretive center features floor-to-ceiling windows with wheelchair-height scopes aimed at the adjacent wetlands. Outside there are level crushed-gravel trails to the boardwalk overlook and Dragon Pond, both of which are only a short distance away. From the boardwalk overlook, you can spot a variety of ducks out on the lake and probably a few snakes and turtles too.

The 2.5 miles of trails around the complex are doable for most wheelchair users in dry weather, however they can be problematic after a rain. If you'd like to tour the whole complex, but don't think you can manage the distance, call ahead and make arrangements for a golf-cart tour. There's no charge for this service, and it's a very accessible way to get a look at the entire site.

Finally, if you want to get a good look at a wide variety of shorebirds, plus some colorful migrants, head on over to the Laguna Madre Boardwalk on South Padre Island. Located just 75 miles from McAllen, the island is the first landfall for birds making that difficult cross-Gulf migration.

The 1500-foot boardwalk overlooks four acres of wetlands near the South Padre Island Convention Center. It features level access and it's a good choice for wheelchair users or slow walkers. A covered shelter is located at the end of the boardwalk, and it's a good place to enjoy the sunset.

Additionally there is a butterfly garden next to the convention center, which tends to attract some colorful migrants. I was thrilled to spot an Indigo Bunting and a Summer Tanager after spending just a few minutes in this small garden. It was a great way to top off my Texas tropics birding tour.

- IF YOU GO
  - World Birding Center, (956) 584-9156, www.worldbirdingcenter.org
  - McAllen CVB, (956) 682-2871, www.mcallencvb.com
  - South Padre Island CVB, (800) 767-2373, www.sopadre.com

TIDE POOLS AND YURTS ON THE OREGON COAST

I have to admit, I have a certain fondness for the rugged Oregon coast. Indeed it's where I go to relax, enjoy nature, kick back and just plain get away from it all. But can a place described as rugged also be accessible? Surprisingly, it can. In fact, my little chunk of heaven is also billed as one of the most accessible wildlife and ocean-viewing venues on the Pacific coast. From wheelchair-accessible tide pools to a first-rate aquarium, there's something for everybody on the rugged Oregon coast.

The crown jewel of Oregon's coastal accessibility is located in the Yaquina Head Outstanding Natural Area, just three miles north of Newport.

This 100-acre coastal headland area was established by Congress in 1980. Several years later, the Bureau of Land Management reclaimed the Yaquina Head rock quarry and converted it to a rocky intertidal area. Over the years, this area, known as Quarry Cove, evolved naturally. Today Quarry Cove supports a wide variety of marine life and includes Oregon's first wheelchair-accessible tide pools.

Wheelchair users can park in the lower parking lot at Quarry Cove and just roll down to the tide pools. The paved paths go right into the intertidal area. There are also raised tide pools, which are just the right viewing height for wheelers. You'll find a wide variety of marine life in the intertidal area, including sea urchins, starfish, anemone, mussels, barnacles, hermit crabs and sculpins. Remember to visit Quarry Cove during low tide, as the whole area is submerged at high tide. The best time to explore the tide pools is in the early morning. Check the local newspaper for a tide table.

To gain access to the lower Quarry Cove parking lot, wheelchair users must first stop at the Yaquina Head Interpretive Center. This gated parking area is reserved for visitors who are disabled, and a ranger must open the gate. The interpretive center also has numerous exhibits that depict the history of the area.

Another must-see attraction is the Yaquina Head Lighthouse. This historic lighthouse dates back to 1873 and has been called one of the most beautiful lighthouses in America. The lighthouse is only accessible by stairs, but you can catch a good view of it from the adjacent asphalt trail. There is also an accessible boardwalk and ocean-viewing platform behind the lighthouse, where you can spot seals, puffins, mures, cormorants and (sometimes) whales in the surf.

For a look at marine life from a different perspective, visit the Oregon Coast Aquarium, located on Yaquina Bay in Newport. This 39-acre site showcases seabirds, marine mammals, fishes, invertebrates and plants native to the Oregon coast.

The aquarium features accessible parking and restrooms, level pathways and barrier-free access to all exhibits. Exhibits range from an aviary filled with puffins to killer sharks in *Passages of the Deep*. And don't miss the twice daily "keeper-talks," which focus on fascinating details about the care and feeding of the resident animals.

. . . .

Wheelchair-accessible tide pools at Yaquina Head Outstanding Natural Area.

Although most of Newport is unremarkable, the Nye Beach area is worth a visit. It's a typical funky beach town with shops and restaurants and tons of ambience. Parking is located near 3rd Street and Coast Drive, and there is a ramp down to the sandy beach area. Some of the old shops are not accessible, but it's a nice place to just sit and watch the ocean.

And if you enjoy the great outdoors, but cringe at the thought of pitching a tent, consider staying in an accessible yurt. These permanent domed structures are furnished and can sleep up to five people. They include plywood floors, framed doors, electricity and skylights, and they rent for a very affordable $35 a night. The two closest accessible yurts to Newport are at Beachside (between Waldport and Yachats) and Beverly Beach (north of Newport). Advance reservations are a must, as the accessible yurts go fast!

- IF YOU GO
  - Yaquina Head Outstanding Natural Area, (541) 574-3100
  - Oregon Coast Aquarium, (541) 867-3474, www.aquarium.org
  - Yurts, (800) 452-5687,
    www.oregon.gov/OPRD/PARKS/rustic.shtml#RUSTIC_YURTS
  - Greater Newport Area Chamber of Commerce, (541) 265-8801,
    www.newportchamber.org

Recommended Reading

Even though I spent years researching destinations for this book, I still consider it a starting point as far as vacation planning goes. It goes without saying that you should contact hotels, restaurants, attractions and transportation providers directly to make sure they can meet your access needs. But beyond that, there are many other good resources out there to help you in the planning process.

Let's start with the free ones.

One of the best free information resources around are the local convention and visitors bureaus (CVBs). These organizations are funded by the tourism industry and they provide free information and services to visitors. I've listed the local CVBs at the end of each chapter. Some are larger than others, so don't expect to get the same services at every CVB. Still, most have plenty of free maps, brochures and guides to dole out. Some guides include limited-access information, but usually it's just the little blue wheelchair pictogram placed next to a few hotels or attractions. Although they are not the best place to go for access information, CVBs are a great resource for general destination information.

On the other hand, some CVBs have teamed up with local disability organizations to publish specialized access guides. San Francisco and San Diego top this list, and hopefully, with the aging population, more destinations will follow suit. So, don't be afraid to ask for access information when you contact a CVB. First off, it's good for them to hear that folks are interested in access issues, and, the more people who inquire about access, the more likely a CVB will be to provide detailed access information at some point in the future. Plus, you just never know; they may have a new access guide or one that just wasn't promoted very well. As I write this, Chicago is wrapping up production on their first access guide, and I'm sure they won't be the last destination to offer this specialized resource.

As far as resources that you have to pay for go, there are many fine books out there that address access issues. There are also many not-so-fine titles on the subject. And believe me, I've read them all. And since I don't like to waste my breath on things I don't like, I'll just give you the run down on the books that I do like. Here, in no particular order, is Candy's recommended reading list.

Easy Access Europe
RICK STEVES AND KEN PLATTNER (2006)

The second edition of this European travel guide includes listings for accessible hotels, restaurants and attractions in London, Paris, Bruges, Amsterdam and Frankfurt. All listings are rated for access, but, because of the off-the-beaten track focus of Steves' titles, the majority of the listings are only appropriate for slow walkers (or those people who can do one or two steps). Still it's a useful resource for budget travelers and for people who can make do with less-than-perfect access. On the plus side, it does include many useful features such as a Tube access map. By Steves' own admission, complete barrier-free access is a rarity in Europe, but this guide helps wheelchair users and slow walkers make informed travel decisions.

Access in London
GORDON COUCH (2003)

Researched by a London-based non-profit organization (Access Project), this handy resource includes information on accessible tourist attractions, toilets, accommodations, recreation and transportation in the London area. The access criteria is clearly defined in the beginning of the book, and most entries also include a brief narrative about their access features. A number of maps and access diagrams are also included. All information in this guide was compiled from site inspections conducted in 2002, so it's best to double-check the information before you head out. Still, the access details included in this title merit it a mention on this list.

Le Quebec Accessible
KÉROUL (2005)

This helpful directory lists more than 1,000 accessible hotels, attractions and restaurants located throughout Quebec province. Grouped by city, each listing features pictograms and notes about accessible services. The accessibility criteria is clearly defined in the beginning of the guide, and detailed access notes are included about any listings that are rated as "fully accessible." Information about local resources, accessible transportation and medical equipment is also included. This title is only available in French, but, because of the use of pictograms, it's still a good resource even if you can't read French. It's a little hard to find in the US, but it can be purchased at Ulysses bookstores in Canada. It's also available directly from Kéroul at (514) 252-3104.

Easy Access Australia
BRUCE M. CAMERON (2000)

First published in 1995, *Easy Access Australia* is packed full of helpful accessibility information. The book is divided by states, and the author lists the major tourist attractions and hotels in each section. This second edition contains approximately 600 accommodations, with 300 bathroom floor plans. Information on accessible transportation is also included, along with lots of contact information, phone numbers and maps. Although this title is pretty old, I still recommend it because of the inclusion of the floor plans and measurements. Generally speaking, floor plans don't change that much, and properties usually don't take out roll-in showers. Unfortunately, this is another title that's hard to find in the US, so your best bet is to contact the author at Easy Access Australia, P.O. Box 218, Kew Victoria 3101, Australia.

The Accessible Guide to Florence
CORNELIA DANIELSON (2004)

This guidebook to Florence contains lots of detailed access information on local tourist sights, transportation, restaurants and accommodations. The access information is presented in a narrative format and includes pertinent details such as the number of steps, ramp locations and threshold heights. An appendix with local resources is also included. The author lives in Florence, which accounts for the attention to detail in this title.

The Practical Nomad: How to Travel Around the World
EDWARD HASBROUCK (2004)

Although this title is billed as a resource on long-term travel and third-world travel, it's really a must-read for all travelers. Now in its third edition, this comprehensive volume includes authoritative information on everything from air and surface transportation to baggage, budgets and health issues. The book contains a few paragraphs and some resources on accessible travel; however, for the most part, it's not an accessible travel title. It should be noted that Mr. Hasbrouck has a very enlightened attitude about accessible travel in third-world countries; an attitude which serves to encourage rather than discourage people from giving it a try. It's an excellent primer for anyone headed overseas.

Wheelchairs on the Go
MICHELLE STIGLEMAN & DEBORAH VAN BRUNT (2002)

This comprehensive guide to accessible fun in Florida includes access information on everything from bicycling and water fun to beaches and accommodations. The information is divided by geographic region and each listing includes a short narrative. Access details on attractions include information on accessible parking, restrooms, entrances and programs. The access criteria is clearly defined in the beginning of the book, and additional details are included with each listing. Accommodations are listed for most every area, and they include very detailed access information such as bed height and the availability of open-platform beds. Complete contact information is also included for all listings. Even though this excellent guide is a bit dated, it's still a good resource because of the authors' meticulous research and attention to detail.

Access Anything Colorado
CRAIG P. KENNEDY & ANDREA C. JEHN (2005)

This resource-filled volume includes detailed information about accessible outdoor fun and activities throughout Colorado. It includes information about adaptive sporting activities for all seasons, from snow skiing and dogsledding to hiking, biking, fishing and camping. Also included are lodging and dining suggestions plus lots of resources. All sites contained in this book were visited and evaluated by the authors.

I Can Do That!
CRAIG P. KENNEDY & ANDREA JEHN KENNEDY (2007)

This second book for Andrea and Craig continues on the active outdoor adventure theme. The meat of the book contains detailed information on 45 adaptive sports. It's not so much of a destination travel guide as it is a how-to guide for adaptive sports. If you want to get active and enjoy the great outdoors, give it a read, as most likely you'll find something that tickles your fancy in this resourceful title. A comprehensive resource list that includes URLs for a bevy of accessible travel and adaptive sports websites is also included.

Watch It Made in the USA
KAREN AXELROD AND BRUCE BRUMBERG (2002)

This handy guide contains detailed information on more than 300 factory tours across the US. Every listing includes general information about the tour plus details on everything from free samples to wheelchair access. The access section specifies if the tour is wheelchair accessible. If the tour is not fully wheelchair accessible, details about the accessible parts (if any) are included. Alternative experiences (such as movies and photo albums) are described in the access section. It's a solid well-researched resource.

A Wheelchair Rider's Guide: San Francisco Bay and the Nearby Coast
BONNIE LEWKOWICZ (2006)

This handy resource includes access details on more than 100 trails and parks in Northern California. All sites included in the guide were visited by author and Access Northern California founder, Bonnie Lewkowicz. "People will be pleasantly surprised at the number and diversity of accessible trails within the Bay Area," says Lewkowicz. And believe it or not, this excellent resource is available free from the California Coastal Conservancy. Just give them a call at (510) 286-1015 or e-mail calcoast@scc.ca.gov to request your copy.

Index

Note: Boldface numbers indicate illustrations.

INDEX

Index

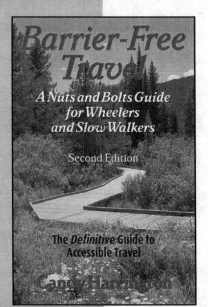

"An essential reference."
— *Midwest Book Review*

"The Bible for barrier-free travel."
— *Ticked.com*

"The brass tacks of accessibility written in Candy Harrington's straight-from-the shoulder style."
— *Mouth Magazine*

Barrier Free Travel continues to be the definitive guide to accessible travel for those who use a wheelchair, walker, or cane, or have any physical ailment that may slow down their gait. This well-researched resource contains detailed information about the logistics of planning accessible travel by plane, train, bus, and ship.

2005   304 pages   Softcover $19.95
ISBN-13: 978-932603-09-5

"A must for anyone who is challenged, needs a wheelchair or is a slow walker."
— *Real Travel Adventures*

"A helpful resource in finding truly accessible bed and breakfast inns."
— *Contra Costa Times*

There Is Room at the Inn is a guide to accessible inns and B&Bs throughout the United States. Through a combination of personal experience, on-site visits, and interviews with innkeepers and other travelers, Candy B. Harrington has discovered the most friendly and accessible properties, and brings her expert recommendations to the reader.

2006   256 pages   Softcover $21.95
ISBN-13: 978-1-932603-61-3

Demos Health
386 Park Avenue South, Suite 301
New York, NY 10016
Tel: 1-800-532-8663
Fax: 212-683-0118
orderdept@demosmedpub.com
www.demosmedpub.com